D0261953

FOLKLORE AND LITERATURE IN THE UNITED STATES

GARLAND FOLKLORE BIBLIOGRAPHIES
(General Editor: Alan Dundes)
Vol. 5

GARLAND REFERENCE LIBRARY
OF THE HUMANITIES
Vol. 392

Garland Folklore Bibliographies

General Editor

Alan Dundes
University of California, Berkeley

1. *South American Indian Narrative: Theoretical and Analytical Approaches: An Annotated Bibliography*
   by Susan Niles
2. *American and Canadian Immigrant and Ethnic Folklore: An Annotated Bibliography*
   by Robert A. Georges and Stephen Stern
3. *International Proverb Scholarship: An Annotated Bibliography*
   by Wolfgang Mieder
4. *Christmas: An Annotated Bibliography*
   by Sue Samuelson
5. *Folklore and Literature in the United States: An Annotated Bibliography of Studies of Folklore in American Literature*
   by Steven Swann Jones

FOLKLORE AND LITERATURE IN THE UNITED STATES

An Annotated Bibliography of Studies of Folklore in American Literature

Steven Swann Jones

GARLAND PUBLISHING, INC. • NEW YORK & LONDON
1984

Library of Congress Cataloging in Publication Data

Jones, Steven Swann, 1949–
Folklore and literature in the United States.

(Garland folklore bibliographies ; v. 5) (Garland reference library of the humanities ; v. 392
Includes index.
1. American literature—History and criticism—Bibliography. 2. Folklore in literature—Bibliography. 3. Folklore—United States—Bibliography. I. Title. II. Series. III. Series: Garland reference library of the humanities ; v. 392.
Z1225.J66 1984 [PS169.F64] 016.81′09′3 82-49182
ISBN 0-8240-9186-8 (alk. paper)

Printed on acid-free, 250-year-life paper
Manufactured in the United States of America

CONTENTS

EDITOR'S PREFACE

The Garland Folklore Bibliographies are intended to provide ready access to the folklore scholarship of a particular country or area or to the scholarship devoted to a specific folklore genre or theme. The annotations are designed to be informative and evaluative so that prospective readers may have some idea of the nature and worth of the bibliographical items listed. No bibliography is ever complete and all bibliographies are doomed to become obsolete almost immediately upon publication as new monographs and articles appear. Still, there is no substitute for a comprehensive, intelligently annotated bibliography for anyone desiring to discover what has been written on a topic under investigation.

Folkloristics, the study of folklore, belongs both to the humanities and the social sciences. Within the humanistic approach to folklore, one major concern is with how folklore inspires, influences, or informs so-called elite creative culture, that is, art, music, and literature. Accordingly, one can choose to investigate such subjects as Bruegel's paintings of proverbs or children's games, Mozart's variations on the tune found in "Twinkle, Twinkle, Little Star" (or "Baa Baa Black Sheep"), or Shakespeare's debt to international folktale type 923, Love Like Salt, for the plot of *King Lear.* Folklore has provided the thematic basis for many of the greatest artists, composers, and writers in the world. The United States is no exception. But if one wished to learn how Nathaniel Hawthorne, Washington Irving, Herman Melville, Mark Twain, or William Faulkner drew upon folklore in their written works, where could one turn to find out? Fortunately, Steven Swann Jones in *Folklore and Literature in the United States: An Annotated Bibliography of Studies of Folklore in American Literature* has given us a valuable source with which to answer that question. Students of American literature with an interest in folklore will henceforth be able to begin their research on a particular author with the citations contained in this volume.

Steven Jones completed his B.A. with honors in English at Haverford College in 1971. After receiving an M.A. in English from the University of California, Davis, in 1974, he completed his doctorate in English and Folklore at the same institution (in cooperation with the University of California, Berkeley) in 1979. His dissertation, "The Construction of the Folktale: 'Snow White'," treated both the folktale and literary versions of it. After serving as assistant professor of Comparative Studies in the Humanities at Ohio State University (1980–1983), Professor Jones joined the department of English at California State University, Los Angeles.

All those who have occasion to consult this important compilation of sources for the study of folklore in American literature will surely be grateful to Professor Jones for all his dedication and diligence.

Alan Dundes, *Editor*
Garland Folklore Bibliographies Series

ACKNOWLEDGMENTS

I would like to thank Alan Dundes for his constant encouragement and invaluable guidance. I would also like to thank Ohio State University and California State University, Los Angeles for their generous support.

INTRODUCTION

I. The Study of Folklore in American Literature: Its Scope and Method

The study of the interconnection of folklore and literature in the United States has been a surprisingly active and yet paradoxically disjointed affair. Numerous scholars have been enticed into analyzing bits and pieces of this field, but historically their methodology and focus have often been more at odds with each other, or in ignorance of each other, than they have been usefully supportive of each other. Many of the past folklore-in-literature studies examine one folk tradition or another as it appears in a given literary text and include two footnotes, one to the literary text and one to some folklore text from which the author derives his or her expertise and documentation of the folkloristic authenticity of the tradition cited. They frequently ignore issues of methodology and just as frequently overlook similar or overlapping studies.

One possible explanation for the provincialism and nearsightedness of many of these studies is the paucity of bibliographical tools to assist the scholars in broadening the range and improving the quality of their scholarship. Folklore-in-literature studies tend to be scattered in various humanities journals and their corresponding bibliographies throughout the library, so that ferreting out the appropriate references is a truly Herculean task. And the two previous bibliographies that have attempted to cover the folklore-and-literature connection have not exactly produced heroic results. Haywood's and Flanagan's bibliographies of folklore include sections devoted to folklore and literature, but even for their circumscribed time periods, 1900–1950 and 1950–1970, they are substantially incomplete.

Furthermore, they lack the indexes essential to assist scholars in locating sources relevant to their particular area of interest.

Curiously, despite these limitations, much of the scholarship concerning folklore in American literature is, nevertheless, enormously revealing. It exposes the intimate connections between the rhetorical strategies of texts and the personal ethics and associations of audiences. Folkloristics is a particularly useful and insightful approach to literary criticism. Identifying the proverbs underlying a Dickinson poem or an Edward Taylor poem, or the use of sea talk in Melville or legends in Pynchon, exposes in a very immediate way the appeal and significance of these texts. These perspectives on the folklore basis of literature reveal the social values, artistic conventions, and archetypal themes that infuse these literary works, and thus these studies of folklore in literature ultimately offer the most direct glimpse into the assumed bond between reader and text, audience and performance.

A variety of scholars, literary, anthropological, and folkloristic, have previously suggested the idea that, to a large extent, the appeal of literature is essentially predicated upon the expression and reworking in literary texts of traditional folk ideas, conventions, plots, motifs, and language. The myth-ritual school, for example, which flourished at the start of the twentieth century, pointed out the mythic parallels and underpinnings in many western literary classics. Scholars in this school such as Stanley Hyman and Richard Chase noted the close relation between cultural anthropology and literature, and they have pointed out that literature is frequently a reworking of mythic concerns for a modern audience. Furthermore, in more recent times, Stanley Fish and the advocates of reader response criticism have justly argued that readers and texts have a dynamic relationship that is fundamentally based upon certain preconceptions about language, behavior, and artistic expression. What Fish and reader response critics are stressing is that it is our cultural make-up that allows us or encourages us to respond to certain works in certain ways. What we like and what we understand in literature is inevitably the product of our cultural heritage, both oral and literate. What is apparently surprising to most students of literature, and as a consequence is relatively neglected in literary scholarship, is the very great extent to which folklore, or oral tradition, contributes to our basic cultural constitution. Folklore, as it turns out, is the very stuff of which we and the literature that we like are made.

Part of the reason for the relative neglect of folklore as a central constituent element of literature is that the concept of folklore itself has been misunderstood. The term was coined in 1846, but it is only in the last decade that a comprehensive and accurate conceptualization of all that "folklore" really includes has emerged. Previous, and now outdated, notions of folklore as quaint and curious customs have unfortunately plagued the study and awareness of this discipline. Because folklore is such an intimate and fundamental part of our daily lives, we seem able to recognize it or appreciate it only in its most exotic and outmoded forms. There are still students of literature today who think of folklore as only those things that are over a century old.

However, folkloristic and anthropological analyses of the ontological nature of folklore, of what this phenomenon *really is* in relation to other forms of culture, have in the last century revised our understanding of what folklore includes. They have pointed out that what all the forms of folklore have in common, whether they be the legends of yore or the ghost stories of today, the peasant garb of Yugoslavia or the lowrider automobiles of California, is that they are cultural traditions created and passed on by individuals or groups through personal communication or example. Thus, our conception of folklore has become greatly widened to include things as general or abstract as folk ideas or worldview (for example, the way a community is laid out, as in the Dogon villages described by Marcel Griaule in *Conversations with Ogotommêli* or the layout of New England farms), as contemporary as urban legends (for example, the story of the rat in the Coca-Cola bottle or the snake in the fur coat from India), as foreign as tribal rituals (for example, the American Indian ritual of Okeepa, where buffalo skulls are hung from the skin of suspended pubescent youths, or Australian aboriginal circumcision rites), or as common as the jokes we hear at work or at school (for example, the jokes circulating after the election of Pope John Paul II or the lightbulb jokes). What all these cultural manifestations have in common is that they have been passed on by word of mouth or personal example in essentially the same form from one person to another. This conception of a specialized form of cultural heritage that includes those beliefs, customs, stories, and practices that have been remembered and repeated by individuals allows us to see the unifying element underlying these disparate traditions; they have all survived the winnowing wind of temporal social life and have been deemed worthy of preserving and recreating. In essence, folklore amounts to a comprehensive portrait of all that has been considered valuable and worth saving by individual people, either historically or contemporaneously.

Defining folklore is no longer the hard part—the hard part is learning the enormous array of materials and traditions that are continually being created, preserved, recreated, and revised. There are, however, some invaluable benefits that accrue from studying folklore. For one reason, knowing the folk cultural heritage of a society is to know the people who live on it or through it. Studying folk traditions can provide us with an accurate reflection of the important social and personal concerns of a given people as well as give us useful insight into the essence of human nature. Furthermore, an awareness of the comprehensive nature of folklore and of all that it includes allows us to recognize the full extent of the interconnection between folklore and literature. It reveals to us the profound extent to which the appeal of a literary work is fundamentally dependent upon its evocation of audience concern and identification through the expression and elucidation of its topic in images, symbols, characters, events, situations, attitudes, expressions, and customs that are the product of folklore. It shows us, for example, that Barth's *Chimera* is based on the legends of Perseus and Bellerophontes, and that Nabokov's *Lolita* draws heavily upon the characters of fairy tales, including princesses, prince charmings, ogre fathers, and jealous stepmothers. Ultimately, our broadened awareness of folklore allows us to realize to what a large degree literate tradition is a superimposed stratum overlying the bedrock of folk tradition. If folklore is how we live day to day, the habits and customs that we acquire from watching our parents and those around us, then literature is to a large extent a documented account of these customs, a written record of human patterns of living.

Ironically, this argument about the implicit connections between the appeal of a text and the folkloristic affiliations of its audience (be they familial, occupational, social, ethnic, national, or universal) serves as an explicit theoretical confirmation of the implicit logic underlying all previous studies of folklore in literature. The underlying assumption of all folklore in literature studies is that by pointing out allusions in a literary text to folk traditions and conventions, they are explicating the underlying appeal of the text. The validity of this methodology has been tested and proven by the multitude of studies of folklore in American literature. These studies as a group convincingly demonstrate the very great extent to which literature relies upon folk traditions to hook and hold its audience and the very real benefits of analyzing these folk connections in literary texts.

Even the early studies that were preoccupied by the item-enumeration approach and that eschewed interpretive analysis still provide enlightening perspectives on the sociological analysis of literature and insightful glimpses into the specific underpinnings of individual literary works. And the preliminary promise of these early studies has blossomed fruitfully in recent folkloristic analyses of literature; the number and quality of studies have risen dramatically. Unsophisticated methodologies have given way to comprehensive, rigorous, scholarly, articulate, and perceptive analyses of the important relationships and parallels between folklore and literature. Scholars are apparently becoming increasingly aware of this vital connection between folklore and literature, and they are becoming increasingly adroit and erudite in the way that they investigate it. These studies as a whole represent the best supporting documentation of the fundamental thesis that literature inevitably relies on folklore.

Accordingly, this bibliography is an attempt to catalog the bulk of these studies of folklore in American literature. Through this bibliographical survey, I hope to encourage a broader conception of the contribution of folklore to American literature and to promote more extensive consultation and use of folklore, and of previous folklore/literature scholarship, in American literary criticism. Furthermore, it is my hope that such a delineation of the relevant studies will not only call attention to this area of research and encourage better scholarship but will also provide a useful preliminary delineation of this field and its concerns. By surveying the topics and methods of the studies listed here, we can acquire a basic appreciation of the essential parameters of the study of folklore in American literature. As a way of anticipating and facilitating such an appreciation, I should like in the following pages to summarize briefly the major methods and conclusions of the studies of folklore in American literature cataloged in this bibliography.

Perhaps the first and most important lesson the survey of previous folklore-in-literature scholarship offers us is *how* to study folklore in literature. From past studies we can glean a valuable understanding of the methodologies that have been found to be appropriate for this field. Three important methodological approaches to the study of folklore in literature have been advanced by scholars in this area.

One fundamental position is that voiced by Richard Dorson who calls for comprehensive documentation of the folkloristic credentials of traditions identified in literary texts; he suggests three criteria for establishing authenticity: biographical evidence, internal evidence, and corroborative evidence. Biographical evidence consists of documentation of an author's actual exposure to authentic folk traditions; internal evidence consists of specific references in the texts to verifiable folk traditions; and corroborative evidence consists of documented traditions outside the text that correspond to the material in the text. The value of this approach to the study of folklore in literature is that it provides a valid basis for analysis and interpretation of the folklore in literary texts; it insures that we recognize the exact folk tradition that the author is incorporating in his text and that we are aware of the actual context and function normally associated with a given example of folklore so that when we deal with it out of its natural context in the literary text, we can reconstruct the specific allusion in its full milieu and with its full significance. This folkloristic documentation of authenticity approach is a fundamental and useful starting point for any study of folkloristic literature, and it is one that has been adopted and successfully employed in numerous studies, for example, Ronald Baker's *Folklore in the Writings of Rowland E. Robinson.*

A second major concern of folklore in literature analysis is that articulated by Alan Dundes, who calls for rigorous interpretation of the purpose and meaning of the folklore found in literature. Dundes argues for folkloristic *explication de text*; this approach attempts to use rhetorical, semiotic, and symbolic analysis to explicate the meaning and function of folklore as it occurs in literary works. The value of this approach is that it attempts to make explicit that which underlies and motivates the incorporation of folklore in a literary text, which in turn reveals the thematic preoccupations of the artist and the work. It uses the clues provided by our familiarity with the social functions and purposes of specific examples of folklore as a springboard into the deeper meanings of literary texts. Numerous scholars have implemented this method, for example, Dan Barnes, in "The Bosom Serpent: A Legend in American Literature and Culture."

The most recent approach to the study of folklore in literature is that suggested by Roger Abrahams, who argues that folklore and literature should be analyzed as performance with all its attendant assumptions, social constraints, and behavioral implications. This folklore and literature as performance school of analysis examines the shared assumptions and strategies for appealing to an audience by folklore, literature, and folkloristic literature alike. It reveals that the bond between audience and artistic product, be it oral or written, is essentially the same, so that familiarity and expertise in the ways that folklore is performed and functions for its audience can be usefully applied to the analysis of literary works and to the folklore in those works. What Abrahams and his school ultimately are suggesting is that the link between folklore and literature is far more essential and fundamental than simply occasional borrowings of folk characters or customs. They reveal dependencies upon identical narrative patterns and basic sociological premises in both folklore and literature. They argue that the rhetorical strategies of both artistic modes of communication are predicated on essentially the same assumptions, so that it turns out that our "willing suspension of disbelief" in reading literature (as literary critics term it) is identical to the mutual contract that governs performer-audience interactions in folklore. In both cases, there is a whole set of acknowledged rules governing the communication: rules of order, syntax, balance, expectation and fulfillment, suitability of subject, etc. And the rules for literary communication are not only similar to folklore, in many cases they are derived from or outright borrowed from folklore. Furthermore, since we generally acquire and develop our sense of these conventions from oral tradition before our exposure to literary tradition (both historically and personally), there consequently exists in literature an inevitable and important folkloristic component. Various scholars have followed up on this approach; for example, Mark Workman's "The Role of Mythology in Modern Literature" develops this line of reasoning as a valuable way to study folkloristic literature.

In addition to teaching us *how* to study folklore in literature, previous scholarship concerning folklore in American literature can also show us *what* that connection includes. Past studies of folklore in American literature can help to provide an answer to the following important questions: What American authors have been most frequently found to incorporate folklore into their works? What kinds of folklore have been most frequently found to underlie and contribute to American literature? What uses of folklore have been made by American authors? The answers to these questions can be gleaned from a survey of past scholarship, and they, in turn, can give us a basic understanding of the folklore/literature connection in America.

Of course, I should qualify these findings by pointing out that in each case the bibliographical results are only a limited approximation of the real answer, limited by their methodological and historical biases. There are authors who use folklore, forms of folklore that are used, and uses themselves that have so far gone unstudied. Summarizing the results of previous scholarship, however, offers us two valuable insights: it gives us a general overview of the current assessment of the vast interconnection of folklore and American literature that otherwise might not be available; and it reveals to us any significant omissions in the scholarship, thereby providing us with directions for future research.

In answering the first question, we find that there are at least one or two studies of folklore's connection to almost every American author. We have ghosts in James, ballads in Emerson, proverbs in Sandburg, mythology in Longfellow, folk speech in

Wolfe, folksongs in Garland, sea slang in Melville, fairy tales in Fitzgerald, tall tales in Twain, witchcraft in Hawthorne, and so on. From the bulk of evidence, one immediate conclusion that we may draw is that literary artistry apparently relies to such degree upon oral conventions and oral materials that there is an inevitable folkloristic contribution to the canon of every American author. Of course, the degree of influence as well as the kind of influence may vary. Certain authors have been found to be especially indebted to folklore; for example, Clemens, Cooper, Ellison, Faulkner, Harris, Hawthorne, Irving, Melville, and Stuart have each been the topic of over a dozen folkloristic studies. Furthermore a good many regional authors have been carefully scrutinized for their debt to folklore. In this group we find authors such as Bill Arp, Rowland Robinson, Charles Russel, John Neihardt, Thomas Bangs Thorpe, Holman Day, George Washington Harris, Henry Clay Lewis, Harry Harrison Kroll, Augustus Baldwin Longstreet, Joseph M. Field, James Hall, Josh Billings and others too numerous to mention. Finally, folklore has been found to be a significant influence for many black American authors, for example, Charles Chesnutt, Imamu Amiri Baraka, Donald L. Lee, Frederick Douglass, Zora Neale Hurston, Toni Morrison, and Alice Walker. For all of these authors, we may conclude that folklore has been found to be an especially important influence in shaping and coloring their art. For the other comparatively less well-studied authors, we may speculate that their folkloristic debt is somewhat less obvious than their well-analyzed counterparts. Consequently, it may take some additional time until their folkloristic heritage is equally well documented.

When we turn to the question of what kinds of folklore have been found to influence American authors, we find from our survey of scholarship that we can identify two primary folkloristic influences appearing in the literature: the contemporary folk influence transmitted through the active traditions of the author's local community and the historical folk influence transmitted through the recorded documents that preserve examples of past folklore. The contemporary traditions include a wide range of folkloristic forms that authors naturally assimilate from their social background; for example, folk beliefs, speech, or customs from an author's past are frequently found to contribute to the author's literary work. The historical folk influence, on the other hand, is acquired from reading and studying the traditions of other cultures, and it often surfaces in literature as mythological characters or legendary exploits that an author will incorporate into his or her work. These two traditions appear and function differently in literature, as we can see, for example, in Twain's use of weather superstitions and Hawthorne's use of Greek mythology, but they both represent significant contributions by folklore to literature.

When we examine what genres of folklore have been found to underlie American literature, we find in our scholarly survey almost every conceivable form of folklore. For example, we find folk language, medicine, music, proverbs, jokes, local legends, rituals, customs, superstitions, gestures, foodways, ghosts, dances, metaphors, and myths embedded in American literature. Given the continuity of conventions between the discourse of literature and the shared communications of folklore, such a comprehensive overlap of traditions is entirely expected. And, as we might also expect, in terms of frequency of noted occurrence, the genres of folk literature are those most commonly identified. The three major categories include folk speech, folk narrative, and folk character, presumably because these are among the most obvious building blocks of literary discourse. We find studies of dialect in Joel Chandler Harris and word lists from Faulkner; fairy tales in Hawthorne and myths in Melville; fairy princesses in Fitzgerald and tricksters in Ellison.

The way that literary works adopt and adapt these folk traditions in order to assure their communication and acceptance is the focus of our final question: What uses of folklore by authors have been identified by scholars? Previous studies that have specifically attempted to define the various uses of folklore in literature have proposed answers that are quite varied; they range from binary divisions of the uses (passive versus active, or transcriptively versus functionally, or stylistically versus structurally) to elaborate matrixes involving degrees of intentionality and artfulness in authorial use of folklore. The uses have been categorized in a tripartite division (metanomic, metaphoric, and metamorphic) or cataloged according to various schools of thought (populist-historical or elitist). Each of these schemas is convincing in its own way, but none is entirely satisfactory. As a matter of fact, in terms of breadth, there appear to be almost as many uses of folklore in American literature as there are authors and texts. However, in terms of depth, we can identify three most commonly discussed uses of folklore in American literature; it is used for *authenticity*, in other words, to make text appear realistic, for *vitality*, in other words to make a work appealing and entertaining, and for *resonance*, in other words, to give a work greater significance or meaning.

Under the rubric of *authenticity*, I include the large number of studies that discuss the verisimilitude created by the incorporation of folklore into a literary work by a given author. For example, studies of folk speech and customs in Jesse Stuart's novels frequently concern themselves with the feeling that the audience is viewing "a real slice of life," which the folklore has helped to evoke. Similarly, Melville's whaling practices have been assessed for their realism and praised for their true-to-life quality. The value of this use of folklore by authors, and correspondingly of studies that examine it, is that these realistic folkloristic allusions are the immediate links that encourage our belief in and identification with the literary texts. Sensing the verisimilitude of the sea life in *Moby Dick* makes us emphathize more deeply with Ishmael's situation. Recognizing the realistic dialect of Twain's characters makes us appreciate more fully the satiric relevance of his commentary. Essentially, the use of folkloric detail makes the literary work come alive for us, and analyzing those details explains the work's immediate appeal.

A second major use of folklore frequently identified by scholars is labeled *vitality*; a great many studies have investigated how an author incorporates folklore into his work in order to enhance his artistry and enliven his style. For example, studies have pointed out how Edward Taylor achieves an important stylistic tension by his incorporation of folk expressions into his poetry, or how Artemis Ward uses folk characters to enliven his dramatic burlesques. In short, these studies generally explain how the folklore contributes to the literary impact of the works. The value of this use of folklore by authors is that it is through these folkloristic techniques that authors catch their listeners' ears.

They weave into their rhetorical style colorful expressions or characterizations that they and their audience have found useful and appealing. Emerson's use of proverbs in developing his essay style, for example, allows us greater access to the method and meaning of his prosaic communication. Correspondingly, the value of studies examining the use of folklore as stylistic embellishment is that they expose the basic mechanisms of literary communication. They reveal how an author's reliance on dialect or tall tale helps to capture his audience's interest and to frame his message. They reveal the basic method behind the literary art.

Finally, the last major use of folklore in literature that has been identified and discussed by scholars is termed *resonance*. This category includes all those studies of the archetypal and mythic meanings engendered by the use of folklore in literature. For example, we have La Belle Dame Sans Merci in Fitzgerald and we have the Grail legend in T. S. Eliot. These studies as a rule investigate the symbolic associations and reverberations generated by the inclusion of folklore in literature. The value of this use of folklore by American authors and, by extension, of the studies that explain it is that it generates a cultural context for the reader. It creates a framework of meaning for the text and for the reader that allows the message of the text to be interpreted in the larger drama of human life. For example, the hero's mission in *Chimera* can be better understood when we realize he is inversely imitating the heroic journey of previous legends. The important philosophical and psychological implications of the message of a specific literary text or the meaning of a particular character's dilemma or course of action are usefully explained by revealing the parallels or correspondences between that text and other familiar figures or narrative patterns from folklore. We understand the literary work better because we know from the folkloristic example what to expect and what we are supposed to understand.

These three uses certainly do not cover all the ways that folklore has been employed in American literature, but they do give us an estimation of the most popular, and perhaps most important, ways that folklore has been found to function in literature. Similarly, the survey of the kinds of folklore found in literature, the authors who use folklore, and the major schools of folkloristic criticism presented earlier in this essay provide a basic introduction to the methods and concerns of this area of research. What this survey of the scholarship of folklore in American literature ultimately teaches us is the wonderful richness and fruitfulness that this field of study can provide. Both in terms of past scholarship and future studies, there is an abundance of insights to be uncovered that can help us understand what is now becoming recognized as a fundamentally crucial connection between folklore and literature. It seems more and more apparent that studying this connection will help us understand the full spectrum of literary art: folk literature, folkloristic literature, and "original" literature.

II. *Operating Assumptions, Premises, and Rationale of this Bibliography*

One faulty premise all too frequently typical of folklore-in-literature studies and literary studies as well is to regard folklore as simply a building block for literature. The implicit logic seems to be that literature is a more refined and highly developed art form, far more worthy than folklore of our analysis and investigation, and that folklore exists simply to be borrowed and reshaped by literature, its more elegant stepsister. This implicit assumption is patently false. The enormous array of folk literature around the world is eloquent testimony to the unsurpassed magic and power of oral tradition. Furthermore, folklore often borrows and reshapes literary materials in as sophisticated and as entertaining ways as literature draws upon folklore. Nonetheless, previous scholarship has often been tainted by a bias towards written literature and has been reluctant to consider folk literature as an equally well developed and appealing form of human expression.

Fortunately, a number of recent studies in narrative theory have begun to reverse this trend and to vindicate folklore's value as an equally significant form of human artistic expression by pointing out how literature and folklore are essentially similar reworkings of fictive materials in very closely related mediums. By breaking down the assumed differences between folklore and literature, by showing how much they have in common, they have begun to show how they are equally impressive forms of human art. It is my hope that this bibliography will contribute to this undoing of past misconceptions about the relative status of folklore and literature by showing to what a large extent our literary masterpieces are in reality folkloristic. This goal is one fundamental motivation and justification of this bibliography.

Of course, once one decides to undertake such a bibliography as this, one has to determine how one is to go about it. If one were to accept the argument advanced in Part I of this essay, that is, recognize the very great extent to which American literature is indebted to folklore—e.g., conventions of language, plot, and characterization; allusions to habits, customs, and beliefs; incorporations of manners, legends, and superstitions; references to archetypal figures, mythic patterns, heroic characters, etc.—if we were to acknowledge this massive interconnection, then it might be argued with equal validity that a vast number of the studies undertaken in American literature are actually studies of folklore's indirect contribution to American literature, unbeknownst of course to the authors of those studies themselves. Since most beliefs, morals, family patterns, etc. found in literature are basically the indirect products of folk culture, studies of these phenomena might be loosely considered folkloristic. Logically, such an understanding of folklore's broad influence could encourage us to regard a wide range of studies as touching indirectly upon the folklore and literature connection. While such a view is sound, it is not particularly practical for the bibliography undertaken here.

The problem is that while, with our widened definition of folklore, we find that a great deal of literary criticism indirectly considers a large cross section of folkloristic concerns, they do not always do so in folkloristically knowledgable or insightful ways; for example, initiation, ritual, play, local color, manners, supernaturalism, myth, and archetype are some key terms and concepts that frequently appear in literary criticism, sometimes in connection with folklore as a serious discipline and sometimes not. As another example, sea quests might be considered a folk narrative plot paradigm, just as the concept of the frontier or of the American dream might be regarded as a folk belief. In addition to these cultural beliefs being folklore, character types, such as the Yankee or Johnny Reb, might be viewed as folkloristic creations. However, while these topics are all to some extent fundamentally a part of folklore, the issue of whether studies of these topics are seriously and fruitfully a part of folkloristic scholarship is another question. The point is, although they treat folklore subjects, they are not necessarily folkloristically sound themselves. The problem then becomes one of extracting the folkloristically competent studies from the mass of general studies available on the subject.

Realistically, we must recognize the enormity of the task—revising the concept of folklore in American literary scholarship and reassessing the folkloristic content and competence of that scholarship—is an undertaking quite beyond the scope of this present project. Rather, this present bibliography has as its objective the less ambitious and more immediate goal of reviewing scholarship directly and primarily concerned with examining folklore in American literature. Accordingly, I have limited this bibliography to studies published as of 1980 that in an explicit and central way examine the influence of folklore upon American literature. As a rule, these studies know that they are considering the impact of a *separate* oral, customary, or material tradition upon American letters. I have included some rare instances where the authors were unknowingly studying folklore as a central part of their argument, or, conversely, I have included studies that by their title purport to study folklore in literature but which turned out to be false leads. For the most part, however, I have attempted to confine this bibliography to that body of scholarship that specifically focuses on the interface between folklore and American literature and that demonstrates clear folkloristic competence.

I have included as an important component of this scholarship the numerous masters and doctoral theses on folklore in American literature. However, as a result of the unavailability in most libraries of the bulk of these manuscripts and the prohibitive cost of ordering them en masse, I have not annotated the masters theses, and I have, for the most part, drawn my annotations for the doctoral theses from *Dissertation Abstracts*.

One of the most problematical areas pertaining to the selection of entries to be included in this bibliography concerns the indiscriminate use in literary criticism of the term myth. All too frequently, the term "myth" is used in a non-folkloristic (and one might say vague or general) sense to refer to abstract narrative patterns, mental processes, or philosophical perspectives that in truth are far removed from folklore or from what folklorists more precisely and technically mean when they refer to myth. Archetypal criticism, for example, uses myth to refer to basic psychological proclivities and not to specific folk cultural traditions. The problem has only continued to worsen, despite numerous acknowledgments by scholars in the field of the present murkiness of the term. In theory, there is nothing wrong with the concept of myth; in folkloristic analysis it usefully describes our basic notions about the cosmos and about the fundamental nature of human experience that have been passed on by personal communication. And as a term, it can efficiently and effectively signify both these basic beliefs and the narratives that paradigmatically illustrate them. The problem arises when scholars with a less-than-precise familiarity with how myth functions in folk tradition take liberties with what is primarily a folkloristic term and misuse it to describe psychological patterns, artistic conventions, and philosophical positions that are not part of folklore. From the point of view of this bibliography, it is tempting to exclude altogether these folkloristically marginal studies of myth and literature. Unfortunately, however, even in its debased form, the concept of myth and its application to literature frequently possesses significant folkloristic implications that cannot be ignored. Accordingly, rather than summarily excluding these marginal studies of myth in literature I have included the most relevant ones, but I have attempted to critique the non-folkloristic applications of the word "myth" in my annotations.

I have similarly chosen for practical reasons to restrict the inclusion of studies from certain related bodies of scholarship produced by the extensive interconnection between folklore and literature. For example, I have excluded analyses of the connection between American literature and Christianity and other formally organized religions, even though these religions have strong and important folk heritages of their own. Studies of this connection would comprise another bibliography of its own. I have included, however, direct examinations of the folkloristic connection between a given religion and American literature. I am also excluding general studies of literary humor, even though humor often has an important oral debt. Once again this related topic requires a bibliography of its own. I have included, though, studies that specifically consider the relationship of folk humor to original literary humor.

The studies remaining within my circumscribed territory, taken as a whole, present perhaps the strongest argument for not sharply narrowing and limiting our conception of folklore's interconnection with American literature. Although they represent but a small portion of what could be done in this field, they already argue persuasively about the pervasive influence of folklore upon the diction, syntax, dialogue, expressions, symbols, attitudes, characterizations, plots, themes, and worldview found in American literature. When we realize, for example, that Emerson's prose style is shaped by his appreciation of proverb esthetics, that Hawthorne's greatest works were inspired by his fascination with witchcraft and New England legend, that Melville's most moving stories are founded upon sea lore, that Dickinson's poetry is based on ballad metrics, that Twain's most popular river tales follow folk plots and are packed with folk customs and beliefs, that Steinbeck's classic novels are accurate accounts of American folklife, and that Faulkner's entire corpus is in essence a record of Southern folkways, then we begin to get a glimpse of the incredibly far-reaching influence of folklore upon American writers. This extensive connection is the ultimate justification for this bibliography.

Folklore and Literature in the United States

BIBLIOGRAPHY

Abrahams, Roger. "Folklore and Literature as Performance." _Journal of the Folklore Institute_ 9 (1972): 75-94.

Argues against the shortcomings of "lore-in-lit" studies that simply identify folk traditions in literature. Suggests instead that there are crucial continuities between the art of life and the art of art in their expression, presentation, and content and that folklore and literature studies should analyze the shared strategies for appealing to the folk and literary audience.

Abrahams, Roger D. "The Literary Study of the Riddle." _Texas Studies in Language and Literature_ 14 (1972): 177-97.

Stresses the importance of analyzing the context and complexity of the subdiscipline folklore-and-literature. Discusses problems in previous studies by Caillois and Huizinga of the riddle, and proposes a more immediate conception of the way riddles are used.

Abrahams, Roger D. "Proverbs and Proverbial Expressions," in Richard Dorson, ed., _Folklore and Folklife: An Introduction_ (Chicago: University of Chicago Press, 1972), pp. 117-24.

Notes parallels between techniques of proverb lore and literature; proverbs share all devices commonly associated with poetry in English: meter, binary construction, balanced phrasing, and rhyme. Gives examples of shared form, but notes that the different mediums produce variations in form and function.

Abrahams, Roger D. and Barbara S. Babcock. "The Literary Use of Proverbs." <u>Journal of American Folklore</u> 90 (1977): 414-29.

Suggests that proverbs are usefully employed in literature because they possess intertextual potential, that is, an ability to re-situate the reader <u>vis-à-vis</u> the impersonal and dissociated text, because they embody their "situation of use."

Abrams, W. Amos. "Time Was: Its Lore and Language." <u>North Carolina Folklore</u> 19 (1971): 40-46.

Calls attention to folklore and folk language in <u>Time Was</u> by John Foster West. Identifies folk remedies, superstitions, rhymes, games, idioms, and sayings in the novel.

Adams, Richard P. <u>Faulkner: Myth and Motion</u>. Princeton: Princeton University Press, 1968. xiv, 260 pp.

Works from the premise that Faulkner knew of and incorporated Eliot's "mythical method" in much of his fiction. Suggests that the purpose of employing myth was to arrest life, to capture and transfix its motion so that it may live again when the literature is read. Points out allusions to Celtic mythology and legendry concerning the Grail as well as Mediterranean mythology concerning Demeter-Persephone-Kore. However, concentrates primarily on the rhetorical devices and images that Faulkner uses to "arrest motion" and analyzes how these are employed in the texts. The folkloristic analysis is limited.

Aderholt, Martha Jo. "The Role of the Plain Folk in the Southern Antebellum Novel." Ph.D. University of Tennessee. 1978. 174 pp. *Dissertation Abstracts International* 39 (1979): 4944A-45A.

The folkloristic perspective is not rigorously explored. Discusses in a general way "the stalwart yeomanry" of Southern fiction and their activities, but no mention is made of their folkloristic heritage or context.

Adkins, Nelson F. "Emerson and the Bardic Tradition." *PMLA* 63 (1948): 662-77.

Points out Emerson's interest in bardic lore and suggests Emerson copied bardic style for a number of his poems, especially "Merlin."

Alexander, Alex E. "Stephen King's *Carrie*: A Universal Fairytale." *Journal of Popular Culture* 13 (1979-80): 282-88.

Notes the similarities between *Carrie* and traditional fairytales such as "Snow White." They begin with the heroine's menstruation and depict her ensuing *rites de passage*.

Ambrosetti, Ronald J. "*Rosemary's Baby* and Death of God Literature." *Keystone Folklore Quarterly* 14 (1969): 133-41.

Points out how the theme of *Rosemary's Baby* is expressed through myth and folklore; references various folk motifs that appear in the novel.

Ammons, Elizabeth. "Fairy-Tale Love and *The Reef*." *American Literature* 47 (1976): 615-28.

Argues that the central theme of Wharton's novel concerns the exposing of deluded female fantasies about love and marriage, visions that have been generated and perpetuated by fairy tales. Points out explicit references in the story of Anna to "Sleeping Beauty" and shows how Wharton ironically reverses the traditional plot by having the Prince Charming not free or save the heroine, but instead enthrall her, in both senses of the word. Also points out allusions to "Cinderella" in the story of Sophy. Concludes that "the fairy-tale fantasy of deliverance by man . . . is a glorification of the status quo: a culturally perpetuated myth of female liberation which in reality celebrates masculine dominance, proprietorship, and privilege" and that Wharton's novel exposes the hypocrisy of the fairy tale formula.

Andersen, David M. "Basque Wine, Arkansas Chawin' Tobacco: Landscape and Ritual, in Ernest Hemingway and Mark Twain." *Mark Twain Journal* 16/1 (1972): 3-7.

Applies Levi-Strauss's ""Principle of Reciprocity," "the exchange of certain items not to secure a profit but to create an air of cordiality and alliance," as an explanation of social ritual in *The Sun Also Rises* and *Huckleberry Finn*. Argues that these daily rituals such as sharing wine or tobacco are used by the authors to illustrate underlying feelings of tension or brotherhood, depending on how the characters are presented in the ritual. Suggests that the trivial bickering of the town loafers over "chawing tobacker" foreshadows the death of Boggs. Concludes that the folkloristic ritual is indicative of the social currents.

Anderson, Hilton. "A Southern 'Sleepy Hollow'." *Mississippi Folklore Register* 3 (1969): 85-88.

Retells Joseph Cobb's "The Legend of Black Creek" in order to point out that it has retained the basic plot and character of Irving's "Legend of Sleepy Hollow."

Anderson, John Q. "Emerson and the Ballad of George Nidever--'Staring Down' a Grizzly Bear." *Western Folklore* 15 (1956): 40-45.

Considers the connection between Emerson and the tall tale of American folklore as suggested by his publication of the ballad of "George Nidiver" (sic), which he collected from Elizabeth Hoar. Concludes that Emerson had some knowledge of frontiersmen and frontier writing and possibly used the folk motif of staring down a bear as a symbol of the power of the human soul.

Anderson, John Q. "Emerson and the Language of the Folk." in Mody C. Boatright, ed., *Folk Travelers: Ballads, Tales, and Talk* (Austin: Texas Folklore Society, 1953), pp. 152-59.

Discusses Emerson's theory of language, that nature was the original source of language, and suggests that his affinity for "the bed-rock quality of common speech" influenced his use of folk speech. Gives examples of folk expressions.

Anderson, John Q. "Folklore in the Writings of 'The Louisiana Swamp Doctor'." *Southern Folklore Quarterly* 19 (1955): 243-51.

Considers briefly the use of the mock oral tales, folk language, and folk medicine in twenty-five humorous sketches by "Madison Tensas, M.D.," the pen name of Henry Clay Lewis. Discusses bear hunting tall tales, "coonskin" similes, folk diction, and screech owl superstitions as they appear in the sketches.

Anderson, John Q. *Louisiana Swamp Doctor; The Life and Writings of Henry Clay Lewis*. Baton Rouge: Louisiana State U. P., 1962. xi, 296 pp.

A biography of a Southern author who made extensive use of folklore in his regional writings. Discusses briefly Lewis's exposure to folk belief, medicine, remedy, dialect, and other material that found its way into his writings.

Anderson, John Q. "Scholarship in Southwestern Humor--Past and Present." *Mississippi Quarterly* 17 (1964): 67-86.

Surveys approaches to Southwestern humor and points out one of the most important topics concerns "the influence of oral folk tradition." Cites Blair, Boatwright, Hudson, Hoale, and Weber as sample studies.

Andes, Cynthia. "The Bohemian Folk Practice in 'Neighbor Rosicky'." Western American Literature 7/1 (1972): 63-64.

Identifies the Bohemian custom of burning crumbs leftover from baking in the orchard to insure a plentiful harvest as functioning in Willa Cather's "Neighbor Rosicky." The protagonist eats a supper in the orchard after the failure of his crops, thus reaffirming "his faith in a plentiful yield for the future," his general optimism, and his belief in the applicability of Old World practices to New World problems.

Andrews, William L. "Moby-Dick and the Legend of Mahuika." American Transcendental Quarterly 42 (1979): 123-27.

Investigates the Polynesian legend of the slaying of Mahuika, the fire god, and the capture of fire by the culture hero, Maui, as an example of Melville's propensity to borrow from the mythology and folk traditions of the world's cultures. Surveys the legend and suggests that "the Maui legend of the homeless younger brother who sets out to find his lost parents and prove his worthiness could have steered Melville's imagination toward the quasi-autobiographical vein of Redburn, White Jacket, and Pierre." Proposes ultimately the possibility that the legend of Mahuika may have shaped the Fishery legends of Mocha Dick, which in turn spawned the myth of Moby Dick, thus giving Moby Dick two generations of folkloristic heritage.

Anon. "The Bear and Huckleberry Finn: Heroic Quests for Moral Liberation." Mark Twain Journal 12 (1963): 12-13, 21.

Identifies a mythic pattern of initiation in Huckleberry Finn and "The Bear" and traces the stories' conformance to the traditional tests experienced by the heroic protagonist.

Ardolino, Frank R. "Life Out of Death: Ancient Myth and Ritual in Welty's 'A Worn Path'." Notes on Mississippi Writers 9 (1976): 1-9.

Argues that "Phoenix's journey with its succession of deaths and resurrections parallels the pagan nature rituals at Eleusis" and creates the theme of life emerging from death. Points out allusions to Eleusian rituals, such as the use of tree imagery, and concludes that through her healing of her grandson's affliction, "Phoenix has brought about the rebirth of the lost god."

Arner, Robert D. "Folk Metaphors in Edward Taylor's Meditation 1.40'." Seventeenth-Century News 3 (1973): 6-9.

Examines satanic imagery in "Meditation 1.40," and asserts that folk resources provided the form and substance of his depiction. Discusses folk imagery, games, and speech as they are employed in the poem. Concludes that Taylor was "the first major American writer who made folk imagination an essential ingredient of his art."

Arner, Robert D. "John Smith, The 'Starving Time,' and the Genesis of Southern Humor: Variations on a Theme." Louisiana Studies 12 (1973): 383-390.

Investigates Smith's humorous tone in recounting legends and anecdotes from colonial Virginia and concludes his use of tall tale style marks him as the father of Southern humor.

Arner, Robert D. "The Legend of Pygmalion in 'The Birthmark'." American Transcendental Quarterly 14 (1972): 168-71.

Sets out to examine "Aylmer's concept of himself as a modern descendent of Pygmalion." Rejects previous interpretations of the motif as illustrating the role of the artist, and instead suggests that Hawthorne"s version is an ironic reversal of the classical myth. "Aylmer's story exactly reverses Pygmalion's, for it ends where the legend began, with a perfect but lifeless idol." Aylmer tries to rise above nature, whereas Pygmalion prays to Venus to have his artistic creation enter the realm of nature. Concludes "in the broadest sense, then, the Pygmalion myth provides Hawthorne with a basic narrative structure as well as certain ironic dimensions of meaning and allusion."

Arner, Robert D. "Of Snakes and Those who Swallow Them: Some Folk Analogues for Hawthorne's "Egotism; or, The Bosom Serpent." *Southern Folklore Quarterly* 35 (1971): 336-46.

Surveys a dozen examples of swallowed snakes taken from newspapers, ballads, and journals and sees them as proof that Hawthorne's tale is based on a folk motif. Considers the accounts also to be illustrations of "the eternal conflict between folk belief and scientific skepticism."

Arner, Robert D. "Proverbs in Edward Taylor's *Gods Determinations*." *Southern Folklore Quarterly* 37 (1973): 1-13.

Examines the important link between Taylor's poetic imagination and the folk mind of the seventeenth century. Discusses the close bond between folk life and Puritan "plain style" as evidenced in Taylor's use of folk metaphors, similes, proverbs, and diction. Views the contrast of elevated subject and homey folk speech in *Gods Determinations* as a stylistic analogue for the tension between heavenly hope and earthly despair.

Arnold, St. George Tucker, Jr., "The Twain Bestiary: Mark Twain's Critters and The Tradition of Animal Portraiture in Humor of the Old

Southwest." Southern Folklore Quarterly 40 (1976): 195-211.

Traces the development of the depiction of animals in Twain's writings and suggests it was drawn from preceding humorists such as Harris and Longstreet as well as from African-American folk traditions.

Arpad, Joseph J. "The Fight Story: Quotation and Originality in Native American Humor." Journal of the Folklore Institute 10 (1974): 141-72.

Considers in some depth examples from American folklore and literature that seem to be remarkably similar and proposes the concept of marginal folk literature, belonging neither to oral or written culture, to describe these items and to describe the influence of print on American folklore.

Arpad, Joseph J. "John Wesley Jarvis, James Kirke Paulding and Colonel Nimrod Wildfire." New York Folklore Quarterly 21 (1955): 92-106.

Traces the development of Colonel Nimrod Wildfire back to a letter from Paulding to Jarvis requesting local color sketches about Kentucky or Tennessee manners.

Arpin, Roger C. "A. B. Gutherie's The Big Sky: The Reshaping of a Myth." Publications of the Arkansas Philological Association 3 (1977): 1-5.

Discusses the Myth of the West which concerns the mythic experience of the mountain man, American civilization's trailblazer, and Gutherie's reshaping of that myth. Suggests that Gutherie illustrates the "ironic quality that this myth has on men who participate in it and on the nature and culture victimized by it." Considers the exploitation of the Indian culture by the mountain man as dramatized by Gutherie.

Arthos, John. "Ritual and Humor in the Writings of William Faulkner." *Accent* 9 (1948): 17-30.

Discusses the presence of rituals in nearly a dozen of Faulkner's best known novels and suggests they represent a religious effort to achieve a sense of conservation. They are the necessary ceremonies for spiritual enlightenment, which Faulkner takes pains to interpret himself.

Attebery, Brian. *The Fantasy Tradition in American Literature*. Bloomington: Indiana Univ. Press, 1980. viii, 212 pp.

Traces the tradition of fantasy from folklore through modern American literature. Identifies many folkloristic characteristics of fantasy that have been adapted by literature, for example, the style and form of the fairy tale. Examines the reliance of many American authors on these conventions, including Irving, Baum, Hawthorne, Lovecraft, Cabell, and Melville.

Aubert, Alvin. "Black American Poetry, Its Language, and the Folk Tradition." *Black Academy Review* 2 (1971): 71-80.

Discusses the incorporation of Afro-American folk creations in black writers. Considers the use of spirituals, sermons, prayers, worksongs, tales, legends, the blues, and jazz in the poetry of Dunbar, Brown, Johnson, Hughes, and Baraka. "In these poems, the folk basis of Afro-American art is affirmed, not only through stylistics, but in terms of imagery and theme as well."

Audhuy, Letha. "*The Waste Land*: Myth and Symbolism in *The Great Gatsby*." *Etudes Anglaises* 33 (1980): 41-54.

Suggests that "Fitzgerald consciously and unconsciously, drew upon *The Waste Land* as a whole, to the point of making it the informing myth of the novel." Traces the parallels between the two works, one important one being their mutual reliance on the Grail story. Points out Fitzgerald's debt to Weston's From Ritual to Romance and Frazer's The Golden Bough and his use of the Fisher King motif. Explains the function of "Owl-Eyes" in Gatsby as a Tiresias figure, emulating the role of the blind soothsayer of Greek legend. Sees also an initiation ritual underlying Gatsby, in that Nick resembles the Grail knight who must ask the meaning of the various symbols displayed in the castle. Concludes that "in Eliot's myths and symbols Fitzgerald found an 'objective correlative' for his uniquely American tale."

Aycock, Wendell M. and Theodore M. Klein, eds. Classical Mythology in Twentieth-Century Thought and Literature. Lubbock: Texas Tech Press, 1980. 235 pp.

A collection of essays focusing primarily on classical literature and mythology and their general influence upon the modern world and modern thinking. Two essays are partly relevant for American literature, Fredericks's "Greek Mythology in Modern Science Fiction" and Gillis's "T. S. Eliot and Classical Tradition." The latter argues that Eliot achieves two ends by levying upon classical myths for allusory material: "a special vein of richness" and a frequent contrast between the heroic past, "especially as it is revealed in classical myth and saga," and the decadent contemporary society.

Babcock, C. Merton. "Americanisms in the Novels of Sinclair Lewis." American Speech 35 (1960): 110-16.

Lists approximately 100 terms and their definitions found in Lewis's novels that were popular folk expressions of the "roaring twenties" and that Lewis helped to preserve.

Babcock, C. Merton. "The Language of Melville's 'Isolatoes'." Western Folklore 10 (1951): 285-89.

Brief survey of some examples of sea talk found in Melville's novels and sea tales. Considers folk expressions, names, sayings, and diction incorporated by Melville to enliven his narratives to be a basic element of his style.

Babcock, C. Merton. "Melville's Backwoods Seamen." Western Folklore 10 (1951): 126-33.

Reviews folk traditions found in Moby Dick, including superstitions, proverbs, customs, and speech. Suggests "a close affinity between the types of traditions among whalemen and the types of traditions among other American frontier peoples."

Babcock, C. Merton. "Melville's Proverbs of the Sea." Western Folklore 11 (1952): 254-65.

Lists over two hundred proverbs, proverbial sayings, and sententia dealing strictly with the sea or the life of seamen found in Melville's sea novels. Argues that these colloquialisms ground Melville's lofty themes and that Melville's use of proverb lore evolved from "direct quotation to conscious paraphrase and imitation, to allusive echoes and verbal synthesis."

Babcock, C. Merton. "Melville's World's Language." Southern Folklore Quarterly 16 (1952): 177-82.

Asserts that Melville in his tales of the sea employed folk language as a means of dramatizing his democratic theme. Surveys colloquialisms, folk beliefs, proverbs, and hyperbolic expressions in Moby Dick, Mardi, and Redburn.

Babcock, C. Merton "Some Expressions from Herman Melville." Publication of the American Dialect Society 31 (1959): 3-13.

Lists ninety examples of regional idioms and locutions in Melville's prose.

Babcock, C. Merton. "The Vocabulary of *Moby Dick*." *American Speech* 27 (1952): 91-101.

Lists 150 vocabulary items, most of which are examples of Melville's use of nautical lore in his writing.

Babcock, C. Merton. "A Wordlist from Zora Neale Hurston." *Publication of the American Dialect Society* 40 (1963): 1-11.

Presents eighty words, idioms, meanings, etc. from Hurston's novels and concludes that Hurston "had the map of Dixie on her tongue," and a sensitivity to the folk patterns, beliefs, and feelings of people of Southern Florida.

Badger, Reid. "The Character and Myth of Hyacinth: A Key to *The Princess Casamassima*." *Arizona Quarterly* 32 (1976): 316-26.

Identifies several parallels between the classical myth of the youth killed by a God's discus and James's story of Hyacinth Robinson. Suggests that "both concern the tragic death of a beautiful youth who had been associating with superhuman or 'superior' persons and ideas." Connects Christina Light to Apollo and "the Western breeze of democratic eqalitarianism and revolution" to Zephyr, the West Wind. Concludes that James uses the classical allusions to argue for the importance of philosophy, poetry, and art over the "socioeconomic arrangements" that temporarily preoccupy the protagonist.

Bailey, Dennis Lee. "The Modern Novel in the Presence of Myth." Ph.D. Purdue University. 1974. 198 pp. *Dissertation Abstracts International* 35 (1975): 7292A-93A.

Develops a theory of myth as "a *structural hermeneutic*" that mediates between man and society. Discusses representative Greek and Hebrew myths, and applies this theory to Faulkner's *A Fable* and Barth's *Giles Goat-Boy*.

Bailey, J. O. "What Happens in 'The Fall of the House of Usher'?" American Literature 35 (1963-64): 445-66.

Suggests the mysterious and malevolent intrigue of "Usher" is built upon vampire lore.

Baker, Houston, A., Jr. "Black Folklore and the Black American Literary Tradition," in Long Black Song: Essays in Black American Literature and Culture (Charlottesville: University Press of Virginia, 1972), pp. 18-41.

Argues that "black folklore stands at the base of the black literary tradition" and surveys the range of important folk traditions underpinning black literature, including folk tales, religious tales, the trickster slave, folksongs, ballads, and proverbs. Suggests these traditions provide the foundation for black literary art, and notes some examples, e.g., Dunbar, Ellison, Wright, McKay, and Brown.

Baker, Ronald L. "Folk Medicine in the Writings of Rowland E. Robinson." Vermont History 37 (1969): 184-93.

Cites potions, drugs, practices used in Robinson's Vermont fiction.

Baker, Ronald L. "Folklore in the Prose Sketches of James Whitcomb Riley." Indiana English Journal 4 (1970): 3-19, 27.

Observes that Riley employed proverbs, superstitions, tales, songs and customs.

Baker, Ronald L. Folklore in The Writings of Rowland E. Robinson. Bowling Green: Bowling Green University Press, 1973. ix, 240 pp.

A comprehensive identification of folklore in the works of Robinson that follows the methodology proposed by Dorson (based on biographical, internal, and corroborative evidence). Includes some analysis as well, though more of an anthropological rather than literary perspective. Finds almost every form of Vermont folklore recorded by Robinson and considers the author to be a zealous preserver of native folklore.

Balmir, Guy-Claude. "Ecrivains et folklores negres du Nouveau Monde." Prescence Africaine 110 (1979): 49-85.

Surveys Afro-American artists, primarily of the Harlem Renaissance, and discusses their incorporation of black folklore. Considers Johnson, Dunbar, Hughes, Brown, Toomer, McKay, among others, and examines their use of spirituals, sermons, blues, folk ballads, and trickster figures. Argues that the folkloristic influence is strong and can be traced back to African heritage. Discusses as an example the relative popularity of the trickster Brer Rabbit among blacks in North and South America, the Caribbean, and Africa. Concludes that, contrary to Dorson's claim, the African connection is quite strong and that it is by studying the transformations of Afro-American folklore into literature that one has the best hope of discovering the essence of "negritude."

Banta, Martha. Henry James and the Occult: The Great Extension. Bloomington: Indiana U. P., 1972. 273 pp.

A study of supernatural phenomena as they are presented in James's works that is grounded in the literary criticism of James; its folkloristic analysis is sketchy, but it does expose the surprisingly important folkloristic underpinning of James's art by the sheer bulk of allusions to ghosts and supernatural activities and by its discussion of folkloristic genres (fairy tales, folktales) and modes (Chapter VII, "The Tale-Teller's Strategies").

Barbour, Dorothy H. "Negro Poetry in American Literature." M.A. English. Ohio University. 1943. 47 pp.

Surveys Black American poetry in order to show folk roots, specifically to folksongs.

Barbour, Frances M. "William Gilmore Simms and The Brutus Legend." _Midwest Folklore_ 7 (1957): 159-62.

Briefly points out the literary historical antecedents (Livy, Shakespeare, Lee) for Simms' use of the legend of the condemned traitorous son in his novel _The Yemassee_. Attributes the influence more to literature than to observation of folk tradition.

Barnes, Daniel R. "The Bosom Serpent: A Legend in American Literature and Culture." _Journal of American Folklore_ 85 (1972): 111-22.

Adopts Dundes's method to "account for what really happens when a serious literary artist appropriates folk materials for his art." Traces the oral heritage of the bosom serpent legends and analyzes its treatment by Thoreau and Hawthorne.

Barnes, Daniel R. "'Physical Fact' and Folklore: Hawthorne's 'Egotism; or the Bosom Serpent'." _American Literature_ 43 (1971): 117-21.

Identifies the folklore roots of Hawthorne's story, suggests it is likely based on oral belief tales, and analyzes Hawthorne's adaptation.

Barnes, Daniel R. "Telling It Slant: Emily Dickinson and the Proverb." _Genre_ 12 (1979): 219-41.

Argues that proverbs were extensively used by Dickinson in her poetry and that her use of them illustrates her poetic strategy of telling it slant. Observes that Dickinson is "prone to periphrasis" and that Dickinson acquired and perfected her poetic preference for oblique and indirect revelation through her exposure to proverbs.

Barnes, Daniel R. "Toward the Establishment of Principles for the Study of Folklore and Literature." Southern Folklore Quarterly 43 (1979): 5-16.

Argues for contextual analysis of folklore in literature and against traditional assumptions that have hampered scholarship. Examples of these faulty assumptions include the "item-centered" approach, the textual preoccupation, the "literature as repository of folklore" fallacy, and the assumption of direct authorial connection to oral tradition based on inadequate documentation.

Barnes, Madeleine. "Joel Chandler Harris's Uncle Remus: The Problem of Origins." M.A. English. University of Kansas. 1965.

Barnett, Louise K. "Alienation and Ritual in Winter in the Blood." American Indian Quarterly 4 (1978): 123-30.

Deals with ritual as "any patterned behavior whose purpose is to induce psychological well-being" and considers, accordingly, personal and communal, original and traditional, secular and sacred rituals in James Welsh's novel. Suggests that the loss of the "ordered and meaningful tribal life" produces a sense of alienation in Winter in the Blood, as illustrated in the ineffectual rituals that have survived.

Barnett, Suzanne Baugh. "Faulkner's Relation to the Humor of the Old Southwest." Journal of the Ohio Folklore Society 2 (1967): 166-179.

Discusses the similarities in technique between the folk humorists of the Southwest and

Faulkner; considers Faulkner's exposure to this tradition and certain coincidences between The Hamlet and As I Lay Dying and Harris's Sut Lovingood's Yarns.

Barrett, Leonora. "The Texas Cowboy in Literature." M.A. English. University of Texas. 1930. 230 pp.

Surveys the history, periodical literature, and dime novels devoted to the cowboy figure.

Barrick, Mac E. "The Hat Ranch: Fact, Fiction, or Folklore?" Western Folklore 34 (1975): 149-53.

Documents an attempt to find the source for a tall tale found in Peter B. Kyne's novel, The Long Chance (1914), in Erle Stanley Gardner's The Case of the Drowsy Mosquito (1943), and in Mark Twain's Roughing It (1872). Barrick has not turned up any strictly oral sources for the tale, and he tentatively concludes that the tale is ultimately literary.

Barrick, Mac E. "Proverbs and Sayings from Gibbsville, Pa.: John O'Hara's Use of Proverbial Materials." Keystone Folklore Quarterly 12 (1967): 55-80.

Lists 200 proverbs found in O'Hara's novels and concludes they form an intrinsic part of his style.

Barry, Nora Baker. "The Bear's Son Folk Tale in When the Legends Die and House Made of Dawn." Western American Literature 12 (1978): 275-87.

Identifies the Bear's son folktale, which underlies Beowulf, as underlying as well as "contemporary" novels where the protagonist is connected to a heroic cultural background." Examines specifically Hal Borland's When Legends Die and N. Scott Momaday's House Made of Dawn and traces the explicit parallels between these stories and the typological description of The Bear's Son. Concludes that the Bear's Son tale becomes a metaphor for the heroes' inner struggles and gives both novels the quality of legend.

Bassof, Bruce. "Mythic Truth and Deception in _Second Skin_." _Etudes Anglaises_ 30 (1977): 337-42.

References some allusions to classical mythology in Hawkes's novel and cites Hawkes's stated intention to make his narrator akin to godlike figures in mythology.

Bayer, John G. "Narrative Techniques and the Oral Tradition in _The Scarlet Letter_." _American Literature_ 52 (1980): 250-63.

Argues that Hawthorne manipulates the reader-narratee relationship by employing the custom-house sketch as a frame that has the rhetorical purpose of winning over his audiences. It serves as "an atavistic reminder of oral modes of composition" and "as an exordium designed to enlist reader cooperation." Suggests that Hawthorne learned this technique of oral narration from his Puritan ministering forebearers. Concludes "that _The Scarlet Letter_ is a fictional exemplar of a residually oral age."

Beard, Anne. "Games and Recreations in the Novels of Edward Eggleston." _Midwest Folklore_ 11 (1961): 85-104.

Cites and annotates eleven folk games and recreations found in seven of Eggleston's major novels. Commends Eggleston for his conscientious devotion to authentic folklore collection.

Beatty, Elsie Fleming. "Washington Irving and the Sources of His Hudson River Legends." M.A. English. Columbia University. 1923. 66 pp.

Beauchamp, Gordon. "The Rite of Initiation in Faulkner's The Bear." Arizona Quarterly 28 (1972): 319-25.

Identifies four steps in the pattern of initiation and argues that "they constitute the pattern of Ike McCaslin's experience in the wilderness." Finds not just a general awakening to the knowledge of evil but a strict pattern of action, a ritual, which is found at the center of primitive religion. Points out how Sam Fathers fulfills the role of guide or priest and that Ike is baptized in the woods. Suggests that Ike's meeting with Old Ben also resembles the rites of circumcision. Concludes, by "his journey into the water-womb of the wilderness with Sam," Ike is purified for his new life.

Beck, Horace. "Melville as a Folklife Recorder in Moby Dick." Keystone Folklore Quarterly 18 (1973): 75-88.

Draws connections between his nine-week experience as a whaleman in 1971 and the whaling activity as it is described in Moby Dick. Concludes that Melville is an accurate folklife recorder.

Behm, Richard H. "A Study of the Function of Myth in the Work of Four Contemporary Poets: Charles Simic, Galway Kinnell, Gary Snyder, and Robert Duncan." Ph.D. Bowling Green State University. 1976. 255 pp. Dissertation Abstracts International 37 (1977): 5118A.

Examines the use of historical myth-systems, and contemporarily practiced religious myth in four modern poets. Finds journey motifs in Simic, cross motifs in Kinnell, Zen and Christian myths in Snyder, and dance rituals in Duncan.

Bell, Bernard. "Folk Art and the Harlem Renaissance." Phylon 36 (1975): 155-63.

Argues that the elder statesmen of the Harlem Renaissance, Dubois, Locke, and Johnson, applied Herder's theory of the folkloristic roots of art to spirituals, sermons, blues, and jazz in order to create their new art. Reviews Du Bois's use of spirituals and his belief in "the importance of folk music as a window into the souls of a people and as the basis of a new nation's formal art." Surveys Locke's belief in the vitality of folk art and its valuable contribution to literature; "the poets of the period 'carried the folk-gift to the attitudes of art'." Discusses Johnson's exposure to Herder's esthetics and his utilization of these concepts in The Autobiography of an Ex-Colored Man, which concerns a songwriter who wishes to write symphonic music based on old slave songs and which includes the folk characters of an old preacher and a singer of spirituals.

Bell, Bernard. The Folk Roots of Contemporary Afro-American Poetry. Detroit: Broadside Press, 1974. 80 pp.

Reviews 1) the distinctions between high art and folk art, 2) the principal theory of folk art that influenced 19th century Anglo-American writers (Herder), and 3) the ideas about and techniques of folk art that influenced modern black writers (including ballads, sermons, spirituals, gospels, blues, and jazz).

Bell, Robert E. "How Mark Twain Comments on Society through Use of Folklore." Mark Twain Journal 10 (1955): 1-8, 24-25.

Investigates Twain's use of the folk hero pattern, the tall-tale pattern, and the supernatural pattern in a number of works; concludes Twain had an active interest in folklore and an intimate connection to the folk traditions of the Mississippi valley, and that Twain used the folk patterning and techniques to critique intrinsic shortcomings in American society.

Belli, Angela. "The Use of Greek Mythological Themes and Characters in Twentieth Century Drama: Four Approaches." Ph.D. New York University. 1965. 280 pp. Dissertation Abstracts International 27 (1967): 3832A.

Identifies four approaches by playwrights in their use of mythological material: psychological metaphors, religious and philosophical expressions, depictions of rebellion, and modern political and social statements. Considers O'Neill, Williams, Eliot, Anderson, and others.

Bennet, Paul L. "Folklore and the Literature to Come." Journal of American Folklore 65 (1952): 23-27.

Sees three relationships of folklore to literature: folklore directly as literature; folklore modified as formal literature; folklore as reference in production of literature. Argues that folklore of the nature and quality of redacted folk-songs, ballads, fables, and myths is synonymous with literature.

Bennett, S. N. "Ornament and Environment: Uses of Folklore in Willa Cather's Fiction." Tennessee Folklore Society Bulletin 40 (1974): 95-102.

Traces the development of Cather's use of folklore--primarily customs--in My Antonia, Death Comes for the Archbishop, and Shadows on the Rock. Argues that Cather learned to re-create folk materials as functioning elements in her novels in order to illustrate the clash of cultures.

Berbrich, Joan D. Three Voices from Paumanok: The Influence of Long Island on James Fenimore Cooper, William Cullen Bryant, and Walt Whitman. Port Washington: Ira J. Friedman, Inc., 1969. xvii, 225 pp.

In surveying the biographical histories of Cooper, Bryant, and Whitman some brief mention is made of the influence of Long Island folklore (e.g., whaling legends and customs) on these authors.

Bewley, Marius. "Scott Fitzgerald's Criticism of America." Sewanee Review 62 (1954): 223-46.

Asserts that Gatsby was a "mythic" character and that Daisy had become a legend in Gatsby's mind. Concludes that The Great Gatsby is a damaging criticism of America because "Gatsby, the 'mythic' embodiment of the American dream, is shown to us in all his immature romanticism."

Bigelow, Gordon E. "Marjorie Kinnan Rawlings' 'Lord Bill of the Suwannee River'." Southern Folklore Quarterly 27 (1963): 113-31.

Points out that Rawlings' character "Lord Bill" is a mixture of part legend, part history, and part fiction, all based on an engaging and memorable character who lived on the Florida frontier.

Blackwell, Louise. "Eudora Welty: Proverbs and Proverbial Phrases in The Golden Apples." Southern Folklore Quarterly 30 (1966): 332-41.

Examines the extensive use of proverbs in "Shower of Gold" as compared to other short works by Welty in The Golden Apples. Concludes that it is evidence of Welty's skillful handling of folk speech to create the character of the first person narrator in the story, Mrs. Katie Rainey.

Blair, Walter. Native American Humor. San Francisco: Chandler Publishing Company, 1960. Revised reprint of Native American Humor (1800-1900) (New York: American Book Company, 1937). 565 pp.

Surveys American humorists in some detail and recognizes their considerable reliance upon folk humor, conventions, and dialect. Discusses tale tall form and exaggeration as important characteristics of American literary humor as evidenced in works by Thorpe, Harris, Twain and others.

Blair, Walter. "Traditions in Southern Humor." American Quarterly 5 (1953): 132-42.

Argues that the best Southern humor is derived in part from Southern folklore, as expressed in the folk's conception of the best jokes, anecdotes, sketches, and tales.

Blake, Susan L. "Folklore and Community in Song of Solomon." MELUS 7 (1980): 77-82

Points out a well-known Gullah folktale that underlies Toni Morrison's novel. Argues that the tale becomes "both the end of, and a metaphor for, the protagonist's identity quest," and that Morrison calls attention through her use of folklore to the relationship between individual identity and community. Both the folktale and the protagonist's quests represent a return to the origins of community. Concludes that Morrison views the concept of political community as perverse because it violates the concept of personal community, the relationships of kin, friends, neighbors, as created and revealed by folklore.

Blake, Susan L. "Modern Black Writers and the Folk Traditon." Ph.D. University of Connecticut. 1976. 207 pp. Dissertation Abstracts International 38 (1977): 260A.

Rejects the idea of a folk tradition in black literature. Argues, instead, that there is a shared subject concerning black oppression that is treated by both folk storytellers and modern writers. Examines the fiction of Chesnutt, Hurston, Hughes, and Ellison, and suggests each has a different understanding of both oppression and the stance of folklore towards it. Suggests that Hurston uses folklore to characterize personal liberation, Ellison fits folklore into a pattern of Western myth, Chesnutt eschews the theoretical method of folk tradition, and Hughes uses it as a force for revolution.

Blake, Susan L. "Old John in Harlem: The Urban Folktales of Langston Hughes." Black American Literature Forum 14 (1980): 100-04.

Observes that Hughes reshapes folklore and makes it work in the present. His character Simple "is the migrant descendent of John the militant slave of black folklore." Points out that Hughes's fictional editorials about Simple follow the pattern of the John tales in characterization and conflict, include traditional motifs, and recreate the relationship between oral story teller and audience. Argues that, like a folk story teller, Hughes speaks of and to the group and that he uses his understanding of folklore "to bind black people together in a real community, united by their recognition of common experience into a force to control." Concludes that "Hughes picks up the folk tradition and carries it on toward the goal of social change in the real world."

Blake, Susan L. "Ritual and Rationalization: Black Folklore in the Works of Ralph Ellison." PMLA 94 (1979): 121-35.

Argues that Ellison uses black folklore in Invisible Man in order to illustrate both the uniqueness and the universality of black experience, especially in their quest for cultural identity. See PMLA, 95 (1980): 107-09 for responses to Blake's argument.

Block, Haskell. "Cultural Anthropology and Contemporary Literary Criticism," in Vickery, ed., Myth and Literature, pp. 129-36. Also in Journal of Aesthetics and Art Criticism 11 (1952): 46-54.

Proposes that the role of cultural anthropology in contemporary literary criticism is of special significance because it provides a cultural index to the great thinkers of our time. Reviews the development of the study of cultural anthropology, especially in the myth-ritual school and the Cambridge school, and then considers the practical applications of anthropology to literary analysis. Suggests we can use folklore to elucidate difficult passages and to "recapture the spirit of now forgotten rites which lend passion and purpose" to life. Concludes that despite the muddiness now associated with the term myth, if we use the term precisely, it can help us understand the origin, structure, and function of literature.

Bluestein, Gene. "'The Arkansas Traveler' and the Strategy of American Humor." _Western Folklore_ 21 (1962): 153-60.

Analyzes the satiric use of "The Arkansas Traveler" by Twain and other Southwestern humorists; suggests the city/country rivalry in the folk versions is expanded into a new world/old world rivalry by the literary authors.

Bluestein, Gene. "Constance Rourke and the Folk Sources of American Literature." _Western Folklore_ 26 (1967): 77-87.

Discusses the theoretical premises underlying Rourke's position and agrees with Rourke that the contribution of American folklore to American literature is what makes it unique.

Bluestein, Gene. _The Voice of the Folk: Folklore and American Literary Theory_. Amherst: University of Massachusetts Press, 1972. 170 pp.

Explains Johann Gottfried von Herder's theories and how they affected Emerson and Whitman. Argues that the essence of a nation's character is in folk tradition, and that the major value of a national literature lies in its ability to recreate the folk tradition. The study is ultimately concerned with showing the Americanness of American folklore and literature and discussing Emerson's and Whitman's utilization of and contribution to this process of Americanization.

Boatright, Mody C. "The American Myth Rides the Range: Owen Wister's Man on Horseback." Southwest Review 36 (1951): 157-63. Published also in Mody Boatright, Folklorist, Ernest B. Speck, ed., (Austin: University of Texas Press, 1973), pp. 80-91.

Discusses the essential qualities of the mythic cowboy hero--prowess and cleverness--and examines how this figure is presented in Wister's fiction. Considers also the folk belief of Anglo-Saxon racial superiority in The Virginian and Philosophy Four.

Boatright, Mody C. Folk Laughter on The American Frontier. New York: Collier Books, 1961. 191 pp.

Reviews a wide variety of frontier folk humor, including tall lying and folk speech, and notes its inevitable influence on journalism and printed literature.

Boatright, Mody C. "The Formula in Cowboy Fiction and Drama." Western Folklore 28 (1969): 136-45.

Identifies the formulaic plots of cowboy fiction and suggests they correspond to traditional heroic patterns.

Bonner, Willard Hallam. "Cooper and Captain Kidd." Modern Language Notes 61 (1946): 21-27.

Suggests that Cooper was not only familiar with the Kidd legend, but that he drew upon it significantly in several tales, especially The Sea Lions and The Water Witch.

Boswell, George W. "The Folklore Basis of Literature." Tennessee Folklore Society Bulletin 27 (1961): 43-45.

Briefly points out that the world's great literature is indebted to folklore and that writers inevitably profit from using folklore.

Boswell, George W. "Folkways in Faulkner." Mississippi Folklore Register 1 (1967): 83-90.

Surveys folk speech, proverbs, songs, customs, beliefs, and medicine in various Faulkner novels and concludes that "Faulkner's life was one extended folkway."

Boswell, George W. "The Legendary Background in Faulkner's Work." Tennessee Folklore Society Bulletin 36 (1970): 53-63.

Points out four separate Faulknerian uses of legend: entertainment, characterization, vitality, and allegory. Distinguishes legend from myth and other folklore; suggests oral culture is deeply embedded in Faulkner's thought, and identifies a great many folkloric legends underlying Faulkner's stories.

Boswell, George W. "Notes on the Surnames of Faulkner's Characters." Tennessee Folklore Society Bulletin 36 (1970): 64-66.

Briefly points out possible folk etymologies for surnames employed by Faulkner.

Boswell, George W. "Traditional Verse and Musical Influence on Faulkner." Notes on Mississippi Writers 1 (1968): 23-31.

Argues that not a little of Faulkner's success is due to his folk roots. Reviews Faulkner's exposure to folk music, folkways, superstitions, tales, folk drama, epic, and mythology and then traces occurrences of folk music and instruments in Faulkner's novels.

Boswell, Jackson Campbell. "Bosom Serpents before Hawthorne: Origin of a Symbol." English Language Notes 12 (1975): 279-87.

Finds strictly literary sources.

Boykin, Carol. "Sut's Speech: The Dialect of a 'Nat'ral Borned' Mountaineer." The Lovingood Papers 1965: 36-42.

Concludes that Sut "talked like" a true East Tennessean and that Harris' variant spellings are phonetically accurate.

Breitkreuz, Hartmut. "John Braine's Proverbs." Western Folklore 31 (1972): 130-131.

Lists proverbs in Life at the Top.

Brewster, Paul. "Jurgen and Figures and Earth and the Russian Skazki." American Literature 13 (1942): 305-19.

Identifies three influences of the Russian skazki on Cabell: similarity in language; direct borrowing of motifs; and borrowings of names.

Bridgman, Richard. The Colloquial Style in American Literature. New York: Oxford University Press, 1966. 254 pp.

Analyzes vernacular grammar and style and then discusses its adaptation by James, Twain, Stein, and Hemingway. Argues that writers first had to learn regional and social dialects and dialogue before they could be refined and stylized in prose.

Brodsky, Sylvia. "The John Brown Legend in American Literature." M.A. English. University of North Carolina. 1943. 126 pp.

Brookes, Stella Brewer. Joel Chandler Harris--Folklorist. Athens: Univ. of Georgia Press, 1950. xv, 182 pp.

Reviews Harris's exposure to folklore as a discipline and concludes that he was one of America's first folklore collectors which led him unsuspectingly into the discipline. Analyzes the occurrence of trickster tales, myths, supernatural tales, proverbs, folkways, dialect, and songs in the Uncle Remus stories.

Brophy, Robert J. Robinson Jeffers: Myth, Ritual, and Symbol in His Narrative Poems. Cleveland: The Press of Case Western Reserve U., 1973. xviii, 321 pp.

Presents detailed readings of six poems by Jeffers and concentrates on his use of myth and ritual patterns. Identifies primarily Biblical, Roman, Greek, and Teutonic allusions which spring from Jeffers' educational background. Notes Jeffers' reliance on "the highly ritualistic pattern of the primitive year-god ritual" and his frequent use of characters, images, plots, and symbols drawn from mythologies of the world. Argues that Jeffers creates his own myth because he has a "sacramental-ritualistic perception," he sees "the same patterns, uniform and repeated endlessly," and that he employs mythological allusions "because they help express his vision with a wealth of corroborating allusion."

Brown, Ashley. "Eudora Welty and the Mythos of Summer." Shenandoah 20/3 (Spring, 1969): 29-35.

Defends The Robber Bridegroom as a beautiful example of romance and suggests that it takes place in a world "where the hero is associated with spring and the enemy with winter and darkness." Considers the work to be a rewriting of a European fairy tale in an American setting. Points out that Welty draws upon the lore of the American frontier rather freely.

Brown, Calvin S. "Faulkner's Use of the Oral Tradition." Georgia Review 22 (1968): 160-69.

Considers Faulkner's reliance upon tall tale, history, folk speech, and comic exaggeration in his writing.

Brown, Carl R. V. "Journey to Ixtlan: Inside the American Indian Oral Tradition." Arizona Quarterly 32 (1976): 138-45.

Argues that the philosophical vision of Don Juan is consonant with American Indian oral tradition and is contrasted with the print and fact oriented perspective of the apprentice and his Western civilization. Presents a general discussion of the premises of oral tradition including the use of silence, the nature of appearance versus reality, the importance of responsibility and ecological concern, the value of dreams, and the meaning of death. The folkloristic discussion remains quite general, however. Concludes that Castaneda's dialectical characterization of the relative merits of oral versus printed culture is alluring, but it is overly simplified, distorted, and biased: "We are capable of synthesizing the oral and literate influence into a truly more wholesome world view."

Brown, Jane Gibson. "The Early Novels of Caroline Gordon: Myth and History as a Fictional Technique." Southern Review 13 (1977): 289-98.

Points out Gordon's reliance on Aristotle and Dante and her allusions to the Trojan War as a counterpart to the Civil War in The Garden of Adonis. Conludes that it is in myth that Gordon unites all the diverse elements of her fiction.

Brown, Sterling A. "Background of Folklore in Negro Literature," in Alan Dundes, ed., Mother Wit From the Laughing Barrel (Englewood Cliffs; Prentice-Hall, 1973), pp. 39-44. Also in Jackson College Bulletin 2 (1953): 26-30.

Examines the prejudicial treatments of Negro folklore by white writers who use folklore to foster stereotypical images and attitudes, for example, Joel Chandler Harris.

Browne, Ray B. "The Affirmation of 'Bartleby'," in D. K. Wilgus, ed., *Folklore International: Essays in Traditional Literature, Belief, and Custom in Honor of Wayland Debs Hand* (Hatboro: Folklore Associates, Inc., 1967), pp. 11-22.

Points out allusions in "Bartleby" to stock national character types, to legendary heroes (Gawain, Launcelot), and to the resurrection of the mythic hero (Christ). Concludes that Melville attempts (not entirely successfully) to make Bartleby into the universal hero-savior of world folklore and mythology and that the story gains great power from its use of mythology and folklore.

Browne, Ray B. "'Popular' and Folk Songs: Unifying Force in Garland's Autobiographical Works." *Southern Folklore Quarterly* 25 (1961): 153-55.

Suggests Garland is note-worthy for his recreation of Middle Border life which is most strikingly dramatized through his use of folk songs. Documents Garland's personal connection to the songs of his era and examines his incorporation of these songs into his novels.

Browne, Ray B. "The Oft-Told *Twice-Told Tales*: The Folklore Motifs." *Southern Folklore Quarterly* 22 (1958): 69-85.

Discusses the similarity to folktales in many of the narratives in *Twice-Told Tales*, and suggests the echoes of other stories enriches these tales.

Browne, Ray B. "Popular Theater in *Moby Dick*," in Ray B. Browne, *et al*, eds., *New Voices in American Studies* (Purdue Univ. Studies, 1966), pp. 89-99.

Points out evidence of the influence of the "spirit of burlesque" in Melville's narrative, for example, in his jokes and dramatic situations which imitated popular theater.

Bruner, Jerome S. "Myth and Identity," in Henry A. Murray, Myth and Mythmaking (New York: George Braziller, 1960), pp. 276-287.

Attempts to reveal the purpose of myth (in general) to create individual identity and suggests modern literature (e.g., Kerouac, Amis, Osborne, Hemingway, Fitzgerald) have taken on this mythic function.

Brunvand, Jan Harold. "From Western Folklore to Fiction in the Stories of Charles M. Russell." Western Review 5/1 (1968): 41-49.

Distinguishes between folklore and fakelore, and then traces the evidence of Western folklore in Russell's forty-four stories. Finds proverbial comparisons, anecdotes, and a basic oral narrative esthetic in Russell's stories.

Brunvand, Jan Harold. "Sailors' and Cowboys' Folklore in Two Popular Classics." Southern Folklore Quarterly 29 (1965): 266-83.

Discusses folk speech, rituals, and habits in Dana's Two Years Before the Mast and Adams' The Log of a Cowboy. Suggests that they have become classics because they are true to the life and folklore of their subjects.

Bryant, Katie. "The Slavery of Dialect Exemplified in Mark Twain's Works." Mark Twain Journal 19/3 (1979): 5-8.

Correlates the dialects assigned to Huck and Jim to their low socio-economic status. Suggests that Twain used the dialect as a way of socially branding his characters and as a commentary on the prejudical treatment of disadvantaged members of society. Concludes that the "unfairness of such a situation was so dreadfully repugnant to Twain, in fact, that he used some of his best-known characters to protest it."

Bryant, Loy Y. "The Pocahontas Theme in American Literature." M.A. English. University of North Carolina. 1935. 151 pp.

A thorough survey of the literary treatments of the folk legend of Pocahontas, primarily by obscure novelists, dramatists, and poets (notable exceptions include Lindsay and Crane).

Brylowski, Walter. _Faulkner's Olympian Laugh: Myth in the Novels_. Detroit: Wayne State University Press, 1968. 236 pp.

Identifies four levels of myth apparent in Faulkner's work: 1) allusion and analogy 2) plot (or mythos) 3) "mythic mode of thought" 4) the "myth of the South." Attempts "to trace a progression through Faulkner's works of his coming to grips with the problem of evil in terms of this mythic mode of thought." Suggests there is an evolving mythic consciousness in the chronological development of Faulkner's works that moves from allusion to myth, to mythic plot, to mythic thought, and examines from this perspective Faulkner's literary canon in some detail.

Budahl, Leon A. "Edwin Arlington Robinson: A Modern Concept of the Arthurian Legend." M.A. Education. Mankato State College. 1963.

Budd, Louis J. "Gentlemanly Humorists of the Old South." _Southern Folklore Quarterly_ 17 (1953): 232-40.

Discusses five Southern humorists and their special link to Southern culture.

Burch, Beth. "Shades of Golden Fleece: "Faulkner's Jason Once Again." Notes on Mississippi Writers 12 (1980): 55-62.

Argues that in The Sound and the Fury Faulkner drew extensively upon myth, specifically "the Eden myth, the Christian myth, and various classical myths such as Semiramis and Euboleus and the swan. Focuses on Faulkner's evoking of the legend of Jason and the Golden Fleece in the characterization of Jason Compson. Suggests that "the stories of both Jason's reiterate the themes of birthright and heritage, sacrifice and acquisition, the interloper and the triumphant female, and exile and sterility." Traces the parallel development of these themes through both stories. Concludes that the use of myth implies a pessimistic reading of The Sound and the Fury and colors the novel with a universality "which obviates time and space."

Burch, Beth and Paul W. Burch. "Myth on Myth: Bernard Malamud's 'The Talking Horse'." Studies in Short Fiction 16 (1979): 350-53.

Observes that Malamud mixes Greek myth and Judaic theology, "creating a crosshatching of mythologies and allusions which are as confounding as they are enlightening." Points out Goldberg's connection to Poseidon and Abramowitz's connection to the unicorn. Concludes that perhaps through the fusion of the myths Malamud indicates the futility of man's relationship with God.

Burke, Kenneth. "Myth, Poetry, and Philosophy." Journal of American Folklore 73 (1960): 283-306.

A wide ranging discussion of the combat myth inspired by Fontenrose's Python; posits this myth as a fundamental formal organization for folklore and literature.

Burkholder, Robert E. "The Uses of Myth in Pat Conroy's The Great Santini." Critique 21/1 (1979): 31-37.

Proposes that in _The Great Santini_ "individual myths seem to consume the characters, functioning as ways of perceiving the world and as cushions against the reality that myths seem to ignore." Suggests that Lillian focuses her Baptist zeal on the icons and rituals of Catholicism in much the same way as Bull focuses his energy on the trappings and traditions of the Marine Corps. Argues that the characters hide behind these rituals and stereotypical role models, behind which lie their most human selves.

Burrison, John A. _The Golden Arm: The Folk Tale and Its Literary Use by Mark Twain and Joel C. Harris_. Atlanta: Georgia State College, 1968. vii, 67 pp.

A short study of the American variant of Tale Type 366. Identifies the folk narrative and traces its influence on both Twain and Harris. Twain used it in _How to Tell a Story and Other Essays_, and Harris presented it in _Nights With Uncle Remus_. Observes that both Twain and Harris reproduced the tale almost exactly as they found it in Negro tradition. Twain uses it to illustrate a story-telling technique, while Harris places it in a natural context of a plantation tale-telling session. "Both writers present the tale for its inherent entertainment value, without any symbolic, allegorical, or propagandistic overtures." Argues that "as a rule, the simpler the intent of the author and the closer that intent is to that of the folklore being used, the better the use is." Concludes, however, that "The Golden Arm" is "ear literature."

Bush, Jr., Sargent. "Bosom Serpents Before Hawthorne: The Origins of a Symbol." _American Literature_ 43 (1971): 181-99.

Examines the bosom serpent tradition and notes its popularity in oral legend, newspapers, obscure medical case histories, and other texts; suggests it was a combination of these influences that encouraged Hawthorne to write "Egotism."

Buxbaum, Katherine Louise. "An Analysis of the Vernacular in Mark Twain's Mississippi Valley Stories." M.A. English. University of Chicago. 1924. 58 pp.

Byers, Kansas. "The Arthurian Legend in American Literature." M. A. English. University of North Carolina. 1924. 104 pp.

Byrd, James W. "Zora Neale Hurston: A Novel Folklorist." Tennessee Folklore Society Bulletin 21 (1955): 37-41.

Gives examples of Hurston's use of folklore, especially folk speech and custom, and evaluates her as one of the most authentic folk novelists of the South.

Cady, Earl Addison. "Folklore in the Works of Donn Byrne." M.A. English. University of Nebraska. 1930. 112 pp.

Callahan, John F. The Illusions of a Nation: Myth and History in the Novels of F. Scott Fitzgerald. Urbana: U. of Illinois Press, 1972. vii, 221 pp.

Presents a loose discussion of myth as the underlying concerns of a nation (for example, Lewis' American Adam) and examines how they are expressed in The Great Gatsby, Tender is the Night, and other novels.

Cameron, Kenneth Walter. "Emerson, Thoreau, Elegant Extracts, and Proverb Lore." Emerson Society Quarterly 6 (1957): 28-39.

Identifies some of Emerson's favorite proverbs as they are found in Elegant Extracts.

Cameron, Kenneth Walter. "Emerson's Arabian Proverbs." Emerson Society Quarterly 13 (1958): 50.

Lists fifty Arabic proverbs that Emerson was apparently fond of.

Campbell, Jeanne. "Falling Stars: Myth in 'The Red One'." Jack London Newsletter 11 (1978): 86-96.

Analyzes London's short story from a Jungian mythic perspective. Concentrates on the archetypal symbolism with no folkloristic documentation.

Campbell, Joseph. The Masks of the God: Creative Mythology. New York: The Viking Press, 1968. 730 pp.

A wide ranging discussion of myth and literature that considers many modern writers who have used myths.

Campbell, Joseph. "Mythological Themes in Creative Literature and Art," in Campbell, ed., Myths, Dreams, and Religion, (New York: E. P. Dutton & Co., 1970), pp. 138-175.

Although mostly a discussion of the functions of myth, it traces evidence of these themes in poems by T. S. Eliot and Robinson Jeffers.

Campbell, Marie. "Witch-Riding in Huckleberry Finn." Journal of the Ohio Folklore Society 2 (1967): 191-99.

Applies Dorson's methodology of studying folklore in literature by documenting the folkloric credentials, as found in various collections, of Jim's account of being ridden by witches in Huckleberry Finn and of using a nickel as a charm; also examines biographical evidence of Twain's exposure to African-American traditions. Concludes that Twain used the folk motif for local color, humor, and as an indication of change in the character of Jim.

Cannon, Agnes Dicken. "Melville's Use of Sea Ballads and Songs." Western Folklore 23 (1964): 1-16.

Documents Melville's autobiographical connection to folk music and argues that Melville uses this traditional material in three ways: to convey realistic description; to indicate a character's state of mind or emotional mood; and to express deeper meaning and symbolism through his reworking of the material. Gives numerous examples.

Carey, George G. "Folk Motifs in the Writings of John Josselyn." M.A. Folklore. Indiana University. 1962. 110 pp.

Carey, George G. "Folklore from the Printed Sources of Essex Country, Massachusetts." Southern Folklore Quarterly 32 (1968): 17-43.

Documents folklore from early 19th century Massachusetts that influenced Whittier, as evidenced by his own published collections of folk legends and beliefs in 1831 and 1846.

Carey, George G. "John Greenleaf Whittier and Folklore: The Search for a Traditional American Past." New York Folklore Quarterly 27 (1971): 113-29.

A biographical sketch that emphasizes the importance of active folk sources for his poems. Discusses legends, supernaturalism, folk beliefs, and rituals underlying Whittier's literary works.

Carey, George G. "Whittier's Roots in a Folk Culture." Essex Institute Historical Collections 104 (1968): 3-18.

Views Whittier in the context of New England storytelling and explains his folk cultural mileau and his motivation behind Legends of New England and The Supernaturalism of New England.

Examines oral storytelling as it was practiced in the Whittier household and discusses its influence on Whittier's writing. Considers also his exposure to folk storytelling on the Isles of Shoals. Analyzes these folk influences on "Snow-bound."

Carkeet, David. "The Dialects in Huckleberry Finn." _American Literature_ 51 (1979): 315-32.

Examines the dialects of the characters in _Huckleberry Finn_ in order to show that there are seven distinct dialects spoken by white characters, just as Twain asserts.

Castille, Philip. "Women and Myth in Faulkner's First Novel." _Tulane Studies in English_ 23 (1978): 175-86.

Argues that in _Soldier's Pay_, Faulkner employs "the mythical method,", i.e., "the use of mythological lore and imagery to create ironic parallels between primitive and modern life," as a way to dramatize his theme of human sterility in the midst of natural abundance. Identifies the myth of Diana and Hippolytus, as described in Frazer's _The Golden Bough_, as a source for Faulkner's narrative. Shows "that Emmy and Donald Mahon resemble Diana and Hippolytus, that Margaret Powers and Cecily Sounders resemble Egeria and Aphrodite, and that all of these relationships are savagely inverted." The ironic inversions of the myths support Faulkner's vision of "man's disjunction from the natural world and his loss of contact with his regenerative powers."

Chambers, Rae. "The Yankee in the American Drama before the Civil War." M.A. English. Brooklyn College. 1940.

Chapin, Helen Geracimos. "Mythology and American Realism: Studies in Fiction by Henry Adams, Henry James, and Kate Chopin." Ph.D. Ohio State University. 1975. 356 pp. _Dissertation Abstracts Internation_ 36 (1975): 3646A.

Analyzes the use of earth mother and goddess archetypes in works by Henry Adams, Henry James, and Kate Chopin. Points out the context of vegetation rituals and seasonal cycles latent in the works, as well as numerous allusions to Greek and Latin myth. Observes that this mythic influence is used to counterbalance the realistic preoccupation of the authors.

Chapman, Arnold. "Pampas and Big Woods: Heroic Initiation in Guiraldes and Faulkner." _Comparative Literature_ 11 (1959): 61-77.

Compares _The Bear_ with _Don Segundo Sombra_ and concludes they are both allegorical stories of initiation rituals employing folk speech and local color.

Chase, Richard. _Herman Melville_. New York: Macmillan, 1949. xii, 305 pp.

A wide ranging biographical and critical study that discusses Melville's use of traditional materials among other topics. Treats his use of legendary frontier folk heroes from America (see especially pp. 64-74) and Yankee pedlars (see pp. 192-96).

Chase, Richard. "Melville's _Confidence Man_." _Kenyon Review_ 11 (1949): 122-40.

Considers _The Confidence-Man_ to be a book of folklore. Sees the main character as a composite of the Yankee pedlar and the Western rustic.

Chase, Richard. _Quest for Myth_. Baton Rouge: Louisiana State U. P., 1949. xi, 150 pp.

Although it does not consider examples from American literature, it represents a fundamental introduction to the study of folklore and literature. Surveys approaches to mythology and considers their relevance to literary criticism.

Chatman, Seymour. "Five Versions of Tristram and Iseult in English and American Literature." M.A. English. Wayne State University. 1949.

Cherry, Fannye N. "The Sources of Hawthorne's 'Young Goodman Brown'." American Literature 5 (1934): 341-348.

Proposes that Hawthorne's tale contains no authentic doctrines of magic and Maleficium from the witch creeds of England and America. The main sources of the tale and its magic are an article on "Witch Ointment" that Hawthorne read and a story by Cervantes.

Chittick, Kathryn A. "The Fables in William Faulkner's A Fable." Mississippi Quarterly 30 (1977): 403-15.

Argues that just as Christian mythology has produced a body of European romance and fable, "whose structures mimic the patterns of the Old and New Testament stories in a non-theological way, so Faulkner has created his own fable by drawing upon the Christ story and other stories sacred to the Western mind." Sees a parallel between the legend of the "golden youth" in the novel and Christ's retreat to the wilderness. States that the story also bears "a striking resemblance to an apocryphal version of the conception of Christ." Sees finally the legend of Lucifer as underlying the presentation of the character of the General, because he tempts the corporal just as Lucifer tempts Christ.

Christensen, Claude Hansen. "The Tristram Story in Edward Arlington Robinson's 'Tristram'." M.A. English. University of Chicago. 1928.

Christiansen, Reidar Th. "Myth, Metaphor, and Simile." Journal of American Folklore 68 (1955): 417-27.

Traces the parallel use of metaphor in folk and literary riddles. Observes that the differences between the metaphors of individual roots and those of folklore are that the latter have been assimilated by tradition and are subject to the laws which determine traditional matter. Concludes the folk and literary riddles are essentially the same, although the latter tend to be characterized by over-elaboration.

Church, Margaret. "Faulkner and Frazer: The Bear." International Fiction Review 7 (1980): 126.

Briefly points out parallels between The Bear and Frazer's accounts of bear sacrifices in primitive tribes.

Clagett, John H. "The Maritime Works of James Fenimore Cooper as Sources for Sea Lore, Sea Legend, and Sea Idiom." Southern Folklore Quarterly 30 (1966): 323-31.

Reviews Cooper's biographical experiences with the sea and then investigates evidence of authentic sea lore in his twelve sea novels. Concludes that Cooper's work is imbued with nautical folklore.

Clark, Charles C. "The Robber Bridegroom: Realism and Fantasy on the Natchez Trace." Mississippi Quarterly 26 (1973): 625-38.

Argues that contrary to critical opinion, Welty's "novella contains much irony, the greatest irony being that what appears to be an amusing fictional amalgam of history, frontier humor, folklore, and fairy tale is actually a statement of the predicament of man." Points out Welty's liberal borrowing from the Brothers Grimm, as well as her use of Baron Munchausen stories, the Cupid and Psyche myth, and Mississippi folklore and legend. Traces these borrowings and parallels through the work and concludes that Welty uses them ultimately to reaffirm the philosophical vision of fairy tales and myths which provide a means of transcending the universal tragedy of man.

Clark, James W. Jr. "Washington Irving and New England Witchlore." New York Folklore Quarterly 29 (1973): 304-13.

Contends Irving's favorite material was New England witchlore, and investigates Irving's main sources, which include Cotton Mather's Magnolia Christi.

Clark, Joseph D. "Burke Davis as Folklorist." North Carolina Folklore 19 (1971): 59-65.

Classifies varieties of folklore (customs, songs, diction, proverbs) in the folksy tales of The Summer Land.

Clark, William Bedford. "A Mediation on Folk History: The Dramatic Structure of Robert Penn Warren's The Ballad of Billie Potts." American Literature 49 (1977-78): 635-45.

Analyzes Warren's treatment of a folk narrative from Kentucky, and identifies the language, similes, characterizations, and plot of Warren's work as folkloric, which makes The Ballad essentially an oral history of the folk.

Clark, William Glen. "Superstition in the Works of Mark Twain." M.A. English. State University of Iowa. 1949. 104 pp.

Clarke, Kenneth. "Jesse Stuart's Use of Folklore," in J. R. LeMaster & Mary Washington Clarke, eds., Jesse Stuart: Essays on His Work (Lexington: Univ. of Kentucky, 1977), pp. 117-29.

Presents a cross-section of folkloristic allusions in Stuart's fiction, including tokens, birdlore, and frog-trouncing. Reveals the variety of folklore elements in Stuart's works and the ways in which it serves the author's literary purposes. Concludes that as a result of Stuart's familiarity with the folklore of Kentucky, he is able to present an authentic American literature.

Clarke, Mary Washington. "As Jesse Stuart Heard It in Kentucky." Kentucky Folklore Record 9 (1963): 75-86.

Identifies over one hundred examples of Stuart's use of folk speech in his novels.

Clarke, Mary Washington. "Jesse Stuart Reflects Kentucky Lore of Tokens and Ghosts." Kentucky Folklore Record 9 (1963): 41-46.

Cites over a dozen examples of Stuart's use of folk legends, superstitions, and supernatural visitations.

Clarke, Mary Washington. Jesse Stuart's Kentucky. New York: McGraw-Hill, 1963. x, 240 pp.

An extensive consideration of the link between the folklore of the Kentucky hill community and the writing of Jesse Stuart. Considers the appearance of a wide range of customs, beliefs, expressions, and oral narratives from Kentucky folk in Stuart's fiction.

Clarke, Mary Washington. "Jesse Stuart's Writings Preserve Passing Folk Idiom." Southern Folklore Quarterly 28 (1964): 157-98.

Lists some 200 examples of folk idiom found in Stuart's prose.

Clarke, Mary Washington. "Proverbs, Proverbial Phrases, and Proverbial Comparisons in the Writings of Jesse Stuart." Southern Folklore Quarterly 29 (1965): 142-63.

Indexes by topic over one hundred proverbial sayings found in Stuart's writings.

Clayton, Lawrence. "Hamlin Garland's Negative Use of Folk Elements." Folklore Forum 6 (1973): 107-8.

Suggests that Garland uses the folk materials in Rose of Dutcher's Coolly and Main-Traveled Roads to provide part of the texture of real life in these works. Argues further that the treatment of this folklore reveals Garland's negative attitude toward rural folklife, which consists in his view of hard work, sore muscles, and bleeding hands.

Cleary, Micheal. "Finding the Center of the Earth: Satire, History, and Myth in Little Big Man." Western American Literature 15 (1980): 195-211.

Examines Berger's novel as a reflection of mythic thought. Focuses upon the satiric conventions of the novel and examines Berger's parody of Western conventions. Specifically exposes Berger's parodic treatment of Indian bravery rituals and cowboy mannerisms in order to invert Indian stereotypes and the Western cowboy hero myth. Concludes that Berger is primarily criticizing white society because it has forgotten what it is to be a human being "at the center of the earth," which is "a Cheyenne concept which expresses one's awareness of the circular nature of things."

Cleveland, William Henry. "American History and Folklore in Vachel Lindsay's Poetry." M.A. English. University of Texas. 1939. 209 pp.

Clipper, Lawrence, J. "Folkloric and Mythic Elements in Invisible Man." College Language Association Journal 13 (1970): 229-41.

Argues that _Invisible Man_ arrives at the truth about the human condition with all the bright magic of a fairy tale. Discusses how closely Ellison's central plot situations parallel the central structural motifs of situations of the typical folktale. Finds a close resemblance between _Invisible Man_ and Propp's morphology. Examines also Ellison's folkloristic context, and discusses his reading of Raglan and his use of Raglan's list of the twenty-two characteristics of heroic legend. Concludes that Ellison uses this folkloristic material to encourage readers to respond sympathetically on the deeper human level of their subconscious.

Coffin, Tristram P. "The Folk Ballad and the Literary Ballad: An Essay in Classification." _Midwestern Folklore_ 9 (1959): 5-18.

Proposes six classifications of ballads that reveal a clearly literary bias (evaluates ballads according to their literary merit). Discusses some literary reworkings of ballads in the last three categories but gives no American examples.

Coffin, Tristram P. "Gatsby's Fairy Lover." _Midwest Folklore_. 10 (1960): 79-85.

Traces the connection between Fitzgerald's Daisy, Keats' _La Belle Dame Sans Merci_, and Aarne-Thompson's _Märchen_ type 561, "Aladdin." Argues that Fitzgerald used the folk character of the fairy lover and the folk plot of "Aladdin" to reveal the impracticality of romantic yearnings in a realistic world, to show that "life is unsentimental, that 'belles dames' are 'sans merci,' and that an America of social and moral traditions is no setting for a _Märchen_."

Coffin, Tristram P. "Harden E. Taliaferro and the Use of Folklore by American Literary Figures." _South Atlantic Quarterly_ 64 (1965): 241-46.

Brief introduction to American literary use of folklore that focuses on Taliaferro's incorporation of Surry County folklore in _Fisher's_

River. Cites it as an outstanding case of successful adaptation.

Coffin, Tristram P. "Real Use and Real Abuse of Folklore in the Writer's Subconscious: F. Scott Fitzgerald," in New Voices in American Studies, Raye B. Browne, et al, eds., (Purdue University Studies, 1966), pp. 102-12.

A revision of "Gatsby's Fairy Lover" that tries to make the point that authors consciously rework folklore in their writing process.

Cohen, Bernard. "Hawthorne and Legends." Hoosier Folklore 7 (1948): 94-5.

Briefly notes the legends underlying a number of Hawthorne's short stories and novels.

Cohen, Hennig. "American Literature and American Folklore," in Our Living Traditions, ed. Tristram P. Coffin (New York: Basic Books Inc., 1968), pp. 238-47.

Suggests that literature is associated with literacy, a printed page, and a fixed text, while folklore is associated with illiteracy, a fluid text, and word of mouth. Argues that folklore appears in American literature in two ways: passively or actively, transcriptively or functionally. Goes on to cite a number of examples of folklore in American literature.

Cohen, Hennig. "Caroline Gilman and Negro Boatmen's Songs." Southern Folklore Quarterly 20 (1956): 116-17.

Briefly notes Gilman's use of Gullah dialect and folklore.

Cohen, Hennig. "Mark Twain's Sut Lovingood." The Lovingood Papers 1962: 19-24.

Traces some parallels between Harris's and Twain's styles, themes, and reliance on traditional motifs.

Cohen, Hennig. "The Singing Stammerer Motif in Billy Budd." Western Folklore 34 (1975): 54-55.

Documents two "cante fables" involving sailors who stammer when talking but can sing fluently. Compares this to Melville's Billy Budd, who stammers when under stress but who "can sing like an angel." Concludes that "Melville might well have heard such cante fables ... [and] used them functionally in Billy Budd as he typically used folklore."

Cohen, Hennig. "Twain's Jumping Frog: Folktale to Literature to Folktale." Western Folklore 22 (1963): 17-18.

Documents Twain's exposure to an oral version of the jumping frog folktale, and traces its use by Twain in his writing and its eventual reoccurrence in oral tradition.

Cohen, Hennig and William B. Dillingham, eds. Humor of the Old Southwest. Athens: University of Georgia Press, 1975. xxiv, 420 pp.

An anthology of folklore influenced literature that includes a useful introduction by the editors that lists the favorite subjects of these humorists and discusses their use of folk conventions and materials, including oral narrative form, vernacular speech, and local character.

Collins, Carvel. "Are These Mandalas?" Literature and Psychology 3 (1953): 3-6.

Interprets the concluding scene of The Bear as corresponding to the mandala, a ritualized experience of synthesis in an ordered setting commonly found in folk ceremony.

Collins, Carvel. "Folklore and Literary Criticism." Journal of American Folklore 70 (1957): 9-10.

Briefly observes folklore's importance for literary criticism and points out some exemplary folkloristic criticism.

Collins, Carvel. "The Interior Monologues of The Sound and the Fury," English Institute Essays 1952 (New York: Columbia U. P., 1953), pp. 29-56.

Discusses Faulkner's use of mythical patterns.

Collins, Carvel. "The Pairing of The Sound and the Fury and As I Lay Dying." Princeton University Library Chronicle 18 (1957): 115-23.

Compares the sociological picture presented in the novels and sees patterns corresponding to the life of Christ and the story of Demeter and Persephone.

Congdon, Wray H. J. "Original Sources of the Hiawatha Legends and Longfellow's Adaptation of Them." M.A. English. Syracuse University. 1915. 43 pp.

Cook, Geneva M. "Rowland Evans Robinson (1833-1900): Portrayer of Vermont Background and Character." M.A. English. University of Vermont. 1931.

Cook, Reginald L. "Big Medicine in Moby Dick," in Vickery, ed., Myth and Literature, pp. 193-200. Also in Accent 8 (1948): 102-109.

Identifies the "magic" in Moby Dick: sea magic, mythic adventure and chase magic, and ultimately Ahab's primitive and shamanistic magic, which infuses the work and gives it its power. Documents Ahab's forswearing of the Christian God and commitment to blasphemous ritual and primitive magic.

Cook, Reginald L. "Emerson and the American Joke." Emerson Society Quarterly 54 (1969): 22-27.

Reveals a native story-telling technique underlying Emerson's humor.

Cookson, William. "Ezra Pound & Myth: A Reader's Guide to Canto II." Agenda 15 (1977): 87-92.

Briefly traces one source of Pound's poem back to Ovid's Metamorphoses and its account of the kidnapping of Dionysus.

Costello, Donald P. "The Language of The Catcher in the Rye." American Speech 34 (1959): 172-81.

Studies Salinger as an example of teenage vernacular. Finds over one hundred slang forms used by Holden.

Cousins, Paul M. Joel Chandler Harris: A Biography. Baton Rouge: Louisiana State U. P., 1968. xiv, 237 pp.

Traces Harris's life and his debt to the folklore of the Negroes in Putnam County.

Cowart, David. "Pynchon's Use of the Tannhauser Legend in Gravity's Rainbow." Notes on Contemporary Literature 9 (1979): 2-3.

Sees a parallel between the legend of Tannhauser, in which a knight consorts with the goddess Venus and thereby loses his soul, eventually to win it back by pious penance, and Pynchon's character Tyrone Slothrup. Points out the explicit connections between the two narratives, and concludes that Tyrone like Tannhauser can only hope for "a distant miracle [that] can make all the difference to him and his 'preterite' kind."

Cowley, Malcolm. "American Myths, Old and New." Saturday Review 45 (1962): 6-8, 47.

Observes that romantic love is not a common theme in American literature and folklore.

Cowley, Malcolm. "William Faulkner's Legend of the South." The Sewanee Review 53 (1945): 343-61.

Uses legend loosely as a descriptive term for Faulkner's quasi-historic, quasi-personal, quasi-visionary chronicle of the South as constructed in his fiction. Not a folkloristic study.

Cox, James M. "Humor and America: The Southwestern Bear Hunt, Mrs. Stowe, and Mark Twain." Sewanee Review 83 (1975): 573-601.

Argues that "Big Bear of Arkansas," Uncle Tom's Cabin, and Huckleberry Finn are all variations on the tall tale tradition of yarn-spinning.

Cox, James M. "Remarks on the Sad Initiation of Huckleberry Finn," In Interpretations of American Literature, ed. Charles Feidelson, Jr., and Paul Brodford, Jr. (New York: Oxford University Press, 1959), pp. 229-43. Also in The Sewanee Review 62 (1954): 389-405.

Suggests that Huck plays the part of Tom Sawyer as an attempt to maintain his independence, but that his initiation is an inevitably sad victory of the society over the individual.

Cox, Louise Hart. "Paul Green's Negro Folk Plays: A Criticism." M.A. English. University of Texas. 1949. 122 pp.

Crane, T. F. "Plantation Folk-Lore." _Popular Science Monthly_ 18 (1880): 24-33. Also in Bruce Jackson, ed., _The Negro and His Folklore in Nineteenth-Century Periodicals_ (Austin: American Folklore Society, 1967), pp. 157-67.

Notes the resemblance of the Uncle Remus stories to Old World fables, especially African folktales, and documents numerous examples.

Crow, John and Richard Erlich. "Mythic Patterns in Ellison's _A Boy and His Dog_." _Extrapolation_ 18 (1977): 162-66.

Sees in Blood, the dog figure in Ellison's novella, a variation of the folk motif of the wise magic animal of folk and fairy tale. Sees also a mythic structural pattern in the story corresponding to formalized rituals of initiation and the task of renewing the waste land. Traces the initiation pattern through the story.

Cuff, Roger Penn. "Mark Twain's Use of California Folklore in His Jumping Frog Story." _Journal of American Folklore_ 65 (1952): 155-58.

Surveys the folk roots of the jumping frog story and concludes that it was erroneously attributed to Greek fable; it can be more accurately traced to California where it appears in a number of different accounts.

Cuff, Roger Penn. _A Study of the Classical Mythology in Hawthorne's Writings_. Nashville, George Peabody College for Teachers, 1936. 7 pp.

A printing of the abstract of Cuff's dissertation. Summarizes the argument that Hawthorne relies significantly upon mythological allusions in his writings. Surveys and enumerates Hawthorne's allusions to various mythologies and observes that Hawthorne's fancy modifies the materials in at least thirty different ways, mixing and matching mythological characters, settings, and events at will. Concludes that classical mythology is not an essential factor in Hawthorne's literary art.

Cutler, Evelyn Starr. "Representation of Maine Dialect in the Work of Sarah Orne Jewett." Ph.D. New York University. 1976. 165 pp. Dissertation Abstracts International 37 (1976): 1515A.

Identifies various phonological, lexical, morphological and syntactic forms of Maine dialect found in Jewett's stories. Verifies these features as ethnographically accurate, and concludes that Jewett's work provides "a permanent picture of the Maine Coast, and a valuable historical record of their speechways."

Dalziel, Margaret. Myth and the Modern Imagination. Dunedin, New Zealand: University of Otago Press, 1967. 124 pp.

The second essay, "Myth in Modern English Literature," includes a discussion of T. S. Eliot's The Waste Land and its connection to the Grail myth and an allusion to Bernard Malamud's recreation of the Grail story in The Natural.

Dance, Daryl. "Following in Zora Neale Hurston's Dust Tracks: Autobiographical Notes by the Author of Shuckin' and Jivin'." Journal of the Folklore Institute 16 (1979): 120-26.

Dance acknowledges his extensive debt to black folklore.

Das Gupta, H. "Ernest Hemingway and the Spanish Bullfight." Indian Journal of American Studies 6 (1976): 55-65.

Suggests that bullfighting provided an emotional substitute for the violence of war. Traces Hemingway's obsession with the mechanics and philosophy of bullfighting, as revealed in

Death in the Afternoon and other fictional works. Concludes with a discussion of the role of bullfighting in The Sun Also Rises and suggests that bullfighting serves as a means of giving Jake "an intensely emotional apprehension of life and death through a definite pattern of action."

Dauner, Louise. "Myth and Humor in the Uncle Remus Fables." American Literature 20 (1948-49): 129-43.

Discusses the folk heritage of the Uncle Remus tales and sees parallels to American Indian and African trickster figures. Analyzes three levels of myth in the stories and various sources of humor.

Davidson, Frank. "Melville, Thoreau, and 'The Apple-Tree Table'." American Literature 25 (1954): 478-88.

Discusses Melville's and Thoreau's reworking of "the story which has gone the rounds of New England," of a bug that eats its way out of a century old apple-tree table.

Davidson, James. "The Post-Bellum Poor-White as Seen by J. W. De Forest." Southern Folklore Quarterly 24 (1960): 101-08.

Details De Forest's description of the folk character of the poor-white; concludes that he portrays these characters sensitively and accurately, with a keen ear for dialect.

Davidson, Levette J. "Folk Elements in Midwestern Literature." Western Humanities Review 3 (1949): 187-195.

Surveys a wide variety of midwestern writers, including Willa Cather, Bret Harte, and Mark Twain, and discusses the local color and ordinary folklife underlying their fiction.

Concludes that "the enduring literature of the Midwest has been based upon the attempt to communicate the actual experiences of the folk."

Davidson, Peter. "Heracles & m'la calata." _Paideuma_ 8 (1979): 413-14.

Notes Pound's use of a classical legend.

Davis, Hestelle Ray. "Regional Elements in the Prose Writing of Jesse Stuart." M.A. English. Miami University. 1953. 138 pp.

Davis, Joseph A. "The Myth of the Garden: Nathaniel Hawthorne's 'Rappaccini's Daughter'." _Studies in the Literary Imagination_ 2/1 (1969): 3-12.

Argues that "only by considering the role that myth plays in the narrative can we grasp the relationship among the seemingly ambiguous parts" of Hawthorne's tale. Suggests that the mythic pattern of "Rappaccini's Daughter" concerns the lost Eden paradise and the task of redeeming this fallen Eden through self-less acts. Analyzes the symbolism of the garden as corresponding to "the Judeo-Christian myth of the Garden of Eden." Suggests that Giovanni is unable to surrender to love and instead succumbs to Dr. Baglioni, "the counterpart of the serpent of the Genesis creation myth," who in this role of ogre or adversary "suggests a type common to all mythologies." Concludes that in mythic terms, "Rappaccini's Daughter" affirms that "man is ever subject to the call of Spirit and that to refuse this call or to fail in the tasks which Spirits set is to 'fall' back into the corrupted condition of the world."

Davis, Joseph A. "The Oldest Puritan: A Study of the Angel of Hadley Legend in Hawthorne's 'The Gray Champion'." _Rackham Literary Studies_ 4 (1973): 25-43.

Reviews the background and history of the Hadley Angel and the Regicide Judges as it filtered its way from folklore into history and eventually into literature. Concludes that Hawthorne's treatment is superior to others and strikes "into the very core of the ambivalent attitudes and beliefs" of all Americans who identified with the symbolic "regicide" of the Revolution.

Davis, Rose M. "How Indian is Hiawatha?" _Midwest Folklore_ 7 (1957): 5-25.

Investigates the authenticity of Longfellow's description of Indian life and customs. Concludes that despite some accuracy in describing folk customs and although Longfellow uses many actual Indian myths, he does not convey the psychological truth about the Indian.

Dawson, Hugh J. "Fathers and Sons: Franklin's 'Memoirs' as Myth and Metaphor." _Early American Literature_ 14 (1979-80): 269-92.

A biographical examination that deals with myth in the general sense of a father-son relation, which motivates and underlies the writing of Frankin's "Memoirs."

Dean, John. "The Sick Hero Reborn: Two Versions of the Philoctetes Myth." _Comparative Literature Studies_ 17 (1980): 334-40.

Examines the mythic underpinnings of two novels by Robert Silverberg, _Philoctetes_ and _Man in the Maze_.

De Caro, Francis A. "Proverbs and Originality in Modern Short Fiction." _Western Folklore_ 37 (1978): 30-38.

Discusses the general functions and meanings of proverbs and posits the premise that authors work with the assumption that readers have preconceived notions about familiar proverbs and the authors take advantage of these preconceptions. Considers the use of proverbs in four stories: Mansfield's "Bliss"; Powers' "The Valiant Woman"; O'Connor's "A Good Man is Hard to Find"; and Suckow's "A Start in Life." Observes that modern writers do not use proverbs directly as did their predecessors, but rather they circumvent the prohibition against using clichéd phrases by either using proverbs ironically or by merely alluding to them obliquely. Explicates the proverbs underlying the four stories.

De Caro, Rosan Jordan. "A Note about Folklore and Literature (The Bosom Serpent Revisited)." Journal of American Folklore 86 (1973): 62-65.

Criticizes Barnes's article for not analyzing sufficiently the function of folklore in its folkloristic context, as well as in its literary context. Suggests we need a methodology that brings folklore materials that are found in literary contexts as well as in a folkloristic context into the same frame of reference. Goes on to discuss the function of bosom serpent legends in oral tradition.

Decker, Philip Hunt. "The Use of Classic Myth in Twentieth-Century English and American Drama, 1900-1960." Ph.D. Northwestern University. 1966. 577 pp. Dissertation Abstracts International 27 (1967): 3536A-37A

Surveys 98 works that substantially rely on classical mythology as their subject matter. Concentrates on the Atreidae myth, the Phaedra-Hippolytus myth, and the Alcestis-Admetur myth which appear in plays by Eliot, H.P. Jeffers, O'Neill, and Rexroth.

DeFalco, Joseph M. "Frost's 'Paul's Wife': The Death of an Idea." Southern Folklore Quarterly 29 (1965): 259-65.

Analyzes the multi-leveled use of "the myth of Paul Bunyan" in Frost's poem. Suggests Frost's intent is to transcend the simple ideals of the folk group that created Paul and to portray in Paul the perennial conflict between man's chthonian nature and his divine spirituality.

DeGruson, Eugene H. "The Gods that Boucher Killed: A Study of the Use of Classical Mythology in the Poetry of Wallace Stevens." M.A. English. Kansas State College. 1958. 67 pp.

Dekker, George and Joseph Harris. "Supernaturalism and the Vernacular Style in _A Farewell to Arms_." _PMLA_ 94 (1979): 311-18.

Investigates the submerged folkloristic motifs of second sight and revenants in _A Farewell to Arms_. Points out the folkloristic underpinnings of Catherine's seeing herself dead in the rain. Sees as well allusions to ballad motifs of lost lovers who return to visit their loved one in Frederic's assuming the place of the English boy killed at the Somme. Notes two other ballad _topoi_ found in _Farewell_. Ballad lovers separated by death may pledge "austerities" such as shorn hair, and the standard mourning period is twelve months and a day; both motifs are suggested at Catherine's and Frederic's first meeting. Observes that the folkloristic games, rituals and patterns that Catherine and Frederic follow enable them to turn their sordid hotel room into a home. Thus, they function in the novel as they do in life, helping to humanize a hostile or uncaring universe. Concludes that Hemingway's use of these folkloristic motifs and themes was probably partially motivated by the examples of Ford, Joyce, Eliot and Pound, who used myth as "a way of . . . giving shape and significance to the immense panorama of futility and anarchy which is contemporary history."

Deming, Robert H. "The Use of the Past: Herrick and Hawthorne." _Journal of Popular Culture_ 2 (1968): 278-91.

Examines "The May-Pole of Merry Mount" and argues that Hawthorne appropriated folk rituals and juxtaposed them with Christianity in order to represent the conflict of the forces of "jollity" (the spirit of life) and "gloom" (the worship of force). Suggests he derived the folk custom of May-pole from written accounts.

Devoto, Bernard. _Mark Twain's America_. Cambridge: Houghton Mifflin, 1932. xviii, 351 pp.

Surveys the historical and biographical background of Samuel Clemens and argues that the author was in essence a frontier humorist. Traces a line from the anonymous frontier story-tellers to the figure of Huckleberry Finn, and suggests that what made Samuel Clemens into the literary person of Mark Twain was his love of the oral anecdote.

Dickinson, Hugh. _Myth on the Modern Stage_. Urbana: U. of Illinois Press, 1969. 359 pp.

Examines modern playwrights employing Greek myths, including Jeffers, O'Neill, Eliot, Williams; considers the playwrights individually and their special use of myth; discusses myth as a form of classical expression, not a folkloristic genre.

Dickson, D. Bruce, Jr. "On Dunbar's 'Jingles in a Broken Tongue': Dunbar's Dialect Poetry and the Afro-American Folk Tradition," in Jay Martin, ed., _A Singer in the Dawn: Reinterpretations of Paul Lawrence Dunbar_ (New York: Dodd, Mead, 1975), pp. 94-113.

Suggests that, despite Dunbar's discomfort at being labeled a dialect poet, he was a good practitioner of the art of recreating dialect and that it accurately captured the way of life of the rural black Southerner in the generation which had gained freedom from slavery. Surveys the positive reaction in black publications to

Dunbar's poetry and assesses his poetry as being vitally concerned with black American issues and folk tradition.

Diez Del Corral, Luis. La Funcion del mito clasico en la literatura contemporena. Madrid: Editorial Credos, 1957. 248 pp.

Chapter Five examines Eliot's treatment of Tiresias and other mythic allusions.

Dinn, James M. "A Novelist's Miracle: Structure and Myth in Death Comes for the Archbishop." Western American Literature 7 (1972): 39-46.

Finds in Cather's Death Comes for the Archbishop a "configuration of images which coalesce in the myth of the questing knight and the related fertility of the land." Traces these symbols in the novel--for example, the Bishop and Jacinto flee to a cave, much like the questing knight finds shelter in the Perilous Chapel--and relates the use of these themes to Christian myth.

Dippie, Brian W. "'His Visage Wild; His Form Exotick': Indian Themes and Cultural Guilt in John Barth's The Sot-weed Factor." American Quarterly 21 (1969): 113-21.

Suggests there is a dark underside to the American consciousness, a negative inversion of its myth of self accomplishment, and that Barth's novel successfully rejects conventional American myths in favor of this darker vision.

Dippie, Brian W. "Jack Crabb and the Sole Survivors of Custer's Last Stand." Western American Literature 4 (1969): 189-202.

States that Little Big Man rests upon a foundation of myth, despite its historical verisimilitude.

Dixon, Melvin. "The Teller as Folk Trickster in Chesnutt's _The Conjure Woman_." _College Language Association Journal_ 18 (1974): 186-97.

Argues that Chesnutt has "consciously created a folk novel that describes a series of adventures of equal importance" and that ultimately focuses on the "clear progression in the character of the teller." It is the folk character of the tale teller that provides the work a sense of unity. Investigates the folkloristic roots of the trickster figure and analyzes its incorporation into _The Conjure Woman_. Concludes that only in the guise of folklore entertainment could Chesnutt, a trickster and tale teller himself, attempt to liberate his audience and his characters from the stereotypical roles of nineteenth century America.

Donaldson, Scott. "'No, I am Not Prince Charming': Fairy Tales in _Tender Is the Night_." _Fitzgerald/Hemingway Annual_ (1973): 105-12.

Examines Fitzgerald's attitude toward sentimental fiction, in which literary fairy tales are included; suggests that it propagates a false view of the world and that it can lead to disastrous results, as illustrated in the conclusion of _Tender is the Night_.

Dorson, Richard M. "Five Directions in American Folklore." _Midwest Folklore_ 1 (1951): 149-65.

One of the directions for promising research is "Folklore as a Tool of Literary Analysis." Reviews some rewarding studies and investigates Hawthorne's folklore connection. Notes that he was exposed to various New England folk traditions, especially the spectral legend, which he put to good use in his writing.

Dorson, Richard M. "Folklore in American Literature: A Postscript." _Journal of American Folklore_ 71 (1958): 158-64. Also in Dorson, _American Folklore and the Historian_ (Chicago: University of Chicago Press, 1971), pp. 204-09.

Reviews additional folklore-and-literature studies; criticizes some studies (Frantz and Rodes) for their lack of folkloristic authentification, and commends others (Reichart, Davis) for their scholarship.

Dorson, Richard M. "The Identification of Folklore in American Literature." Journal of American Folklore 70 (1957): 1-8. Also in Dorson, American Folklore and the Historian (Chicago: University of Chicago Press, 1971), pp. 186-203.

Proposes a methodology for the study of folklore in literature that involves identifying three kinds of evidence to authenticate the presence of folklore in literature: biographical, internal, and corroborative. Stresses the importance of verifying an author's exposure to actual folk traditions.

Dorson, Richard M. Jonathan Draws the Long Bow. Cambridge: Harvard University Press, 1946. viii, 274 pp.

Documents the existence of New England folktales and legends from a variety of sources. Chapter VI, "Literary Folktales," considers literary borrowings of folktales by Whittier and other less well known New England writers.

Dorson, Richard M. "Print and American Folktales." Western Folklore 4 (1945): 202-15. Also in American Folklore and the Historian (Chicago: University of Chicago Press, 1971), pp. 173-85.

Tackles the tricky question of printed dissemination of oral tales, and attempts to clarify the basis for distinguishing between true folklore and literary adaptation of folk material (cites Thorpe, Simms, Twain, Benet, Hawthorne, and Irving as examples). Suggests oral style, internal clues, and external evidence can provide a basis for differentiation.

Dorson, Richard M. "The Use of Printed Sources," In Richard Dorson, ed., Folklore and Folklife (Chicago: University of Chicago Press, 1972), pp. 465-77.

Discusses the ways folklore and literature may be intertwined. Categorizes the types of printed sources that include folklore. Draws a distinction between folk matter and artistic use of folk matter.

Dotterer, Ronald L. "The Fictive and the Real: Myth and Form in the Poetry of Wallace Stevens and William Carlos Williams," in McCune, ed., The Binding of Proteus (Lewisburg: Bucknell U. P., 1974), pp. 221-48.

Deals with myth in a general way as the causing of something to come into being according to certain form. Not sufficiently rigorous to be useful.

Doubleday, Frank. "Hawthorne's Use of Three Gothic Patterns." College English 7 (1946): 250-62.

Notes that one of the three gothic patterns in Hawthorne's writing is his use of witchcraft. Discusses Hawthorne's successful use of witchcraft in "Young Goodman Brown" and The Scarlet Letter.

Dow, Janet. "Ahab: The Fisher King." Connecticut Review 2 (1969): 42-49.

Notes archetypal parallels between Moby-Dick and the Grail legend, specifically the wounded king and the questing hero.

Doyle, Mary Ellen. "In Need of Folk: The Alienated Protagonists in Ralph Ellison's Short Fiction." College Language Association Journal 19 (1975): 165-72.

Traces the alienation of a number of Ellison's characters and shows how they alleviate that alienation through participation in folk group experiences, for example, Mr. Parker's singing with Welshmen in "In a Strange Country." Concludes that Ellison's protagonists "find human connection with the world primarily and inevitably through the folk," revealing Ellison's belief "that folklore preserves and protects Negroes' wisdom" and humanizes the world.

Drake, Carlos G. "Literary Criticism and Folklore." Journal of Popular Culture 5 (1971): 289-97.

Argues that studying folklore is valuable for literary criticism because it instructs students as to their relation to literary art.

Dundes, Alan. "African and Afro-American Tales." Research in African Literatures 7 (1976): 181-99.

Discusses the African heritage of Afro-American traditions, one example of which includes African folktales in Uncle Remus stories.

Dundes, Alan. "The Study of Folklore in Literature and Culture: Identification and Interpretation." Journal of American Folklore 78 (1965): 136-42.

Delineates the proper methodology for studying folklore in literature, which includes two steps: the identification of the exact traditional context of the folklore allusion, and the interpretation of its significance in the literary text.

Dundes, Alan. "Washington Irving's Version of the Seminole Origin of the Races." Ethnohistory 9/3 (1962): 257-64.

Compares four versions of the Seminole folk narrative concerning the origin of the races, and concludes that Irving might have altered the tale to make it more palatable to an all-white audience of Knickerbocker readers.

Eaton, Clement. "The Southern Yeoman: The Humorists' View," in The Mind of the Old South (Baton Rouge, 1964), pp. 101-118.

Discusses the Southern humorists' use of colloquialisms and folk customs (e.g., fiddling, revival meetings) to depict the Southern mind.

Eby, Cecil D., Jr. "Americanisms in the Down-East Fiction of George D. Wasson." American Speech 37 (1962): 249-54.

Finds an untapped reservoir of American words and phrases. Cites some eight examples.

Eby, Cecil D., Jr. "Faulkner and the Southwestern Humorists." Shenandoah 11 (1959): 13-21.

Examines the setting, characters, and episodes of The Hamlet in comparison to the regional humorists in order to show how Faulkner conforms to the folk tradition utilized by the early Southern writers. Suggests the characters in The Hamlet fall into categories developed by the humorists.

Eby, Cecil D., Jr. "Ichabod Crane in Yoknapatawpha County." Georgia Review 12 (1962): 465-69.

Argues that Faulkner reworks the legend of Ichabod Crane in The Hamlet and that both are regionalistic rejections of outsiders.

Edmondson, Munro S. Lore: an Introduction to the Science of Folklore and Literature. New York: Rinehart and Winston, 1971. xv, 456 pp.

An overly ambitious attempt to redefine and reclassify all of literature and folklore; the theoretical model of the relationship of folklore and literature is questionable, but it does point out some similarities between those two art forms.

Edson, Elina A. "To What Extent is Mythology Used by the Leading Modern British and American Poets?" M.A. Education. New York University. 1932. 58 pp.

Engel, Grace Margaret. "Pocahontas in American Literature." M.A. English. Columbia University. 1937. 92 pp.

Ericson, Eston Everett. "Burial at the Cross Roads." _Folk-Lore_ 47 (1936): 374-5.

Identifies the folk custom of burying suicides at a cross-roads as a contribution of Slavic folk tradition to _My Antonia_.

Eulice, Daphne. "Folk Motifs in Guy Owen's _Journey for Joedel_." _North Carolina Folklore_ 24 (1976): 111-14.

Contends that Owen most sensitively recreates the mood and lifestyle of folklife in rural 1930's North Carolina. Points out local expressions that flavor the language of his characters, superstitions and tales that color their beliefs, and regional customs that shape their lifestyles. Argues that "the eastern North Carolina folklore enriches, both structurally and descriptively, the story of Joedel Shaw and his family."

Evard, Isabel. "Nathaniel Hawthorne's Use of Folklore." A.M. English. Saint Louis University. 1936. 63 pp.

Evers, Lawrence J. "Further Survivals of Coyote." _Western American Literature_ 10 (1975): 233-36.

Gives examples of Native American coyote lore in contemporary Western American literature.

Fackler, Herbert V. "Multiple Myth and Folklore in H. Allen Smith's Picaresque Satire *Mister Zip*." *Satire Newlstter* 6 (1968): 35-42.

Argues that in *Mister Zip*, Smith weaves together the Don Quixote myth, frontier folklore, the Hollywood folktale formula, and Boy Scout folklore.

Fahy, Joseph. "Thomas Pynchon's *V.* and Mythology." *Critique* 18 (1977): 5-18.

Argues that mythology provides a solution to the irregularities apparent in the novel, because Pynchon employed the mythology of Graves and Frazer. Suggests that Pynchon presents V. as "a representation of the White Goddess as Graves has described her." Points out similarities between the two, and concludes that Pynchon evolved "an intricate mythology fundamentally based on Frazer's *The Golden Bough* and Graves' *The White Goddess*" that expressed his view of the world's movement into a new age of Armageddon.

Fairing, Robert Lewis. "The Sources of Longfellow's *The Song of Hiawatha*." M.A. English. Pennsylvania State University. 1933. 60 pp.

Farmer, Betty Catherine Dobson. "Mythological, Biblical, and Literary Allusions in Donald Barthelme's *The Dead Father*." *International Fiction Review* 6 (1979): 40-48.

Observes that Barthelme "accomplished the 'cosmopolitanization' or global application of the Dead Father figure by comparing him to the Judeo-Christian concept of God; the Greco-Roman concepts of Zeus, Orpheus, and Jason; the Serpent-god of Indian mythology; the All-Father, Odin of Norse mythology, and the Norse pessimism expressed in the belief in the Day of Ragnarok or 'Twilight of the Gods'; the German 'voivode' (voevode) or 'devil'; and the Medieval English vegetation myths of the dying god and the Fisher King." Traces these allusions through the story, and concludes that in filling in the Dead Father's grave, Barthelme is "calling for the interment of all world idols."

Faulkner, Howard. "The Uses of Tradition: William Melvin Kelley's A Different Drummer." Modern Fiction Studies 21 (1975-76): 535-42.

Identifies Kelley's reliance upon the traditions of the folktale, the tall tale, and Southern and Western folk humor and satire.

Feder, Lillian. Ancient Myth in Modern Poetry. Princeton, N.J.: Princeton University Press, 1971. xiv, 432 pp.

Uses a thorough consideration of the nature of myth as the starting point for extended discussion of myth in the works of four major poets: Pound, Eliot, Auden, and Yeats. Other American poets cited include Conrad Aiken, Allen Ginsberg, Robert Lowell, Sylvia Plath, and John Crowe Ransom. Primarily interprets the philosophical and unconscious meanings of individual works and their connection to traditional myths.

Feldman, Burton, and Robert D. Richardson, eds. The Rise of Modern Mythology, 1680-1860. Bloomington: Indiana University Press, 1972. xxvii, 564 pp.

A large collection of essays considering the significance, impact, influence, and use of mythology.

Ferguson, J. Kelancey. "The Roots of American Humor." American Scholar 4 (1935): 41-49.

Argues that most of American folklore found in literature has its roots in Europe, including proverbs and folk characters.

Ferguson, Robert C. "Folklore References in Faulkner's The Hamlet and As I Lay Dying." Journal of the Ohio Folklore Society 1 (1972): 1-10.

Points out similarities between incidents in Faulkner's novels and episodes from American folk narrative, including horse trading and selling one's soul to the devil.

Ferrell, Margaret Jean. "Hawthorne's Use of Four Myths." M.A. English. University of Oklahoma. 1963. 96 pp.

Field, Bettye. "William Faulkner and the Humor of the Old Southwest." M.A. English. Vanderbilt University. 1953. 85 pp.

Field, Leslie A. "Wolfe's Use of Folklore." New York Folklore Quarterly 16 (1960): 202-15.

Surveys American folklore, especially folk characters and yarn spinning, in Wolfe's The Hills Beyond, which is "pregnant with American folklore as none of Wolfe's other works are."

Figh, Margaret Gillis. "Folklore and Folk Speech in the Works of Marjorie Kinnan Rawlings." Southern Folklore Quarterly 11 (1947): 201-9.

Examines Rawling's use of superstitions, sayings, and similes in portraying the Florida Cracker and suggests these characterizations help portray both the stoical fatalism and earthy humor of this folk type.

Figh, Margaret Gillis. "Folklore in Bill Arp's Works." Southern Folklore Quarterly 12 (1948): 169-75.

Observes that Arp enlivened his sketches with superstitions, tales, folk games, rhymes, and local customs.

Figh, Margaret Gillis. "Folklore in the 'Rufus Sanders' Sketches." Southern Folklore Quarterly 19 (1955): 185-95.

Identifies tales, folk ways, and dialect in Lloyd's Sketches of Country Life.

Figh, Margaret Gillis. "Tall Talk and Folk Sayings in Bill Arp's Works." Southern Folklore Quarterly 13 (1949): 206-12 (in issue 4, which is mis-paginated).

Lists examples of folk speech employed in his writing; concludes Arp had "a keen ear for folk speech."

Figh, Margaret Gillis. "A Word List from 'Bill Art' and 'Rufus Sanders'." Publications of the American Dialect Society 13 (1950): 3-15.

Culls a word-list from two cracker barrel columnists whose works reflect the everyday work speech of Southerners.

Firebaugh, Joseph H. "Inadequacy in Eden: Knowledge and 'The Turn of the Screw'." Modern Fiction Studies 3 (1957): 57-63.

Points out that the Man from Harley Street functions somewhat as the Old Testament God who sets up Eden and then withdraws to heaven. Argues that James uses this folkloristic model to illustrate the inadequacies of "ancient identifications of knowledge of sin." Concludes that the "young efforts" of Miles and Flora "to know have been forced in the pattern of Original Sin," which results in hysteria and death.

Fisher, Dexter, & Robert B. Stepto, eds. Afro-American Literature: The Reconstruction of Instruction. New York: MLA, 1979. viii, 256 pp.

A useful collection of essays by O'Meally, Gates, Williams, and Hemenway about the folkloristic contribution to Afro-American literature. The articles are referenced individually in this bibliography.

Flanagan, John T. "The Fiction of Jessamyn West." Indiana Magazine of History 67 (1971): 299-316.

Analyzes the appeal of West's fiction and points out her use of folk speech, proverbs, and superstitions.

Flanagan, John T. "Folk Elements in John Brown's Body." New York Folklore Quarterly 20 (1964): 243-56.

Identifies folk history, superstitions, sayings, songs, and myths in Benet's poem.

Flanagan, John T. "The Folk Hero in Modern American Drama." Modern Drama 6 (1964): 402-16.

Traces the depiction of American folk characters on the stage, including John Henry and Paul Bunyan.

Flanagan, John T. "Folklore in Faulkner's Fiction." Papers on Languages & Literature 5 (1969): 119-144.

Discusses examples of Faulkner's use of rituals, proverbs, beliefs, tricksters, and tall tales, especially in The Hamlet, Go Down Moses, and The Reivers. Argues that the folklore provides verisimilitude and archetypal resonance.

Flanagan, John T. "Folklore in Five Middlewestern Novelists." Great Lakes Review 1 (1975): 43-57.

Discusses the fiction of Kirkland, Garland, Quick, Stuart, and J. West.

Flanagan, John T. "Folklore in the Novels of Conrad Richter." Midwest Folklore 2 (1952): 5-14.

Traces Richter's indebtedness to folklore (idioms, proverbs, superstitions) culled from old settler's diaries and journals.

Flanagan, John T. "Folklore in the Stories of James Hall." Midwest Folklore 5 (1955): 159-68.

Examines the use of Indian legend and frontier superstition in the writings of an early nineteenth century Ohio lawyer and author. Concludes that he uses folklore in a deliberate, contrived, and sly way, like Irving.

Flanagan, John T. "The Impact of Folklore on American Literature." Jahrbuch für Amerikastudien 7 (1962): 67-72.

Argues that folklore has significantly influenced American literature; cites as examples Franklin, Sandburg, Faulkner, Hawthorne, Melville, Twain, Irving, Poe, Lindsay, and Benet.

Flanagan, John T. "John G. Neihardt, Chronicler of the West." Arizona Quarterly 21 (1965): 7-20.

Discusses Neihardt's depictions of traditional legendary figures from the American west, including Mike Fink, in his Cycle of the West.

Flanagan, John T. and Arthur Palmer Hudson. The American Folklore Reader: Folklore in American Literature. New York: A. S. Barnes and Co., 1958. Reprinted as Folklore in American Literature (Evanston: Row, Peterson, and Co., 1958). 511 pp.

An anthology of literary selections having folkloristic content; illustrates the artistic use of folklore by American authors. Includes a brief analytical introduction and a bibliography (pp. 504-506).

Fleck, Richard F. "Mythic Buds in Thoreau's Journal." Ariel 7 (1976): 77-86.

Uses myth in a very general way to describe "the mystical process of spiritual analogizing" as seen in Thoreau's seasonal, fluvial, and animal descriptions and accounts.

Fleck, Richard F. "Thoreau as Mythologist." Research Studies 40 (1972): 195-206.

Argues that Thoreau must be considered a mythologist, even though he relied primarily on poetic and intuitive insights into the nature of myth, rather than on linguistic and anthropological data. Suggests Thoreau believed classical mythology to be inspired by more ancient folklore and that all mythology still speaks eloquently to moderns. Reviews Thoreau's pronouncements on the nature and uses of mythology, and concludes that Thoreau believed that nature lies at the core of myth.

Fleck, Richard F. "Thoreau's New England Mythology." Thoreau Journal 4 (1972): 1-9.

Suggests Thoreau's works "partake of the qualities of myth."

Fleming, Robert E. "'Playing the Dozens' in the Black Novel." Studies in Black Literature 3 (1972): 23-24.

Identifies the use of the dozens by three black novelists.

Flusche, Michael. "Joel Chandler Harris and the Folklore of Slavery." Journal of American Studies 9 (1975): 347-63.

Uses the slave folktales recorded by Harris to recreate the world view of the slaves. Observes that the folktales were selectively chosen and heavily bowdlerized, but they still reveal much about the early black community.

Foeller, Elzbieta. "The Mythical Heroes of John Barth and John Gardner." *Kwartalnik Neofilologiczny* 27 (1980): 183-97.

Investigates Barth's and Gardner's use of "received" stories from classical, Germanic and Arabic mythology. Argues that both authors use this material consciously in order to shape and give meaning to their fiction. States that Barth uses the classical myths underlying *Lost in The Funhouse* "to explore the nature of artistic and specifically literary endeavor, of which myth is the first and most enduring source and product." Finds Barth to be an ironic rewriter of myths. Interprets Gardner's *Grendel* as an affirmation of myth's potential for providing meaning and order to an otherwise "mechanical chaos of casual, brute enmity." Concludes that the mythical heroes of Barth and Gardner are doubting protagonists who cling to the mythic pattern as a guideline in the bewildering experience of life.

"Folklore in Literature: A Symposium." *Journal of American Folklore* 70 (1957): 1-24.

Includes essays by Dorson, Collins, and Hoffman, which are individually referenced in this bibliography.

Folks, Jeffery J. "Folk Humor in the Stories of Ellis Parker Butler." *Tennessee Folklore Society Bulletin* 45 (1979): 79-84.

Documents the folklore influence in the work of an early twentieth-century writer from Iowa. Uses the criteria established by Dorson to point out that Butler was well familiar with Midwestern rural or small town folklore and that he used this familiarity to an advantage in his stories. Concentrates on tall tales and folktales that flourished in mid-America and that contributed entertainingly to Butler's narratives.

Fontenot, Chester J. "Mythic Patterns in *River Niger* and *Ceremonies in Dark Old Men*." *MELUS* 7 (1980): 41-49.

Identifies in Afro-American drama a tension between the linear and the mythic conceptions of history. In the mythic vision, the Black historical past (e.g., exploitation by Whites) is constantly recreated in contemporary life; whereas, in the linear view, a developmental progress characterizes Black history. Sees the conflict between these two visions illustrated in Walker's River Niger and Lonne Elder's Ceremonies in Dark Old Men.

Fontenrose, Joseph. John Steinbeck; An Introduction and Interpretation. New York: Holt, Rinehart, and Winston, 1963. ix, 150 pp.

Discusses among other topics Steinbeck's use of the Grail Legend and the Waste Land theme in Cup of Gold, To a God Unknown, Tortilla Flats, and The Pearl.

Ford, Thomas W. "Ned Brace of Georgia Scenes." Southern Folklore Quarterly 29 (1965): 220-27.

Suggests the best sketches in Longstreet's Georgia Scenes are derived from oral material; identifies Ned Brace as a Southern-born Yankee trickster figure.

Foster, Carolyn Emily. "Folklore in Mary Webb's Novel Precious Bane: A Catalog and Discussion of Folklore Material with Comparative References to the Author's Other Novels." M.A. English. University of Maryland. 1956. 96 pp.

Foster, Charles W. "The Phonology of the Conjure Tales of Charles W. Chesnutt." Publication of the American Dialect Society 55 (1971): 1-43.

Examines Chesnutt's dialect tales and praises them for their accurate and artistic use of black folk speech.

Foster, Charles W. "The Representation of Negro Dialect in Charles W. Chesnutt's *The Conjure Woman*." Ph.D. University of Alabama. 1968. 258 pp. *Dissertation Abstracts International* 29 (1969): 3596A-97A.

Examines field tapes for the Linguistic Atlas for the South Atlantic States to demonstrate the authenticity of Chesnutt's dialect. Concludes that Chesnutt is remarkably accurate.

Foster, George R. "What is Folk Culture?" *American Anthropologist* 55 (1953): 159-173.

In a larger general discussion of folk culture, he considers the symbiotic relationship of folk arts and sophisticated arts. Postulates a circular flow of cultural contact between folk and sophisticated art.

Fox, Velda Mae. "The Development of the Pocahontas Story in American Literature. 1607-1927." M.A. English. State University of Iowa. 1927.

Franklin, H. Bruce. *The Wake of the Gods: Melville's Mythology*. Stanford: Stanford Univ. Press, 1963. 236 pp.

Written originally as a doctoral dissertation at Stanford University in 1962. Argues that "Melville's mythology determines and defines large parts of the structure and meaning" of his major works. Analyzes most of Melville's major works for the pagan and Christian mythic influence and interprets Melville's use of these myths. Suggests that Melville surreptitiously appropriates these myths, "thus taking advantage of unconscious psychological values . . . inherent in mythic patterns." Points out that Melville was well versed in his mythology, and finds abundant mythological allusions in the fiction.

Frantz, Ray William "The Place of Folklore in the Creative Art of Mark Twain." Ph.D. University of Illinois. 1955. 261 pp. Dissertation Abstracts International 16 (1956): 1126.

Surveys Twain's developing use of folklore, from his travel books, to his historical books, to his Hannibal books. Suggests folklore permeates all Twain's work, but his later treatment of it became more sophisticated. Argues that the folk materials perform a great variety of important functions and that Huckleberry Finn is Twain's greatest folklore achievement. Concludes that the folklore represents a basic writing method for Twain as well as the kernel of his work.

Frantz, Ray W., Jr. "The Role of Folklore in Huckleberry Finn." American Literature 28 (1956): 314-27.

Argues that the folklore in Huckleberry Finn is "organically important to the novel" and assists in developing structure, theme, plot, and character. Analyzes Twain's use of folklore forecasting and superstition as an organizational pattern in the novel.

Franz, Eleanor. "Hunting the Hunter: Nat Foster Today." New York Folklore Quarterly 20 (1964): 270-75.

Historical survey of the folk character reputed to be the model for Cooper's Leatherstocking.

Frazer, Timothy C. "A Note on Mark Twain's Use of Dialect in Earlier Writings." Mark Twain Journal 20 (1980): 8-9.

Comments on Twain's representation of South Midland and South dialect in "The Dandy Frightening the Squatter" and "Letter from Thomas Jefferson Snodgrass." Identifies the regional dialects that Twain employs, and finds Twain's treatment, "though enhanced by the use of eye dialect and rusticisms, as regionally accurate."

Freeman, Gordon Query. "Climbing the Racial Mountain: The Folk Elements in the Works of Three Black Writers." Ph.D. University of New Mexico. 1977. 442 pp. Dissertation Abstracts International 38 (1977): 3641A-42A.

Uses Dundes's methodology to examine the folklore in works by Hughes, Wright, and Ellison. Analyzes Hughes's use of textual jazz rhythms in his poetry, Ellison's use of jazz as a structuring device in Invisible Man, and Wright's use of folklore to create a proletarian literature. Suggests Hughes uses folklore to portray Black folklife and its transformation to urban communities, Wright uses folklore as a means of coping with racial prejudice, and Ellison uses folklore to reveal the discrepancy between American ideals and American life.

French, Florence Healy. "Cooper the Tinkerer." New York Folklore Quarterly 26 (1970): 229-239.

Examines Cooper's variations of traditional proverbs. Suggests Cooper varies the proverbs to illustrate his political convictions and for stylistic effect.

French, Florence Healy. "Cooper's Use of Proverbs in the 'Anti-Rent' Novels." New York Folklore Quarterly 26 (1970): 42-49.

Discovers 206 proverbs in three novels by Cooper and argues that Cooper drew them from oral tradition and used them to support his belief in Jeffersonianism.

Frenz, Horst. "Ironic Use of Myth in The Hairy Ape." The Eugene O'Neill Newsletter 1/3 (1978): 2-4.

Proposes that in The Hairy Ape O'Neill subverts and parodies the myth of Dionysus. Points out that the plot is derived from a legend concerning Dionysus's capture and imprisonment by pirates. Suggests that Yank is a Dionysus, but stripped of all his power, revealing O'Neill's attitude towards modern life. "Yank, O'Neill is saying, represents contemporary man dispossessed of godhead and self-harmony through the workings of a perverted social consciousness." Concludes that by "inverting the heroic pattern of Dionysian myth, O'Neill expresses through irony his own wasteland vision of a materialistic culture ignorant of its roots in myth and drama."

Fridy, Wilford E. "Robert Penn Warren's Use of Kentucky Materials in His Fiction as Basis For His New Myths." Ph.D. University of Kentucky. 1968. 250 pp. Dissertation Abstracts International 30 (1969): 1523A

Suggests that Warren creates a fictional world out of Kentucky history, legend, biography, and folklore. Focuses on the "mythos" or "weltanschauung" that results from Warren's construct, which reveals man's fundamental dependence on his community.

Friedman, Albert B. The Ballad Revival: Studies in the Influence of Popular on Sophisticated Poetry. Chicago: The University of Chicago Press, 1961. 375 pp.

While the main thrust of the book is on English poets' interest in ballads and using of ballad conventions, the epilogue mentions several American poets and American ballads: Robert Frost; Robert Penn Warren; Stephen Vincent Benet; Emily Dickinson; Marianne Moore; Vachel Lindsay; William Rose Benet; T. S. Eliot; E. E. Cummings; and Hart Crane.

Friedman, Arthur Bernard. "A Historical Study of the Yankee Comic Character in American Drama from 1787 to 1947." M.A. Drama. University of Southern California. 1947. 175 pp.

Friesen, Paul. "The Use of Oral Tradition in the Novels on Conrad Richter." Ph.D. Texas Tech. University. 1978. 241 pp. Dissertation Abstracts International 39 (1979): 5511A.

Observes that Richter relied heavily on folk character types and traditions to provide realistic detail and color. Investigates the character types of the Yankee, the woodsy, and the Earth-Mother, rituals of initiation and maturation, familiar folktales, myths, and legends, superstitions, customs, and medical cures, folksongs, ballads, and rhymes, and frontier dialect, including idioms, folk names, and folk vocabulary, in Richter's complete works. Concludes that Richter presents an authoritative and accurate picture of frontier folk life as the result of diligent research and conscientious craftmanship.

Frizzel, John Henry. "Proverbial Philosophy in American Literature." M.A. English. Pennsylvania State University. 1912. 48 pp.

Frye, Northrop. Anatomy of Criticism: Four Essays. Princeton: Princeton University Press, 1957. x, 383 pp.

The "Third Essay" entitled "Archetypal Criticism: Theory of Myths" is a compendious attempt to classify literature in its relationship to myth. Suggests that myth is "one extreme of literary design; naturalism is the other and in between lies the whole area of romance." Views literature as attempts, in varying degrees, "to displace myth in a human direction."

Frye, Northrop. "New Directions from Old," in Henry A. Murray, ed., Myth and Mythmaking (New York: George Braziller, 1960), pp. 115-131.

A general discussion of literary artists as cosmologists which considers, among others, some American writers (e.g., Pound, Eliot); points out some folkloristic images and symbols employed by those writers.

Furlow, Cartim. "Folklore Elements in the Florida Writings of Marjorie Kinnan Rawlings." M.A. English. University of Florida. 1963. 97 pp.

Gabbard, Lucina P. "Albee's Seascape: An Adult Fairy Tale." Modern Drama 21 (1978): 307-17.

Observes that the method of Seascape duplicates the method of fairy tales as described by Bettelheim. References Jung, Campbell, Henderson, Freud, and Brown as well, and identifies the archetype of initiation and symbols of transcendence in Seascape.

Gaddy, C. F. "James Russell Lowell's Knowledge and Use of Classical Mythology." M.A. English. University of North Carolina. 1925. 48 pp.

Gale, Robert L. "Henry James's Dream Children." Arizona Quarterly 15 (1959): 61-63.

Observes that James frequently refers in his figures of speech to numerous fairy tales.

Gallacher, Stuart A. "Franklin's Way to Wealth: A Florilegium of Proverbs and Wise Sayings." Journal of English and Germanic Philology 48 (1949): 229-51.

Is concerned with identifying the source of Franklin's proverbs. Divides them into three groups: those which were in print before Franklin's Way, those which appear elsewhere after the publication of his text, and those which have no other parallels. Surveys the proverbial expressions and concludes that Franklin did not hesitate to draw on his earlier reading material for his expressions. "His new material is not abundant" and his Way to Wealth "is not a creation of expressions" but a folkloristic collection.

Garret, George Palmer. "The Function of the Pasiphae Myth in Brother to Dragons." Modern Language Notes 74 (1959): 311-13.

Proposes that Warren uses the myth of Pasiphae coupling with a bull to illustrate the brute reality of the inner evil in man. Sees the labyrinth which hides the minotaur as a metaphor for the psychological concept of the concealed id at the heart of the psyche. Sees the function of Daedalus as ironically parallel to the function of Warren in constructing the work of art. Concludes that the Pasiphae myth serves as an appropriate symbolic background for "the terrible potential of mankind for irrational ecstasy, good or evil" that Warren depicts in his tale.

Garrison, Daniel H. "Melville's Doubloon and the Shield of Achilles." Nineteenth Century Fiction 26 (1971): 171-84.

Notes some striking similarities (shape, features, structural placement in the narrative) between Ahab's doubloon and Achilles' shield.

Garrison, Theodore Roosevelt. "John Greenleaf Whittier: Pioneer Regionalist and Folklorist." Ph.D. University of Wisconsin. 1960. 536 pp. Dissertation Abstracts International 21 (1960): 621-22.

Re-evaluates Whittier's regional writings and asserts that they are based on New England folklore. Discusses Whittier's biographical connection to the area, and surveys Whittier's developing efforts to record and incorporate folklore in his writings. Points out that Whittier used folk belief and supernaturalism extensively, especially in Legends of New England and The Supernaturalism of New England, and analyzes a variety of uses to which he put the folk materials, including championing social tolerance and expanding religious philosophy.

Gaston, Karen C. "'Beauty and the Beast' in Gail Godwin's Glass People." Critique 21 (1980): 94-102.

Suggests that Godwin reworks two fairy tales in her novel: "Sleeping Beauty" in reverse, where the prince puts the princess to sleep, and "Beauty and the Beast." Argues that Godwin depicts "the strain of being loved only for one's physical appearance and the invisible barriers to growth and self-discovery." Concludes that while some women writers eschew fairy tales because they apparently entrap women in stereotypical roles, Godwin uses mythology as a structural and thematic source and as a means for ironic commentary.

Gates, Henry-Louis, Jr. "Dis and Dat: Dialect and the Descent," in Dexter Fisher & Robert B. Stepto, eds., <u>Afro-American Literature</u> (New York: MLA, 1979), pp. 88-119.

Discusses the use of dialect as a mask for deeper meanings in the works of Afro-American poets. Traces the different attitudes towards and uses of dialect by Johnson, Dunbar, McKay, Brown, and Hughes. Argues that "because dialect was an independent form, it could carry 'independent' meaning--a distinctly black meaning."

Gerber, A. "Uncle Remus Traced to the Old World." <u>Journal of American Folklore</u> 6 (1893): 245-57.

Traces numerous African and European antecedents for motifs found in Uncle Remus. Tries to prove that the majority of those tales were imported from the Old World.

Getz, John R. "Irving's 'Dolph Heyliger': Ghost Story or Tall Tale?" <u>Studies in Short Fiction</u> 16 (1979): 67-68.

Argues the ambiguity of "Dolph Heyliger" prevents definitive assessment of its veracity. Suggests that Irving incorporates conventions of both the ghost tale and tall tale.

Gidmark, Jill Barnum. "Melville's Sea Vocabulary: A Commentary and a Glossed Concordance." Ph.D. University of North Dakota. 1978. 711 pp. Dissertation Abstracts International 39 (1979): 5511A-12A.

The folkloristic connection is not specifically examined, although the influence is inevitable. Traces nautical language usage in general and concludes that semantically, Mardi and Moby-Dick make best use of sea vocabulary and are the most magnificent of his sea novels.

Gillis, Everett A. "Southwestern Literary Balladry." New Mexico Folklore Record 8 (1953-54): 1-5.

Surveys examples of ballad poems.

Gillmore, Frances "Southwestern Chronicle: From Report to Literature." Arizona Quarterly 12 (1956): 344-51.

Suggests that collectors, anthropologists, and novelists can effectively turn folklore into literature.

Gingerich, Willard. "The Old Voices of Acoma: Simon Oritz's Mythic Indigenism." Southwest Review 64 (1979): 18-30.

Notes that Ortiz employs the figure of coyote and the speech patterns and rhythms of his ancestors; concludes that he uses the weight of tradition to sustain his poetry; however, it is "not folkloric innocence, but clairvoyant sophistication that sees the continual rebirth of spirit in all things."

Ginsberg, Elaine. "The Female Initiation Theme in American Fiction." Studies in American Fiction 3 (1975): 27-38.

Examines initiatory motifs in fiction by Cooper, Rowson, Welty, Porter, McCullers, etc.

Glassie, Henry. "The Use of Folklore in _David Harum_." _New York Folklore Quarterly_ 23 (1967): 163-85.

Discusses Westcott's artful use of folk speech, especially proverbs in _David Harum_. Documents 71 examples; suggests they are authentic central New York folklore and they illustrate the author's knowledgeable use of folklore in literature.

Goering, Melva Ruth. "American Folk Materials in the Fiction of Marjorie Kinnan Rawlings, Elizabeth Madox Roberts, and Ruth Seukow." M.A. English. University of Pittsburgh. 1950. 63 pp.

Goodwyn, Frank. "A Proposed Terminology for Clarifying the Relationship Between Folklore and Literature." _Southern Folklore Quarterly_ 14 (1950): 143-49.

Considers the theoretical, definitional, and terminological relationship of folklore and literature and proposes "folkloristic literature" as the name for literary treatments of folkloric plots.

Gornto, Eleanor F. "A Study of the Influence of the Fairy Tale on the Fiction of Henry James." Ph.D. University of Illinois at Urbana-Champaign. 1973. 154 pp. _Dissertation Abstracts International_ 34 (1974): 7754A.

Suggests that the fairy tale through its motifs and melodramatic elements offered James an exaggerated fictional reality against which to measure his essential realism. Points out James's apparent preoccupation with the fairy-tales of "Sleeping Beauty" and "Cinderella."

Gould, Eric. _Mythical Intentions in Modern Literature_. Princeton: Princeton U.P., 1981. ix, 279 pp.

Presents a general discussion of theoretical approaches to the study of myth in literature, and applies these theories to Joyce, Lawrence, and T.S. Eliot. Argues that in The Waste Land, Tiresias is Eliot's "most important" person "because he represents in myth the ideal unity of the sexes."

Gray, Richard. "Signs of Kinship: Thomas Wolfe and His Appalachian Background." Appalachian Journal 1 (1974): 309-19.

Points out mountain legends and traditions in The Hills Beyond.

Gray, R. J. "Southwestern Humor, Erskine Caldwell, and the Comedy of Frustration." Southern Literary Journal 8 (1975-76): 3-26.

Suggests that Caldwell's popularity is similar to the appeal of the Southwestern humorists; they both present intimate portraits of country folk, either as caricaturists or mythologizers.

Green, Mary K. "Edwin Arlington Robinson and the Arthurian Legend." M.A. English. George Peabody College for Teachers. 1930. 85 pp.

Greenberg, Alvin. "Shaggy Dog in Mississippi." Southern Folklore Quarterly 29 (1965): 284-87.

Points out the underlying narrative technique of the shaggy dog formula of Light in August and Old Man (the narrative doubles back on itself in the end) and suggests the technique underscores Faulkner's moral vision.

Greene, Burton J. "Joseph C. Lincoln and the Triumph of the Little Man: A Defense of Popular Culture." Journal of the Ohio Folklore Society 4 (1969): 90-102.

An examination of popular folk values and stereotypes in three Lincoln novels about Cape Cod.

Greet, Thomas Young "The Southern Legend in Yoknapatawpha Fiction of William Faulkner." M.A. English. University of North Carolina. 1950. 150 pp.

Grimes, Geoffrey A. "'Brandy and Water': American Folk Types in the Works of Artemus Ward." <u>New York Folklore Quarterly</u> 25 (1969): 163-74.

Illustrates how Ward used the New England Yankee, the Southern Negro, the backwoods man, and the American Indian to enliven his dramatic burlesques.

Grimes, Geoffrey A. "'Muels', 'Owls', and Other Things: Folk Material in the Tobacco Philosophy of Josh Billings (Henry Wheeler Shaw)." <u>New York Folklore Quarterly</u> 26 (1970): 283-296.

Surveys folk sayings, poems, and stories adopted by Shaw in his depiction of Billings.

Grimes, Johanna Lucille. "The Function of Oral Literature in Selected Afro-American Fiction." Ph.D. Northwestern University. 1980. 233 pp. <u>Dissertation Abstracts International</u> 41 (1980): 2604A.

Investigates the use of folklore in Zora Neale Hurston, Leon Forrest, Albert Murray and Toni Morrison. Discusses customs and folk setting in Hurston and their contribution to her character and theme development. Focuses on the storytelling and sermonizing voice in Forrest, and on various motifs. Examines folk character in Murray and his use of heroic formula. Analyzes folk rhyme, blues, folk belief, and folksong in Morrison, and argues that she exploits the literary potential of these folk materials. Concludes that oral tradition provides an important contribution to Afro-American fiction.

Grobman, Neil R. "Melville's Use of Tall Tale Humor." Southern Folklore Quarterly 41 (1977): 183-94.

Examines five examples of tall tales incorporated into Moby-Dick and discusses other instances of Melville's imitation of the tall tale genre. Concludes that Melville must have been intimately familiar with tall tale telling from his own whaling experiences.

Grobman, Neil R. "A Schema for the Study of the Sources and Literary Simulations of Folkloric Phenomena." Southern Folklore Quarterly 43 (1979): 17-37.

Surveys theoretical classifications of the uses of folklore by writers and then proposes his own model of twelve varying kinds of use ranging from indigenous to borrowed sources and selective recreation to symbolic imitation.

Grobman, Neil R. "The Tall Tale Telling Events in Melville's Moby-Dick." Journal of the Folklore Institute 12 (1975): 19-27.

Documents Melville's exposure to tall tale telling and then traces evidence of tall tale characteristics in five stories in Moby-Dick. Concludes that Melville used folklore to magnify his depiction of the "essential Truth" and not to represent accurately folk traditions.

Gross, Seymore L. "Hawthorne and the Shakers." American Literature 29 (1958): 457-63.

Discusses Hawthorne's exposure to Shaker customs and lifestyle and his incorporation of these traditions into two tales, "The Canterbury Pilgrims" and "The Shaker Bridal."

Guereschi, Edward. "Ritual and Myth in William Faulkner's Pylon." Thoth 3 (1962): 101-110.

Argues that Faulkner's treatment of ritual and myth in Pylon suggests that modern man lacks belief in religious values. Suggests that Faulkner employs the folkloristic motif of the Wasteland and the myth of the Fall to illustrate this theme. Concludes that Faulkner ultimately uses myth to point the way towards a Christian reconciliation to the existential conditions of life.

Gunew, Sneja. "Mythic Reversals: The Evolution of the Shadow Motif," in Joseph D. Olander & Martin Harry Greenberg, eds., Ursula K. Le Guin (New York: Taplinger, 1979), pp. 178-99.

Suggests that Le Guin has a mythopoeic impulse and that she revolutionizes the symbols of the old mythology in order to create a new mythology. Illustrates this argument with a discussion of the shadow motif as it is used in a dozen of Le Guin's novels. The mythological sources are not explored however.

Haber, Edythe C. "Nabokov's Glory and the Fairy Tale." Slavic and East European Journal 21 (1977): 214-24.

Points out Nabokov's fondness for fairy tales and argues that, of his Russian novels, Glory most clearly contains a pattern of allusions to fairy tales. The pattern of allusions reveals Nabokov's dichotomized vision of the opposition of the world of imagination and the "real" world.

Hall, Larry Joe. "The Development of Myth in Post-World-War-II American Novels." Ph.D. North Texas State University. 1974. 253 pp. Dissertation Abstracts International 35 (1975): 6139A.

Discusses the use of myth by Morris, Heinlein, Vonnegut, Ellison, Kesey, Pynchon, and Bellow. Argues that these novels indicate a trend toward a reformation of the basic mythological structures of Western man. This new mythology is an archetypal consciousness that "recognizes the threat of death as the face the universe shows during initiation."

Hall, Wade. "Humor and Folklore in Vinnie Williams' Walk Egypt." Southern Folklore Quarterly 26 (1962): 225-31.

Discusses the author's use of colorful folk sayings, names, and humor of the South.

Hamer, Marcelle Lively. "Anecdotal Elements in Southwestern Literature." M.A. English. University of Texas. 1939. 118 pp.

Hammond, John Francis. "The Monomythic Quest: Visions of Heroism in Malamud, Bellow, Barth, and Percy." Ph.D. Lehigh University. 1979. 224 pp. Dissertation Abstracts International 39 (1979): 6130A.

Argues that The Natural, Henderson the Rain King, Giles Goat Boy, and Lancelot are recreations of either the search for a holy grail or a symbolic journey to the underworld. Generalizes these different myths into a monomythic pattern of the rites of passage: separation, initiation, return. Traces this pattern through the four novels, and concludes that it is used to show the inescapability of the human condition.

Hancock, Joyce Ann. "Kurt Vonnegut and the Folk Society." Ph.D. University of Kentucky. 1978. 222 pp. Dissertation Abstracts International 39 (1978): 3580A.

Explains the form and meaning of Vonnegut's fiction by returning to Redfield's "The Folk Society," an article published in 1947 by a professor who greatly influenced Vonnegut as a graduate student. Argues that Vonnegut uses the concept of an ideal folk society as an ironic cultural counterpoint to the apathy and insanity of modern life. Suggests that Vonnegut's treatment of the ideal folk societies in his fiction reveals his belief that they are antithetical to modern lifestyles and the modern temper. He relocates them to distant worlds or places them in a fragile position in this world to illustrate the limitations and social criticisms of our divided society. Concludes that through his fictional attempt to find an audience, Vonnegut attempts to create his own ideal folk society.

Handy, Deirdre Cathleen. "Family Legend in the Stories of Katherine Anne Porter." M.A. English. University of Oklahoma. 1953. 102 pp.

Hansell, William H. "Black Music in the Poetry of Langston Hughes: Roots, Race, Release." <u>Obsidian</u> 4 (1978): 16-38.

Examines a number of Hughes' poems with the intention of demonstrating that Hughes' poetry was in large part modeled on black music. Discusses a variety of allusions to jazz, blues, spirituals, and gospels, and analyzes how Hughes uses these folkloristic forms to convey his attitudes about blacks and whites, which included optimism about the black future and satirical criticism of white exploitation of black culture.

Hansen, Chadwick. "The Metamorphosis of Tituba, or Why American Intellectuals Can't Tell an Indian Witch from a Negro." <u>The New England Quarterly</u> 47 (1974): 3-12.

Traces the history of a West Indian witch and her evolution as a literary character employed by Longfellow, Williams, and Arthur Miller. Suggests the faulty characterization of her as part Negro is a reflection of our racist culture that associates the practice of magic with Negro tradition. Points out that the witchcraft employed by Tituba is English in origin.

Harder, Kelsie B. "Hemingway's Religious Parody." New York Folklore Quarterly 26 (1970): 76-77.

A brief discussion of Hemingway's parody of the Paternoster and the Ave Maria in "A Clean, Well-Lighted Place"; concludes the parody illustrates the ritualistic attitude of the characters.

Harder, Kelsie B. "Proverbial Snopeslore." Tennessee Folklore Society Bulletin 24 (1958): 89-95.

Calls attention to the distorted proverbial sayings by I. O. Snopes, and suggests Faulkner uses them to illustrate I. O.'s character--"I. O. does not think, he speaks." Contends that Faulkner successfully exploits the folk idiom.

Harding, Walter. "Another Source for Hawthorne's 'Egotism; or The Bosom Serpent'." American Literature 40 (1969): 537-38.

Notes an article in Yeoman's Gazette on the bosom serpent legend.

Hardy, Panspy Leavitt. "The Influence of the Southern Nevada and Southern Utah Folklore on the Writings of Dr. Juanita Brooks and Dr. LeRoy R. Hafen." M.A. English. Brigham Young University. 1965. 160 pp.

Harris, Lillian. "The Character of the Yankee as Culled from American Dramas, from 1787-1839." M.A. English. Columbia University. 1933. 60 pp.

Harris, Norman. "Politics as an Innovative Aspect of Literary Folklore: A Study of Ishmael Reed." Obsidian 5 (1979): 41-50.

Argues that Reed uses folklore for practical and theoretical purposes. Practically, it advances the plot, provides structure, and raises questions about society. Theoretically, it provides "a vast and largely untapped reservoir of African and Afro-American history, folklore, and myth" which asserts an alternative view of history. Suggests that Reed's political literary folklore also seeks to offer alternatives to existing reality. Examines primarily Reed's use of "La Bas," a term associated with HooDoo, to describe "the confluence of history's external realities and myths' internal or subjective realities."

Harris, Trudier. "Ellison's 'Peter Wheatstraw': His Basis in Black Folk Tradition." Mississippi Folklore Register 9 (1975): 117-26.

Suggests that Wheatstraw epitomizes the black folk tradition. Points out a number of uses of the trickster folk figure and argues that Wheatstraw attempts to initiate the narrator into that disguise. Examines the folk speech employed by Wheatstraw and concludes that he is a true representative of black oral tradition. Assesses the narrator as not yet ready to accept his folk heritage.

Harris, Trudier. "Folklore in the Fiction of Alice Walker: A Perpetuation of Historical and Literary Traditions." Black American Literature Forum 11 (1977): 3-8.

Points out that Alice Walker employs folklore in her fiction "for purposes of defining characters and illustrating relationships between them as well as for plot development." Notes Walker's use of the conjure woman character in her books, as well as other folk materials. Concludes the Walker feels that folk culture is an inseparable part of black folk.

Harris, Trudier. "The Tie That Binds: The Function of Folklore in the Fiction of Charles Waddell Chesnutt, Jean Toomer and Ralph Ellison." Ph.D. Ohio State University. 1973. 277 pp. Dissertation Abstracts International 34 (1973): 2489-A.

Examines various kinds of folklore used by Chesnutt, Toomer, and Ellison, including folktales, folksongs, myths, legends, folk heroes, superstitions, stereotypes, and signs, and explores the historical, social, and political reasons for using this folklore. Argues that the writers used the folklore to characterize, provide structure, advance plot, and comment on existing social conditions. Suggests that Chesnutt uses folklore most directly, while Toomer and Ellison tend to alter it for artistic purposes. Concludes that Chesnutt uses folklore to show the vibrant traditions of blacks, Toomer uses it to define his racial heritage, and Ellison uses it to demonstrate the continuity of human tradition.

Harrison, Robert. "Faulkner's 'The Bear': Some Notes on Form." Georgia Review 22 (1966): 318-27.

Regards "The Bear" as myth and discusses archetypal material underlying the story. Argues that Faulkner has drawn the formal substance of "The Bear" from folk myth and primitive initiation rites and that Ike is guided through his rites of passage by his spiritual father, Sam Fathers.

Harry, A. Leslie. "Myth as Structure in Toni Morrison's Song of Solomon." MELUS 7 (1980): 69-76.

Argues that Morrison uses myth to make her story speak to those who do not share her characters' background or experiences. Observes that Morrison fuses Afro-American myth with the beliefs of Judeo-Christian and Greco-Roman heritages to fashion her own myth. Points out that Milkman's search for self-identity in the face of social obligations follows the clear pattern of birth and youth, alienation, quest, confrontation, and reintegration common to mythic heroes as disparate as Moses, Achilles, Beowulf, and Oedipus. Traces this heroic pattern through Morrison's novel.

Hart, John E. "_The Red Badge of Courage_ as Myth and Symbol," in Vickery, ed., _Myth and Literature_, pp. 221-28.

Sees the novel as a version of the myth of self discovery. Henry is the eternal youth who is transformed through a series of rites and revelations into a hero.

Hatley, Donald W. "Folklore in the Fiction of Barry Benefield." _Mississippi Quarterly_ 21 (1967-68): 63-70.

Discusses folk characters from East Texas that enliven Benefield's fiction.

Havard, William C. "Mark Twain and The Political Ambivalence of Southwestern Humor." _Mississippi Quarterly_ 17 (1964): 95-106.

Traces Twain's evolution from his origins as a folk humorist "who revelled in the tall tale" to his political and philosophical alienation at the end of his career.

Havens, Charles Buford. "Mark Twain's Use of Native American Humor in His Principal Literary Works." Ph.D. Vanderbilt University. 1954. 368 pp. _Dissertation Abstracts International_ 14 (1954): 1080.

Surveys Twain's exposure to Native American humor in "his variegated career as printer's apprentice, a Mississippi steam boat pilot, and an inquiring traveler," but focuses on the influence of literary precursors on his work.

Hays, Peter L. "_Gatsby_, Myth, Fairy Tale, and Legend." _Southern Folklore Quarterly_ 40 (1977): 213-23.

Differentiates myth, legend, and fairy tale in order to show how Fitzgerald employs these genres to create contrasting worlds in _Gatsby_.

Concludes that Fitzgerald uses the qualities of legend and fairy tale in Gatsby to mock the American dream.

Hays, Peter L. The Limping Hero: Grotesques in Literature. New York: New York U.P., 1971. vii, 248 pp.

A comprehensive examination of maimed figures in Western myth and literature. Includes lengthy discussions of the ritual backgrounds of this motif and its appearance in works by Malamud, Eliot, Bellow, Albee, Hemingway, Ford and Wharton. Considers the symbolic significance of this motif as an expression of human limitations (as related to the Devil's traditional description) and of human sexuality (as illustrated by the Fisher King).

Heath, Margaret Eleanor. "The Sources for Longfellow's The Song of Hiawatha." M.A. English. University of Colorado. 1961. 76 pp.

Heimer, Jackson W. The Lesson of New England: Henry James and His Native Region. Muncie: Ball State University, 1967. x, 26 pp.

Asserts that James drew his conceptions of American character and lifestyle from his sojourn in New England, but provides little cultural or folkloristic evidence.

Helterman, Jefrey. "Gorgons in Mississippi: Eudora Welty's 'Petrified Man'." Notes on Mississippi Writers 7 (1974): 12-20.

Traces direct allusions, puns, oblique and transferred references, and mythic incidents in Welty's story to the legend of Perseus. Argues that Welty uses this mythic substructure as a means to present a "symbolic dissection of three loveless women." Points out the numerous parallels, and concludes that the resonance of the classical myth with the inner workings of the human mind allows Welty to employ a specificity of mythic detail to enrich and clarify her psychological character studies of three sterile women.

Hemenway, Robert E. "Are You a Flying Lark or a Setting Dove," in Dexter Fisher, ed., _Afro-American Literature_ (New York: MLA, 1979), pp. 122-52.

Argues against simplistic analysis of Afro-American literature as sociological dogma and for concentration on aesthetic forms and patterns. Proposes that "the most profound and persistent aesthetic forms of Afro-American writing arise from the traditional poetic performances . . . called folklore." Reviews the history of the study of folklore in literature and advocates a contextual approach to folkloristics; "what one studies is folklore _and_ literature," not an author's use of folklore, but his adaptation or transformation of phenomena that previously existed as folklore. Proposes a six step analytical method that focuses both on the original social context and the subsequent literary treatment of folklore. Emphasizes the literary text because "one always begins and ends" with the literary text. Analyzes Hurston's _Jonah's Gourd Vine_ and focuses on her use of a courting ritual. Concludes that the "paradigm of folklore as a communication process opens up the novel to a special kind of literary analysis."

Hemenway, Robert E. "The Functions of Folklore in Charles Chesnutt's _The Conjure Woman_." _Journal of the Folklore Institute_ 13 (1976): 283-309. See also _Journal of the Folklore Institute_ 14 (1977): 197-200.

Attempts to build from the methodology proposed by Dundes and Barnes by considering Chesnutt's use of folklore.

Hemenway, Robert E. _Zora Neale Hurston: A Literary Biography_. Urbana: U. of Illinois Press, 1977. xxvi, 371 pp.

Investigates the inevitable connection between Hurston's folklore research and her fiction. Chapter 8, "Plough Up Some Literary," which discusses Hurston's writing of Jonah's Gourd Vine, and Chapter 9, "Crayon Enlargements of Life," which discusses Their Eyes Were Watching God, consider the folklore contribution underlying these works.

Hendricks, William O. "Folklore and the Structural Analysis of Literary Texts." Language and Style 3 (1970): 83-121.

Examines major theories of structural analysis of folklore (Propp, Olrik) in order to demonstrate its wider applicability to literature. Argues that the structural principles underlying the composition of folk narratives are similar--if not identical--to those underlying literary narratives.

Hepp, Ralph A. "Myth and Realism in Frank Norris' 'Blix,' 'Moran of the Lady Letty,' and 'McTeague.'" M.A. English. University of South Dakota. 1963. 40 pp.

Herman, Judith B. "Plath's 'Daddy' and the Myth of Tereus and Philomela." Notes on Contemporary Literature 7/1 (1977): 9-10.

Details an allusion to the cutting out of Philomela's tongue in Plath's poem, in which the heroine cannot talk to her father to tell him of her outrage.

Hernandez, Fances. "Isaac Bashevis Singer and the Supernatural." CEA Critic 40/2 (1978): 28-32.

Reviews Singer's interest in folkloristic descriptions of supernatural experiences and his preoccupation with this theme in his fiction. Surveys Singer's presentation of these materials in numerous stories.

Hess, Judith W. "Traditional Themes in Faulkner's 'The Bear'." Tennessee Folklore Society Bulletin 40 (1974): 57-64.

Attempts to document the connection to folklore in "The Bear" by pointing out two folkloric themes: the strong man overcoming all adversaries and the initiation of a young man into adulthood. Traces these themes in Crockett's and Thrope's tales of bear hunting, which are related to frontier lore.

Higgins, John C. "The Lumberjack in American Literature: His Life and Customs, His Slang, His Ballads, and Shanties, and His Folk-Epic of Paul Bunyan." M.A. English. University of Southern California. 1935. 147 pp.

Highet, Gilbert. The Classical Tradition: Greek and Roman Influences on Western Literature. New York: Oxford U.P., 1949. 763 pp.

Surveys the historical development of the extensive contribution of classical tradition to western literature. However, its consideration of both classical folklore and American literature is surprisingly sketchy.

Hildebrand, Reuben Paul. "Whittier's Treatment of New England History and Legend." M.A. English. University of Pittsburgh. 1929. 84 pp.

Hill-Lubin, Mildred A. "'And the Beat Goes On': A Continuation of the African Heritage in African-American Literature." College Language Association Journal 23 (1979): 172-87.

Traces evidence of African folk tradition, especially music, surfacing in Afro-American literature. Considers folksinging in Douglass's My Bondage and My Freedom, blues and the call response pattern in Hughes's Not Without Laughter as well as in The Autobiography of Malcom X, and competition and improvisation in dancing in

Baldwin's _Go Tell It on the Mountain_ and Angelou's _I Know Why the Caged Bird Sings_. Concludes that these uses of folk music serve to underscore the fundamental philosophies of the texts in which they appear.

Hill, Mildred A. "Common Folklore Features in African and African-American Literature." _Southern Folklore Quarterly_ 39 (1975): 111-33.

Points out parallels in the narrative techniques and uses of folklore between African writers, such as Achebe and Tutuola, and Afro-American writers, such as Bontemps, Chesnutt, Ellison, Johnson, and Hurston. Some of the common features include: the dozens, signifying, magic, superstition, trickster figures, and folk sayings. Gives examples of the use of these features in both traditons. Concludes that despite reluctance by Black authors to acknowledge the importance of Black American folklore, it represents a significant philosophical heritage that can be traced back to African oral tradition and it contributes significantly to Afro-American literature. Includes a bibliography.

Hiller, Anna K. "The Life of the Ozarks Seen Through the Literature of the Region." M.A. English. Miami University. 1940. 190 pp.

Hines, Joyce R. "The Arthurian and Grail Themes in the Poetry of Charles Williams." M.A. English. Columbia University. 1952. 156 pp.

Hlavsa, Virginia V. "_Light in August_: Biblical Form and Mythic Function." Ph.D. State University of New York at Stony Brook. 1978. 599 pp. _Dissertation Abstracts International_ 39 (1979): 6130A-31A.

Concentrates on Faulkner's use of the Gospel according to St. John and Frazer's _Golden Bough_ in _Light in August_. Points out specific ties with the Bible, with myth, and with primitive practice and belief. Constructs a concordance to follow clusters of words, which reveal the full extent of Faulkner's borrowings. Argues that Faulkner elaborates and elucidates the important concepts and themes in John and Frazer. Notes structural and stylistic correspondences as well. Concludes that Faulkner's treatment in _Light in August_ provides new enlightenment for old myths.

Hlavsa, Virginia V. "St. John and Frazer in _Light in August_: Biblical Form and Mythic Meaning." _Bulletin of Research in the Humanities_ 83 (1980): 9-26.

Argues that interpretive problems associated with _Light in August_ can be resolved if the book is viewed as an artfully structured parallel of the 21 chapters of the St. John Gospel; suggests further that Faulkner develops the stories "by incorporating mythic figures, primitive practice, and folk belief from Sir James Frazer's complete _Golden Bough_." Points out the detailed parallels between _light_ and John and the links between Faulkner's story and the rituals described by Frazer. Sees connections between Lena and Isis the Corn-Mother, between Lucas and Osiris, and between the ritual acquisition of the golden bough and Joe's ordeal. Concludes that Faulkner reworks the Christian myth and pagan rituals in an attempt to humanize then, to invest them with a contemporary and naturalistic reality.

Hoadley, Frank M. "Folk Humor in the Novels of William Faulkner." _Tennessee Folklore Society Bulletin_ 23 (1957): 75-82.

Maintains that Faulkner uses all the devices of frontier humor--tall tale, hyperbole, understatement, trick situations, and stereotyping. Not well supported by the evidence however.

Hoag, Ronald Wesley. "A Second Controlling Myth in John Updike's _Centaur_." _Studies in the Novel_ 11 (1979): 446-53.

Identifies Caldwell as "a sharply defined Sisyphus figure." Points out the parallel motif of exposure to privileged sexual knowledge shared by Sisyphus and Caldwell, which results in their parallel tormented conditions. Notes the resemblance between Sisyphus's task and Caldwell's teaching, between Sisyphus's rock and Caldwell's buick. Concludes that Updike modifies the myth slightly by suggesting the possibility of human success through faith and brotherhood.

Hoffman, Daniel G. "Folklore in Literature: Notes Toward a Theory of Interpretations." Journal of American Folklore 70 (1957): 15-24.

Considers the relationship of folklore and literature both as independent forms of expression and as hybrid mixtures. Identifies three approaches to folklore in literature, three patterns in literary use of folklore, and three levels of significance in the literary use of folklore.

Hoffman, Daniel G. Form and Fable in American Fiction. New York: Oxford U. P., 1961. 368 pp.

Shows the shaping role of folklore in ten of the most important American tales and romances by Irving, Hawthorne, Melville, and Twain. Identifies native characters, idioms, and attitudes contributed by American folklore to these stories; considers as well the mythic vision of the New World that influenced the literature. A major critical study that examines the richness and complexity of folklore's contribution to American fiction in order to trace some common themes concerning the American hero and his philosophical position.

Hoffman, Daniel G. "Irving's Use of American Folklore in 'The Legend of Sleepy Hollow'." PMLA 68 (1953): 425-35.

Argues that Irving is "the first important American author to put to use the comic mythology and popular traditions of American character which . . . had proliferated widely in oral tradition." Concentrates especially on the clash of regional characters--the Yankee vs. the backwoodsman.

Hoffman, Daniel G. "Myth, Romance, and the Childhood of Man," in _Hawthorne Centenary Essays_, ed. Roy Harvey Pearce (Columbus: Ohio State U.P., 1964), pp. 198-219.

Examines Hawthorne's recasting of Greek myths in _A Wonder-Book for Girls and Boys_ and _Tanglewood Tales_. Suggests that Hawthorne not only garnishes these tales, but recasts them in an attempt "to provide his native land with a moralized mythology." Discusses the continued influence of classical myth on Hawthorne's later works. Concludes that "like the myths which they clothe with the morality and the manners of their age, these tales . . . have became a permanent part of our inheritance."

Hoffman, Daniel G. _Paul Bunyan: Last of the Frontier Demigods_. Philadelphia: University of Pennsylvania Press, 1952. xiv, 213 pp.

Traces the successive treatment of Paul Bunyan material from its possible folk sources to its subsequent adoption by literary artisans, including Sandburg, Frost, and Auden. Considers the folk tradition of Paul Bunyan authentic though sparse, and details the literary revisions it underwent in its written versions.

Hoffman, Daniel G. "Robert Frost's Paul Bunyan: A Frontier Hero in New England Exile." _Midwest Folklore_ 1 (1951): 13-18.

Investigates Frost's use of the Bunyan legend in "Paul's Wife"; concludes that Frost borrows some motifs from oral literature but reworks it into a pattern of his own illustrating the inviolability of the individual.

Hoffman, Daniel G. "Sandburg and 'The People': His Literary Populism Reappraised." Antioch Review 10 (1950): 265-278.

Claims that Sandburg in The People, Yes resurrects the dying folklore of a vanishing way of life. Details the folk motifs underlying "Who Made Paul Bunyan" and concludes that Sandburg sentimentally attempts to return to a romantic depiction of American life and that his poetry relies upon unpolished borrowings of popular jokes and proverbs.

Hoffman, Daniel G. "Thoreau's 'Old Settler' and Frost's Paul Bunyan." Journal of American Folklore 73 (1960): 236-38.

Notes a parallel metaphor in Thoreau's Walden and Frost's "Paul's Wife," and suggests they both have their roots in older folk motifs.

Hoffman, Daniel G. "Yankee Bumpkin and Scapegoat King," in John B. Vickery and J'nan M. Sellery, eds., The Scapegoat: Ritual and Literature (Boston: Houghton Mifflin, 1972), pp. 132-42.

Identifies folk themes in Hawthorne's "My Kinsman, Major Molineux." Points out the story reenacts the ancient ritual of the deposition of the Scapegoat King. Suggests furthermore that Robin resembles the folk characters of Yankee yarn and folklore and that the experience serves as a rite of passage for the youth.

Horowitz, Floyd Ross. "Ralph Ellison's Modern Version of Brer Bear and Brer Rabbit in Invisible Man." Midcontinent American Studies Journal 4 (1963): 21-27.

Characterizes the narrator of Invisible Man as possessing bear-like attributes and traces the elaborate parody of the folklore motif of the Brer Bear/Brer Rabbit competition as it is revealed in the interactions of the protagonist with the other characters.

House, Kay Seymour. Cooper's Americans. Columbus: The Ohio State U. P., 1965. viii, 350 pp.

Follows Rourke's argument and examines a variety of popular character types in Cooper's fiction, including the Indian, the Dutchman, the Negro, the Yankee, and the frontiersman, most of which have folkloric roots. "Such characters think and act in accord with their communal affiliation; and while they themselves may be unaware of their own group's history, they bear its identifying marks."

Hovet, Theodore R. "'Once Upon a Time': Sarah Orne Jewett's 'A White Heron' as a Fairy Tale." Studies in Short Fiction 15 (1978): 63-68.

Applies Propp's morphology to Jewett's short story and notes that it "follows the linear sequence of the first twenty functions." Argues also that the symbolic imagery and function of fairy tales is used by Jewett "to explore parabolically the social and sexual tensions in nineteenth-century America," to convert regional materials into universal themes, and to advocate the nurturing power of nature over the materialistic exploitation of industrial America.

Howard, L. "Walt Whitman and the American Language." American Speech 5 (1930): 441-51.

Analyzes Whitman's use of slang, aboriginal names, and popular speech as a way of keeping his poetry, and America, vital.

Howell, Elmo. "Faulkner's Sartoris and the Mississippi Country People." Southern Folklore Quarterly 25 (1961): 136-46.

Argues that Faulkner in Sartoris draws heavily on the folk habits of Mississippi people; surveys some characters and scenes that illustrate the folksy quality of the novel, and concludes that Faulkner gives his novel an archetypal significance by employing these folk memories.

Howell, Elmo. "William Faulkner's 'Christmas Gift'." Kentucky Folklore Record 8 (1967): 37-40.

Explains Faulkner's allusion in The Sound and The Fury to the Southern greeting "Christmas Gift" as an illustration of his feeling about the passing of old values and as an explanation for Quentin Compson's suicide.

Howell, Elmo. "William Faulkner's Mule: A Symbol of the Post-War South." Kentucky Folklore Record 15 (1969): 81-86.

Discusses the role of the mule in Southern folk traditions and its symbolic appeal for Faulkner as a metaphor for the ability of the Southern people to endure hardship and for the right combination of humility and stubborn pride.

Howell, John Michael. "The Waste Land Tradition in the American Novel." Ph.D. Tulane University. 1963. 128 pp. Dissertation Abstracts International 24 (1964): 3337.

Explores the influence of Eliot's poem and his mythical method on The Great Gatsby, The Sun Also Rises, The Sound and the Fury, and The Catcher in the Rye. Points out the "Waste Land" and "Grail" motifs in these novels and discusses their philosophical significance.

Hubbel, Jay. "The Smith-Pocahontas Story in Literature." Virginia Magazine of History and Biography 65 (1957): 275-300.

Discusses the folkloristic qualities of the Pocahontas legend and reviews its adaptation by aspiring American writers.

Huddleston, Eugene L. "Depictions of New York in Early American Poetry." New York Folklore Quarterly 24 (1968): 275-293.

Discusses folk traditions, local color, and naturalistic scenery as it is presented in a selection of early American poetry.

Huddleston, Eugene L. "Place Names in the Writings of Jesse Stuart." Western Folklore 31 (1972): 169-77.

Notes that authentic Kentucky place names in Stuart's novels are most abundant and successful.

Hudson, Arthur Palmer. "The Impact of Folklore on American Poetry," in A Tribute to George Coffin Taylor, ed. Arnold Williams (Chapel Hill: University of North Carolina Press, 1952): 132-47.

Discusses the mixing of folklore in works by Frost, Longfellow, Whittier, Holmes, Harte, Sandburg, Stevens, among others, and concludes that folklore has always been one of the main ingredients of American poetry.

Hudson, Arthur Palmer. "The Singing South: Folksong in Recent Fiction Describing Southern Life." Sewanee Review 44 (1936): 3-30.

Surveys Southern fiction from 1923-1932 and finds 161 folksongs in 25 novels and 46 folksongs in 22 short stories. Discusses four uses to which these folksongs have been put in the literature: to document historicity, to describe local color, to assist thematic development, or to illustrate professional interest.

Hudson, Arthur Palmer. "Some Versions of The King of the Cats." Southern Folklore Quarterly 17 (1953): 225-31.

Brief reference to Irving's and Benet's use of the folktale "The King of the Cats."

Hudson, Tommy. "William Faulkner: Mystic and Traditionalist." Perspective 3 (1950): 227-35.

Tradition as folklore is not discussed.

Hughes, Elaine Wood. "Development of a Mythic Consciousness in John Barth, the Novelist." Ph.D. University of Alabama. 1979. 354 pp. Dissertation Abstracts International 41 (1980): 251A.

Traces the development of a mythic consciousness in Barth's writings through his use of the myths of Narcissus, Dionysus, and Orpheus. Argues that there is an archetypal progression apparent in Barth's fiction, "a logical development of the individual which strives for total self-hood." Draws connections between Barth's first two novels and the myth of Narcissus, his second two novels and Dionysus, and his next two novels and Orpheus.

Huguenin, Charles A. "The Truth About the Schooner Hesperus." New York Folklore Quarterly 16 (1960): 48-53.

Details Longfellow's poetic license in revising the facts of the wreck of the Hesperus; it may have been drawn in part from accounts of other wrecks.

Hume, Kathryn. "Robert Coover's Fiction: The Naked and the Mythic." Novel 12 (1979): 127-48.

Discusses two primary facets of Coover's fiction, the "naked," which describes his concern for the concrete details of life, his humor, and his vividness, and the "mythic," which means the "wide variety of patterns that refer implicitly or explicitly to an extrinsic meaning-giving system." Points out Coover's use of games, magic, folktales, and jokes. Concludes that the combination of these dual aspects of Coover's fiction are what mark his writing as especially deserving of our appreciation.

Hunter, Grace. "The Tristram Legend in English and American Poetry Since 1850." M.A. English. University of Kansas. 1929. 190 pp.

Hurst, Richard Maurice. "Snakelore Motifs in the Writings of J. Hector St. John de Crevecoeur." M.A. Folklore. Indiana University. 1962. 84 pp.

Hutchison, Earl R., Sr. "Antiquity and Mythology in The Scarlet Letter: In the Primary Sources." Arizona Quarterly 36 (1980): 197-210.

Notes an allusion in the character of Hester Prynne to Aphrodite and Hetaira Phryne, and argues that it reveals a major theme in Hawthorne's novel--"paganism and an earthy, healthy love of life." Points out the ironic contrast between the trial in the Eleusinian Mysteries of the courtesan Hetaira, who is ultimately acquitted of impiety toward the gods for her prostitution, and Hester, who is found guilty and punished for her single transgression of the Puritan code. The irony is sustained by the parallel emphasis on the heroine's bosom and by the role of their lovers. Suggests also that "the triangular affair of Aphrodite, Hephaestus, and Ares that produces Harmonia correlates exactly with Hester, Roger, Arthur, and Pearl."

Hyde, Stuart W. "The Ring-Tailed Roarer in American Drama." Southern Folklore Quarterly 19 (1955): 171-78.

Traces the depiction of the backwoods folk character of "the ring-tailed roarer" in a variety of early American dramas.

Hyman, Stanley Edgar and Ralph Ellison. "The Negro Writer in America: An Exchange," in Alan Dundes, ed., Mother Wit From The Laughing Barrel (Englewood Cliffs: Prentice-Hall, 1973), pp. 46-64. Also in Partisan Review, 25 (1958): 197-222.

Hyman's essay, entitled "The Folk Tradition" examines the influence of Negro folklore on Negro literature, with examples from Ellison, Hurston, Wright, Fisher, and Baldwin. Views Negro folklore as having a similar message and influence upon Negro literature as Western folklore had on Western literature. Considers especially the trickster figure and blues.

Ellison's essay, entitled "Change the Joke and Slip the Yoke," rejects Hyman's position that the trickster figure is a true Negro hero in either folk or literary tradition. The characters are too aware of their temporal woes and limitations to be merely archetypal representations. Gives examples from Invisible Man and other black literature.

Inge, M. Thomas, ed, High Times and Hard Times. Nashville, Tennessee: Vanderbilt U. P., 1967. x, 348 pp.

Briefly considers, in the introductory essays, Harris's command of American vernacular and his use of local color in his Sut Lovingood stories.

Inge, M. Thomas. "Literary Humor of the Old Southwest: A Brief Overview." Louisiana Studies 7 (1968): 132-43.

Identifies the folk custom of telling stories as being crucial for the creation of the literature of the Southwestern humorists.

Inge, M. Thomas. "William Faulkner and George Washington Harris; In the Tradition of Southwestern Humor." Tennessee Studies in Literature 7 (1962): 47-59.

Suggests that Faulkner, like Harris, acquired his ribald humor from the tall tales and anecdotes told on porches and street corners. What distinguishes Faulkner is that he uses the material for more serious artistic end. Compares adaptations of folk materials in both authors' writings.

Ives, C. B. "James's Ghosts in The Turn of the Screw." Nineteenth-Century Fiction 18 (1963): 183-89.

Examines the appearance and possible source of the ghosts (from after dinner scare stories heard by James) and concludes the inconsistency between James's account in the Preface and the actual occurrence of the ghosts supports the non-supernatural interpretation of the ghosts.

Ives, Sumner. "The Phonology of the Uncle Remus Stories." Publication of the American Dialect Society 22 (1954): 3-59.

Reviews the literary dialect employed by Harris and concludes that it is consistent and accurate representation of genuine folk speech.

Ivey, Saundra Keyes. "Aunt Mahalia Mullins in Folklore, Fakelore, and Literature." Tennessee Folklore Society Bulletin 41 (1975): 1-8.

Recounts the history of a local folk character, Mahala Mullins, the legends attached to her, and her appearance in literary texts by Henry Wiltse, James Aswell, Mildred Haum, and Jesse Stuart.

Jackson, Nancy-Dabney Roosevelt. "Edward Albee: Myths for Our Time." Ph.D. Columbia University Teachers College. 1978. 136 pp. Dissertation Abstracts International 39 (1979): 6399A-400A.

Views Albee as a shaman and guardian of a body of cultural myths. Suggests he reworks the Adam figure, uses classical and Christian symbolism, employs a stereotypical and patriarchal attitude towards women, and incorporates a Puritan vision of pre-industrial America as Eden in his plays. Traces these four ideas through the plays, and concludes that by spectacles, ritual, music, and incantation, Albee re-defines our shared traditions and reproduces our ancient myths, somewhat like "a modern medicine man."

Jaskoski, Helen. "Power Unequal to Man: The Significance of Conjure in Works by Five Afro-American Authors." Southern Folklore Quarterly 38 (1974): 91-108.

Identifies the body of lore and custom called conjure that is African in inspiration and outside Anglo-American culture, and examines its use in writings by Douglass, Chesnutt, McClellan, Perry, and Gaines.

Jeffe, David. "Some Origins of Moby-Dick: New Finds in an Old Source." American Literature 29 (1957): 263-77.

Notes that Melville found in a narrative account of a South-sea expedition material for Queequeg's depiction. The appearance, background, beliefs, manners, and customs of Queequeg appear to be drawn from this early ethnographic survey, especially its description of one local chief.

Johnson, Guy B. "Folk Values in Recent Literature on the Negro," in Folk Say: A Regional Miscellany 1930 (Norman: University of Oklahoma Press, 1930), pp. 359-72.

Points out instances of "the treatment of Negro Folk life by recent Southern authors," including Adams, Bradford, Heyward, Odum, Peterkin, and Sale.

Johnson, Lemuel A. "'Ain'ts,' 'Us'ens,' and 'Mother-Dear': Issues in the Language of Madhubuti, Jones, and Reed." Journal of Black Studies 10 (1979): 139-66.

Identifies a tradition of word play in Afro-American literature that is derived from the techniques and mode of perception in the oral tradition of the blues, toasts, signifying, dozens, and sermons. Suggests that Afro-American authors use these oral dimensions of language to introduce new meaning and perspectives to their works.

Johnson, Patricia A., & Walter C. Farrell, Jr. "How Langston Hughes Used the Blues." *MELUS* 6 (1979): 55-63.

Suggests that Hughes transformed the idioms of blues and jazz into poetic verse in *Fine Clothes to a Jew* and then abandoned this ethnocentric style of indigenous poetry for fifteen years, when he turned to more political and socio-economic concerns. He returned to the blues, however, for *Shakespeare in Harlem*. This later work incorporates the blues style, but it focuses more heavily on economic determinants of the blues, and it is more narrative in development, achieving thus "a smooth flow of meaning from verse to verse . . . and a greater sense of organic unity."

Johnson, Susan Emily. "Joel Chandler Harris Without 'Uncle Remus': A Critical Study of J. C. Harris as a Writer of the Mountaineer and the Georgia Cracker." M.A. English. University of Georgia. 1943. 86 pp.

Jones, Alexander E. "Mark Twain and Freemasonry." *American Literature* 26 (1954-55): 363-73.

Part of the essay deals with "the echoes of lodge ritual which are present in *Innocents Abroad*."

Jones, Bartlett C. "American Frontier Humor in Melville's *Typee*." *New York Folklore Quarterly* 15 (1959): 283-88.

Observes that Melville's stylistic borrowings from American frontier humor, especially the use of tall tales, braggadocio, exaggerated language, rustic figures of speech, etc., have contributed to the undermining of the reception of his novel _Typee_ as truthful.

Jones, Bayard Hale. "Hawthorne and German Romance: Hawthorne's Artistic Relationship to Hoffman, Tieck, and Musaus; Based on a Comparison of 'Volksmärchen' and 'Kunstmärchen'." M.A. English. University of California at Berkeley. 1912. 98 pp.

Jones, Charles W. "Knickerbocker Santa Claus." _New York Historical Society Quarterly_ 38 (1954): 357-83.

Suggests that Irving created his image of St. Nicholas from folk legends and from materials acquired from the New York historical society.

Jones, Kyra. "Myth in _The Winter of Our Discontent_," in Wilson M. Hudson, ed., _Diamond Bessie & the Shepherds_ (Suskin: Encino Press, 1972), pp. 93-102.

Argues that Steinbeck used multilayered Biblical parallels in an effort to depict in his narrative the contrast of sacred myth and profane reality. Ultimately, the myth vanquishes the reality, stressing Steinbeck's appreciation for "living mythologically."

Jones, Michael Owen. "'Ye Must Contrive Allers to Keep Jest the Happy Medium Between Truth and Falsehood': Folklore and the Folk in Mrs. Stowe's Fiction." _New York Folklore Quarterly_ 27 (1971): 357-69.

Contends that Mrs. Stowe used folklore to create memorable fiction by relying heavily on folk characters, plots, expressions, and other story-telling techniques. Examines _The Pearl_, _Oldtown Folks_, and _Fireside Stories_.

Jones, Steven Swann. "The Enchanted Hunters: Nabokov's Use of Folk Characterization in *Lolita*." *Western Folklore* 39 (1980): 269-83.

Argues that Nabokov employs the folk characters of the jealous mother, the fairy princess, the prince charming, and the old ogre in *Lolita* in order to borrow their magical appeal as well as to parody the romantic and optimistic perspective of fairy tales.

Jones, Steven Swann. "The Legend of Perseus and John Barth's *Chimera*." *Folklore Forum* 11 (1978): 140-151.

Investigates the question of literature's use of "adulterated" folklore (folklore preserved by print). Observes that such folkloristic materials are commonly employed by authors, and argues that a comprehensive understanding of these folklore source materials contributes significantly to our understanding of the literary text, as illustrated by a representative examination of Barth's use of the Perseus legend in *Chimera*.

Jones, William M. "Eudora Welty's Use of Myth in 'Death of a Traveling Salesman'." *Journal of American Folklore* 73 (1960): 18-23.

Examines Welty's 'mythical method" in "Death of a Traveling Salesman"; she recasts traditional materials in modern guise, as illustrated by allusions to the Hercules myth in the story.

Jones, William M. "Name and Symbol in the Prose of Eudora Welty." *Southern Folklore Quarterly* 22 (1958): 173-85.

Traces the use of folklore (especially allusions to mythic figures, e.g., the Phoenix, Clytie, Perseus) in Welty's works and suggests she takes the whole world of folk knowledge and compresses it into the modern South.

Kagan, Sheldon S. "'Going' Down the Road Feelin' Bad': John Steinbeck's The Grapes of Wrath and Migrant Folklore." Ph.D. University of Pennsylvania. 1971. 190 pp. Dissertation Abstracts International 32 (1972): 4507A.

Examines materials collected from California migrant camps in 1940 in order to determine the versimilitude of Steinbeck's fiction. Concludes that Steinbeck displays an accurate eye and ear for his subject.

Kamenetsky, Christa. "In Quest of Virtue: Popular Trends Reflected in Children's Literature in Nineteenth Century Michigan." Keystone Folklore Quarterly 10 (1965): 63-85.

Finds that folk values and beliefs greatly influence the children's literature of Michigan.

Karem, Suzanne Story. "Mythology in the Works of Eudora Welty." Ph.D. University of Kentucky. 1977. 181 pp. Dissertation Abstracts International 39 (1978): 3581A.

Focuses on Welty's use of vegetation and fertility myths to illustrate her belief in the necessity of accepting and understanding the cycle of nature. Points out her use of the vegetation and initiation rites associated with the Demeter-Persephone myth and Eleusinian mysteries, and argues that she consciously incorporates Eliot's mythical method. Traces these solar and agrarian myths through Welty's fiction, and finds numerous parallels to the ancient vegetation myths of the dying god or goddess who is reborn with the return of plant growth in the spring. Concludes that the myths of death and rebirth in nature provide Welty her primary means of ordering her vision of life in the South and of expressing her view of the ultimate nature of human existence.

Keefer, T. Frederick. "William Faulkner's Sanctuary: A Myth Examined." Twentieth Century Literature 15 (1969): 97-104.

Uses myth loosely to describe the erroneous belief "that Faulkner himself considered Sanctuary to be a potboiler," which is "completely without basis." No folkloristic analysis.

Keiser, Albert. The Indian in American Literature. New York: Oxford University Press, 1933. 312 pp.

Points out that much of the impact of Indians upon American literature is folkloristic. Surveys treatments of Indian myths, legends, customs, and beliefs by Cooper, Paulding, Simms, and Longfellow.

Kennedy, Sally P. "The Wandering Jew in Nathaniel Hawthorne's Short Fiction." M.A. English. University of Tennessee. 1964. 78 pp.

Kent, George E. Blackness and the Adventure of Western Culture. Chicago: Third World Press, 1972. 210 pp.

Two essays deal with folklore and literature: "Langston Hughes and Afro-American Folk and Cultural Tradition" (pp. 53-75) and "Ralph Ellison and Afro-American Folk and Cultural Tradition" (pp. 152-63).

Kent, George E. "Langston Hughes and Afro-American Folk and Cultural Tradition," in Langston Hughes: Black Genius--A Critical Evaluation (New York: William Morrow, 1971), pp. 183-210.

Argues that Hughes's use of folklore requires us to analyze the significance of "folk literature and art that derives from centuries of confrontation of black lives with the ambiguities of their universe and that of American culture." Suggests that black folklore possesses a number of qualities that Hughes takes advantage of in his own writing. Discusses Hughes's incorporation of blues, sermons, gospels, and folk values into his art.

Kent, George E. "Ralph Ellison and Afro-American Folk and Cultural Tradition." College Language Association Journal 13 (1970): 265-76.

Surveys Ellison's pronouncements on the use of folklore in his fiction and argues that the folklore provides added dimension to Ellison's work. Examines how Ellison incorporates themes from Black folklore, such as oppression and castration, into his narrative through the use of allusion and analogy to black traditions. Identifies Black folk figures and jokes underlying Invisible Man. Concludes that to a self-conscious artist like Ellison, black folk tradition is not an end in itself, it is a means to the communication of his message.

Kent, George E. "Self-Conscious Writers and Black Folk and Cultural Tradition," in The Humanity of English: NCTE 1972 Distinguished Lectures (Urbana: National Council of Teachers of English, 1972), pp. 73-93.

Contrasts the individualism of self-conscious writers with the group identity of folk culture. Argues that "the strongest black writers have . . . found themselves involved in profiting by resources of folk-tradition." Points out evidence of folk identity in Dunbar, Chesnutt, Johnson, Hughes, and Brown.

Keyser, Samuel Jay, & Alan Prince. "Folk Etymology in Sigmund Freud, Christian Morgenstein, and Wallace Stevens." Critical Inquiry 6 (199): 65-78.

Defines folk etymology as the process whereby unfamiliar terms are made into familiar ones by providing traditional accompanying explanations, anecdotes, or mythologies based on a presumed division of the word into its smaller components. Suggests that in this activity, the word is made to enact the world. Identifies this proclivity in Egyptian mythology, American political history, and Genesis. Analyzes its use by

Stevens in "Infanta Marina" and shows that Stevens emulates the folk etymological process by renaming his title in his poem and by providing a table explaining the derivation of the new name. Concludes that in Stevens, this principle of folk etymology has the same major status as the mythic principle of creation-through-language illustrated in Egyptian mythology, Genesis, and the Torah.

Killheffer, Marie. "The Development of the Yankee Character in American Drama from 1787 to 1861." M.A. English Language and Literature. University of Chicago. 1927. 77 pp.

Kime, Wayne R. "Washington Irving and Frontier Speech." American Speech 42 (1967): 5-18.

A glossary of over seventy examples of frontier speech in Irving's three western works.

Kirby, David K. "The Princess and the Frog: The Modern American Short Story as Fairy Tale." Minnesota Review 4 (1973): 145-149.

Briefly notes the similarity between short stories by Malamud, Capote, and Calisher and certain Grimms' fairy tales.

Kissane, James. "Imagery, Myth, and Melville's Pierre." American Literature 26 (1955): 564-72.

Criticizes Moorman's mythic reading of Pierre. Suggests instead that there is a dramatic movement toward disillusionment and a search for truth.

Kleiman, E. "The Wizardry of Nathaniel Hawthorne: Seven Gables as Fairy Tale and Parable." English Studies in Canada 4 (1978): 289-304.

Suggests that _Seven Gables_ is a parable dressed up as a fairy tale because the artist's role is like that of the magician or wizard, casting spells to enchant an audience. Hawthorne uses the familiar materials and forms of fairy tale, moral parable, classical fable, and Biblical tradition to create "his portrait of the Western Eden." The story includes an enchanted garden, a wicked ogre, puppets dancing to an organ-grinder's music, magical red blossoms, witchcraft, spells, phantoms, a magic mirror, and a Merlin figure at work within his tower.

Kliger, Samuel. "Hebraic Lore in Maxwell Anderson's _Winterset_." _American Literature_ 18 (1946): 219-32.

Examines the Hebraic concept of a final Judgment Day and the Jewish Messianic belief, and discusses their function in Anderson's play.

Klotman, Phyllis R. "An Examination of the Black Confidence Man in Two Black Novels: _The Man Who Cried I Am_ and _dem_." _American Literature_ 44 (1973): 596-611.

Points out the tradition of the confidence man in American literature, and suggests Kelley's and Williams' recent novels deal with the confidence man in unique ways.

Knox, George. "The Totentanz in Ellison's _Invisible Man_." _Fabula_ 12 (1971): 168-78.

Examines Ellison's use of the medieval Dance of Death motif in _Invisible Man_ and concludes that the author took the social forms and events of contemporary American life and welded them with attenuated forms of myth and ritual (in particular the _Totentanz_ genre) in order to construct a combined Afro-Anglo-American symbology.

Kolker, Robert P. "Toward a Definition of Myth in Literature." _Thoth_ 5 (1965): 3-21.

Generally analyzes myth as a fundamental, recurring pattern of human experience and considers how literature is a form of myth. Argues that the poetic process repeats the primal process of myth-making. Concentrates on William James's attempts to shift the focus of philosophical thought away from realms of abstract reasoning and onto the basic stuff of life as an approach to the identification of archetypes. Discusses the prevalence of the quest pattern in Western literary history.

Kosok, Heinz. "'A sadder and a wiser boy': Herman Melville's _Redburn_ as _Novel of Initiation_." _Jahrbuch für Amerikastudien_ 10 (1965): 126-52.

A lengthy article written in German that argues that the theme of visitation is central to the story of Redburn. Traces the examples of initiatory experience that occur during the protagonist's journey, and concludes that the story may be viewed as a _Bildungsroman_.

Kreyling, Micheal. "Myth and History: The Foes of _Losing Battles_." _Mississippi Quarterly_ 26 (1973): 639-49.

Views Welty's novel as a depiction of the dialectical struggle in human consciousness between concern for the timeless and preoccupation with the temporal, between myth and history. Examines primarily Welty's role as the creative artist manipulating place, character, plot, symbol into a coherent whole, above myth and history.

Kroll, Harry Harrison. "How I Collect Proverbial Materials for my Novels." _Tennessee Folklore Society Bulletin_ 23 (1957): 1-5.

Recounts his folk heritage and his master's thesis on folk speech and explains how he employs folklore in his novels to develop character.

Kroll, Judith. <u>Chapters in a Mythology</u>. New York: Harper and Row, 1976. xvi, 303 pp.

Argues that there is one overriding concern in Plath's poetry, "the problem of rebirth or transcendence," and that it is expressed through her mythic system. The mythic system involves a mythologizing of autobiographical events, which provides the author with a sense of detachment by presenting the material through mythic motifs and plots. The general mythic motifs of rebirth, the Moon-muse, the dying god, metamorphosis, ritual sacrifice and exorcism are traced through Plath's poetry, but the specific folkloristic connections and sources are not explored.

Kuklick, Bruce. "Myth and Symbol in American Studies." <u>American Quarterly</u> 24 (1972): 435-50.

Argues that the myth and symbol approach taken in Smith's <u>Virgin Land</u> may have value "for determining the significance <u>to us</u> of certain texts," but "it does not tell us what the authors meant, what they intended to say about the world." Concludes that "if myth-symbol generalizations have any substance, they must be subject to falsification by the conclusions of 'lower level' historical research."

Kumar, P. Shiv. "Marionette in Taleysin: Yiddish Folkfigures in Two Malamud Stories." <u>Indian Journal of American Studies</u> 8 (1978): 18-24.

Identifies a group of Yiddish folkfigures in Malamud's and Bellow's fiction, including the <u>schlemiel</u>, the <u>schnorrer</u>, the <u>luftmenschen</u>, and the <u>shadkhn</u>. Focuses on the <u>schnorrer</u> anbd the <u>luftmenschen</u> as quintessential Jewish archetypes and discusses their appearance in "The Last Mohican" and "The Magic Barrel." Concludes that Malamud recognizes and takes advantage of his Jewish heritage in creating his fiction.

LaBudde, Kenneth. "Cultural Primitivism in William Faulkner's 'The Bear'." <u>American Quarterly</u> 2 (1950): 322-28.

Points out the resemblances of Faulkner's description of the bear to primitive customs and attitudes towards totemic animals.

Langford, Beverly Young. "History and Legend in William Faulkner's 'Red Leaves'." Notes on Mississippi Writers 6 (1972): 19-24.

Investigates Faulkner's treatment of legendary material concerning Indians in "Red Leaves." Suggests the narrative was drawn from oral history.

LaRosa, Ralph Charles. "Emerson's Proverbial Rhetoric: 1818-1838." Ph.D. University of Wisconsin. 1969. 259 pp. Dissertation Abstracts International 30 (1969): 1140A.

Investigates the thetorical principles underlying the form and content of Emerson's journals and notebooks, which explains Emerson's distinctly proverbial style.

LaRosa, Ralph Charles. "Henry David Thoreau: His American Humor." Sewanee Review 83 (1975): 602-22.

Argues that Thoreau used the stereotypical stances of the Yankee and the frontiersman (as identified by Rourke) to present his humor. "His humor captured the pervasive tone of the native monologue typical of folk raconteurs."

LaRosa, Ralph Charles. "Invention and Imitation in Emerson's Early Lectures." American Literature 44 (1972): 13-30.

Discusses Emerson's appreciation for the common proverbs and his invention and imitation of proverbs in his lectures.

LaRosa, Ralph Charles. "Necessary Truths: The Poetics of Emerson's Proverbs," in Mid-Nineteenth

Century Writers: Eliot, De Quincey, Emerson, eds. Eric Rothshein and Joseph Wittreich (Madison: U. of Wisconsin Press, 1976), pp. 129-216.

Discusses Emerson's style and shows how it imitates proverbial rhetoric. Argues that even when Emerson changes proverbs and invents new ones, he maintains "a certain proverbial realism."

Lattin, Vernon E. "The Quest for Mythic Vision in Contemporary Native American and Chicano Fiction." American Literature 50 (1979): 625-40.

Treats mythic vision as sacred vision, not oral tradition.

Laughlin, Rosemary M. "Attention, American Folklore: Doc Craft Comes Marching In." Studies in American Fiction 1 (1973): 220-27.

Identifies a character in James Alan MacPherson's "A Solo Song; For Doc" as based on occupational folk heroes in the Negro dining car tradition.

Leach, MacEdward. "Folklore in American Regional Literature." Journal of the Folklore Institute 3 (1966): 376-97.

Examines the regionality of American culture and posits eight overlapping ways that American regional writers have used folklore.

Leary, Lewis. "The Adventures of Captain John Smith as Heroic Legend," in Joseph A. Leo Lemay, ed., Essays in Early Virginia Literature Honoring Richard Beale Davis (New York: Franklin, 1977), pp. 13-33.

A historical biography of Smith that equates his writing impulse with that of Whitman and suggests his style corresponds to classical heroic fiction. Draws comparisons to the stories of Odysseus, Siegfried, and Aeneas, and evaluates

Smith's autobiography according to the twenty-two typical incidents in the career of the mythic hero as defined by Raglan. Notes that Smith scores nine and concludes that Smith's story remains so irresistible because it is "legend certified by heroic adventure the world over, since legend began." Notes other elements of traditional lore also appear in Smith's *True Travels*, e.g., the Jonah story and the quest motif.

Lechlitner, Ruth N. "Arthurian Story Retold by Edwin Arlington Robinson." Ph.D. English. State University of Iowa. 1926. 113 pp.

Lee, Hector H. "Tales and Legends in Western Literature." *Western American Literature* 9 (1975): 239-54.

Observes that it is the tales and legends of the West that give Western literature its distinctive characteristics. Discusses the definition and form of Western folk narratives, and surveys the use in Western literature of folk legends, themes, characters, beliefs, and folk tales. Focuses ultimately on the legendary narrative of "The Shadows from Lookout Bridge" as an illustration of the common ingredients of the Western story.

Lee, Valerie Gray. "The Use of Folktalk in Novels by Black Women Writers." *College Language Association Journal* 23 (1979): 266-72.

Argues that Hurston, Morrison, and Jones use folktalk to communicate their philosophy, to entertain their audience, and to capture the subtle dynamics of black life. Analyzes the language and metaphors in passages from *Their Eyes Were Walking God*, *Sula*, and *Corregidora* and shows how the folk allusions illuminate the authors' themes.

Leeds, Josephine. "Longfellow's Use of Indian Lore." M.A. English. Columbia University. 1929. 83 pp.

Leisy, Earnest E. "Folklore in American Literature." College English 8 (1946): 122-29.

A brief survey of major American authors who use folklore, e.g., Irving, Cooper, Poe, Hawthorne, etc.

Leisy, Ernest E. "Literary Versions of American Folk Materials." Western Folklore 7 (1948): 43-49.

Continues his survey of American writers employing folklore, including Irving, Cooper, Poe, Whittier, Simms, Hall, Harris, Dos Passos, Wolfe, and Faulkner, and cites evidence of folk narratives, customs, and proverbs found in their writings.

Leonard, Raymond E. "Witchcraft and Hawthorne." M.A. English. Brown University. 1946. 106 pp.

Lerfald, Robert Allan. "Hemingway's Search for the Sacred: A Study of the Primitive Rituals of a Twentieth-Century American Adam." Ph.D. University of Minnesota. 1976. 323 pp. Dissertation Abstracts International 37 (1977): 7752A.

Uses Eliade's universal Myth of the Eternal Return to argue that Hemingway's philosophy emulated primitive religious ontology. Both personally and artistically, he created a set of rituals that enabled him to experience what he considered the sacred; his Wilderness Garden was a version of the Edenic myth, and it included hunting, fishing, and writing rituals, which were sacred. Analyzes "The Last Good Country" as the best mythopoeic expression of initiation into the Edenic Myth, Green Hills of Africa as the most comprehensive mythopoeic expression of his sacred hunting rituals, and The Old Man and the Sea as the ideal mythopoeic expression of his fishing rituals. Concludes that Hemingway's suicide was the rational plan of a man dedicated to primitive religious truth.

Leverence, W. John. "Cat's Cradle and Traditional American Humor." Journal of Popular Culture 4 (1972): 955-63.

Identifies sixteen traditional aspects of American humor present in Cat's Cradle: e.g., the tall tale, the unreliable narrator, the Negro minstrel, incongruous language, anecdote, satire, the Western character, etc.

Levesque, George A. "Le Roi Jones' Dutchman: Myth and Allegory." Obsidian 5 (1979): 33-40.

Identifies the stereotypes in Jones's drama and focuses primarily on Lula. Lula is seen as "a tainted Eve in the corrupted American Eden, eating apples and tossing them over her shoulder carelessly," and as an inverted version of the fairy tale character of Snow White. She offers Clay the apple and she is like a sorceress. Concludes that this characterization contributes to the allegorical function of Jones's play which demonstrates that Lula as a mythic representation of white womanhood and white society does not accept Clay as a human being.

Levin, David. "Shadows of Doubt: Specter Evidence in Hawthorne's 'Young Goodman Brown'." American Literature 34 (1962): 344-52.

Argues that Hawthorne knew the facts and lore of Salem witchcraft and that he used them liberally in his story.

Levin, Harry. "Some Meanings of Myth," in Henry A. Murray, ed., Myth and Mythmaking (New York: George Braziller, 1960), pp. 103-114.

A broad discussion of myth's role in culture and literature that alludes obliquely to Emerson, Cooper, Whitman as users of myth.

Lewis, Mary Ellen B. "The Study of Folklore in Literature: An Expanded View." Southern Folklore Quarterly 40 (1976): 343-51.

Discusses three levels of folklore (situation, medium, and product) all of which require analytic consideration when discussing folklore's appearance in literature. Discusses the methodology involved with each level of analysis.

Lewis, Mary Ellen B. "Why Study Folklore and Literature?" Folklore Forum 11 (1979): 163-75.

Suggests that folklore and literature, as parallel cultural expressions, mutually illuminate one another and gives examples, mostly from Huckleberry Finn.

Lewis, R. W. B. The American Adam: Innocence, Tragedy and Tradition in the Nineteenth Century. Chicago: U. of Chicago Press, 1955. 272 pp.

Sees a pervasive cultural view or "myth" of America crystallizing in the literary works of American writers from 1820 to 1860, (e.g., Holmes, James, Whitman, Cooper, Hawthorne, Melville). Regards the Biblical figure of Adam before the Fall as an archtypal pattern (a folk character model) for 19th century American writers.

Lewis, R. W. B. "The Hero in the New World: William Faulkner's The Bear." Kenyon Review 13 (1951): 641-60. Also in Charles Feidelson, Jr. and Paul Brodtkorb, Jr., eds., Interpretations of American Literature (New York: Oxford University Press, 1959), pp. 332-48.

Identifies _The Bear_ as a _Bildungsroman_ and "a canticle or chant relating the birth, baptism, and early trials of Isaac McCaslin." Analyzes this ceremonious quality in the style and structure of the story.

Lewis, Ruth Neeley. "Nathaniel Hawthorne's Versions of Greek Myths." M.A. English. University of Maryland. 1963. 60 pp.

Lidoff, Joan. "Another Sleeping Beauty: Narcissism in _The House of Mirth_." _American Quarterly_ 32 (1980): 519-39.

Suggests that the appeal of Wharton's novel is drawn from the fairy tale characterization of its heroine Lily, which taps the nexus of primordial feelings associated with narcissistic impulses. Identifies Lily's characterization as narcissistic in that it focuses on her fantasies and libidinal imagery of wish fulfillment. Identifies a variety of fairy tale allusions which serve to underscore the narcissistic appeal of the text.

Light, Kathleen. "Uncle Remus and the Folklorists." _Southern Literary Journal_ 7 (1974-75): 88-104.

Investigates the "ethnological considerations" provoked by Harris's publication of his Remus tales and their subsequent influence upon Harris and his writing.

Light, Martin. "Lewis's 'Scarlet Sign,' Accommodating to the Popular Market." _Journal of Popular Culture_ 1 (1967): 106-13.

Argues that Lewis introduced "a startlingly substantial number of motifs which are characteristically found in folktales" in his fiction, but that he comprised his material by tailoring it for the demands of the popular market.

Lindahl, Carl. "On the Borders of Oral and Written Art." Folklore Forum 11 (1978): 94-123.

Identifies two traditional approaches to the study of folklore-and-literature, and attempts to determine "what distinguishes written from oral art." Considers eight possible differentiating characteristics; compared to literature, folklore is considered: oral, fixed, less complex, more structured, traditional, communally produced, spontaneously composed, and performed for a live audience. Points out parallel examples of these characteristics in both folklore and literature (some American examples are included) and concludes that only fixity of text and performance for audience genuinely mark the boundary between the printed and the spoken work of art.

Lindberg-Seyersted, Brita. "The Ode Familiar: A Colloquial Diction and Its Uses," in The Voice of the Poet: Aspects of Style in the Poetry of Emily Dickinson (Cambridge: Harvard University Press, 1968), pp. 59-117.

Examines Dickinson's use of regionalistic vocabulary and concludes that although she uses only a small percentage of distinctly regional words, they reveal that "the Squire's daughter was socially secure in her speech habits," that seeing "New Englandly" came naturally to her.

Linville, Jane Jessup. "A Study of Some of the Literary and Legendary Sources of Poe's 'Gold Bug'." M.A. English. Columbia University. 1947. 68 pp.

Lisca, Peter. John Steinbeck: Nature and Myth. New York: Crowell, 1978. viii, 245 pp.

A biographical survey of Steinbeck's life and literary canon. Identifies the major themes underlying each work; some themes are related to folklore such as the Cain and Abel story in East of Eden, and the Christ legend in Of Mice and

Men. Discusses the influence of Lao-Tze on Cannery Row as well. Not primarily a folkloristic study however.

Litzinger, Boyd. "Myth Making in America: 'The Great Stone Face' and Raintree County." Tennessee Studies in Literature 8 (1963): 81-84.

Views Lockridge's Raintree as an elaboration of the mythical elements in Hawthorne's "The Great Stone Face "; mythic materials include the Johnny Appleseed story, the Lincoln legend, and the John Brown saga.

Long, E. Hudson. "Social Customs in O. Henry's Texas Stories," in A Good Tale and a Bonnie Tune, ed. Mody C. Boatright et al. (Dallas: SMU Press, 1964), pp. 148-67.

Describes O. Henry's two years on a Texas ranch and his exposure to their customs and lore, and traces this influence in his fiction.

Loomis, C. Grant. "Bret Harte's Folklore." Western Folklore 15 (1956): 19-22.

Briefly surveys California anecdotes, tall tales, superstitions, and Spanish-American lore in Harte's writings.

Loomis, C. Grant. "Emerson's Proverbs." Western Folklore 17 (1958): 257-262.

Lists 105 proverbs from Emerson's writing.

Loomis, C. Grant. "Folk Language in William MacLeon Raine's West." Tennessee Folklore Society Bulletin 24 (1958): 131-48.

Alphabetically lists 186 proverbs and 201 proverbial expressions from over 80 western novels by Raine. Briefly discusses formulaic patterns of action as well.

Loomis, C. Grant. "Henry David Thoreau as Folklorist." Western Folklore 16 (1957): 90-106.

Gives examples from Thoreau's journals and publications of tales, characters, customs, and folk speech that he recorded.

Loomis, C. Grant. "Sylvester Judd's New England Lore." Journal of American Folklore 60 (1947): 151-58.

Gives lengthy quotations illustrating Judd's partiality to folk belief, song, and proverb.

Lord, Albert B. "A Comparative Analysis," preface to Merlin Ennis, compiler and translator, Umbundy: Folktales from Angola (Boston: Beacon Press, 1962).

Discusses characteristic compositional devices of oral style, the role of common phrases, recurring incidents, and groups of incidents in the repertoire of oral storytellers as the mark of oral versus written literature.

Lovecraft, H. P. Supernatural Horror in Literature. New York: Dover Publications, 1973. 106 pp.

Traces the development of literature based on "horror-lore," "the dark heritage, both of random folklore and of academically formulated magic and cabbalism." Chapters 7 and 8 focus specifically on Poe and American literature and their incorporation of the supernatural, both artistically and folkloristically.

Lowery, Dellita Martin. "Selected Poems of Nicolas Guillen and Langston Hughes: Their Use of Afro-Western Folk Music Genres." Ph.D. Ohio State University. 1975. 280 pp. Dissertation Abstracts International 36 (1975): 1487A-88A.

Points out that Hughes uses the rhythms, the overlapping call-and-response structure, and the folk language associated with the blues and jazz. Analyzes these African-derived oral traditions of the New World in The Weary Blues, Fine Clothes to a Jew, and Montage of a Dream Deferred.

Lucas, Dolores Dyer. Emily Dickinson and Riddle. Dekalb: Northern Illinois University Press, 1969. v, 151 pp.

Dickinson's apparently cryptic quality is viewed as an outgrowth of her love of riddles, which are prevalent throughout her poetry; Dickinson's poetic riddles are surveyed and analyzed.

Lucente, Gregory L. The Narrative of Realism and Myth: Verga, Lawrence, Faulkner, Pavese. Baltimore: Johns Hopkins U.P., 1979. xi, 189 pp.

Presents a theoretical analysis of the contrasting realistic and mythic modes of literary expression. Discusses the philosophical responses of Plato, Aristotle, and Vico to the mythic mode. Investigates the interaction of the realistic and mythic. Analyzes in "Southern Literature/Southern History: Flem in Hell or 'The Trickster Tricked" Faulkner's incorporation of overtly mythic elements from classical and preclassical Greek, Eastern, and Germanic mythology, as well as fabulist elements from Aesop, American Indian tales, European fables, and Southern folklore.

Ludovici, Paola. "The Struggle for an Ending: Ritual and Plot in Recent American Indian Literature." Ph.D. American University. 1979. 52 pp. Dissertation Abstracts International 40 (1979): 854A.

Explores the conflict between oral, tribal tradition and Western modernism in the novels of four American Indian writers (Leslie Silko, Hyemeyotists Storm, N. Scott Momaday, and James Welch).

Lutwack, Leonard. Heroic Fiction: The Epic Tradition and American Novels of the Twentieth Century. Carbondale: Southern Illinois U.P., 1971. xiv, 174 pp.

Considers solely prose epic tradition, with little or no discussion of a comparison to oral epic tradition; as a consequence, the definition and concept of epic is somewhat vague and general.

Lydenberg, John. "Nature Myth in Faulkner's 'The Bear'." American Literature 24 (1952): 62-72. Reprinted in Vickery, Myth and Literature.

Sees two kinds of myth in "The Bear"--the myth of the South and the myth of primitive nature. Examines the latter and argues that the story is a "magical role enacted by superhuman characters" in which religion, magic, legend and ritual combine to demonstrate the eternal struggle between Man and Nature. Sees the narrative as concerning "the hunting of the tribal god, whom they dare not, and cannot, touch, but whom they are compelled to challenge."

Lynch, James J. "The Devil in the Writings of Irving, Hawthorne, and Poe." New York Folklore Quarterly 8 (1952): 111-31.

Describes the "kind of devil that Irving, Hawthorne, and Poe inherited from Massachusetts" and the different treatments of him by those authors.

Lynn, Kenneth S. "Huck and Jim," in Huckleberry Finn: Text, Sources, and Criticism (New York, 1961), pp. 231-37.

Views Huck's life as similar to "the Mosaic saga of an infant who 'died' and was reborn in the river" and as unfolding "in a series of initiations."

Lynn, Kenneth S. _Mark Twain and Southwestern Humor_. Boston: Little, Brown and Co., 1959. 300 pp.

Analyzes the careful craftsmanship and social background of the Southwestern humorists, up to Twain, whose tradition relied heavily on oral frontier materials.

Lynn, Kenneth S. _Visions of America: Eleven Literary Historical Essays_. Westport: Greenwood Press, Inc., 1973. 211 pp.

The essays consider a number of folklore-influenced works by Thoreau, Stowe, Twain, Norris, and Crane; the final essay, "Violence in American Literature and Folklore," pp. 189-205, concerns the use of violent humor by London, Twain, Melville, and Wright and their sources in the Southwestern humorists and folk humor.

Lytle, Andrew. "The Working Novelist and the Myth-making Process," in Henry A. Murray, ed., _Myth and Mythmaking_ (New York: George Braziller, 1960), pp. 141-156.

A brief description of some folkloristic themes (Biblical motifs) in _The Velvet Horn_, by its author.

MacDonald, Duncan, Jr. "The 'Uncle Remus Stories': One of the few American Classics of World Literature." _Fabula_ 1 (1957): 159-61.

Brief reference to Harris's use of fable and dialect in his stories. Points out the dialect is from 17th century England.

Machann, Virginia Sue Brown. "American Perspectives on Women's Initiations: The Mythic and Realistic Coming to Consciousness." Ph.D. University of Texas at Austin. 1979. 553 pp. _Dissertation Abstracts International_ 40 (1979): 1470A.

Investigates the American variations on the traditional initiatory pattern (separation, trial, communication of communal secrets, return to community) in six autobiographies (Bradstreet, Ashbridge, Fuller, Mead, Lindbergh, and McCarthy) and two novelists (Hawthorne and James). Investigates the wide variety of self-definitions depicted in these works, and notes the continuity of the initiatory structure itself, which follows either a coming of age or a coming to consciousness pattern. Points out the mythic point of view in The Scarlet Letter and Mead's literary use of vegetation myths and contrasts these with the historical, personal, and artistic preoccupations of the other works. Concludes that the initiatory patterning is a reflection of the culture in which the literary work is created, and in its implementation for women we can trace the muted opposition of the intensely individualistic American myth of self-realization and the traditional communal associations and ties of women.

Maclachlan, John M. "Folk and Culture in the Novels of Erskine Caldwell." Southern Folklore Quarterly 9 (1945): 93-101.

Considers Caldwell's novels as sociological documents and examines the social mores presented there.

Maclachlan, John M. "Folk Concepts in the Novels of Thomas Wolfe." Southern Folklore Quarterly 9 (1945): 175-186.

Argues that Wolfe used his folk heritage from the Appalachians to create the cultural context of his novels.

Maclachlan, John M. "William Faulkner and the Southern Folk." Southern Folklore Quarterly 9 (1945): 153-67.

Examines the pattern of culture, castes, and folk groups in Faulkner's novels and concludes that the novels can best be understood in the context of group interaction and sociological representation.

Madden, David. "Let Me Tell You the Story: Transforming Oral Tradition." Appalachian Journal 7 (1980): 210-29.

Discusses his own use of folklore in writing fiction.

Major, Mabel and Pearce, T. M. Southwest Heritage: A Literary History with Bibliographies. Albuquerque: U. of New Mexico Press, 1972. 165 pp.

Includes relevant chapters on "Literary Folktales" (IV) and "Humor and Tall Tales" (II) that survey the connection between folklore and southwestern literature.

Malin, Irving. William Faulkner: An Interpretation. Stanford: Stanford U. P., 1957. viii, 103 pp.

Sees the traditional and archetypal patterns underlying Faulkner's fiction; interprets "The Bear" as "the submission of the son (Isaac) to the priest (Sam-Abraham) and of both the priest and the sacrificial victim to the wilderness."

Malone, Ted. "Edwin W. Fuller and the Tall Tale." North Carolina Folklore 22 (1972): 36-41.

Identifies the use of tall tales in Fuller's North Carolina novel, Sea Gift. Discusses definitions by Fuller and Botkin of tall tales.

Marcus, Mordecai. "What Is an Initiation Story?" Journal of Aesthetics and Art Criticism 19 (1960): 226-27.

Surveys Faulkner's primitive and psychological rituals in "The Bear" and finds them convincing.

Marsh, Philip M. "Indian Folklore in Freneau." New Jersey Historical Society Proceedings 71 (1953): 125-135.

Argues that Freneau was a romantic follower of Rousseau and that he was a "speculative primitivist" who advocated the environment and customs of the American Indian. Discusses Freneau's essay "The Pilgrim" which reveals his leaning toward Indian values and details in subsequent poetry Freneau's numerous allusions to Indian tradition.

Marshall, W. Gerald. "Mark Twain's 'The Man That Corrupted Hadleyburg' and the Myth of Baucis and Philemon." Mark Twain Journal 20 (1980): 4-7.

Points out the interesting parallels between the myth of the virtuous, hospitable old couple who receive Jupiter graciously and are rewarded for it and the basic plot of "Hadleyburg." In both narratives, the central actor decides to punish a town for its immoral behavior, but decide to spare one couple because of their kindness towards him. Argues, however, that Twain's treatment of the myth is ironic. "He suggests that the universal values of charity and faith inherent in the myth have essentially vanished in the modern world," because the old couple in Hadleyburg are not truly deserving; they are tormented by the knowledge of their inner greed. Also, Stephson does not act with the same moral justification and wisdom as his mythic counterpart, Jove; rather, he is somewhat vengeful and satanic. Concludes, finally, that "the myth of Baucis and Philermon is used in the story as a context through which contemporary society can measure what it has lost."

Martin, Dale Frederick. "Robert Frost: The Poet as Mythmaker." Ph.D. Southern Illinois University at Carbondale. 1978. 146 pp. Dissertation Abstracts International 40 (1979): 854A-55A.

Suggests that Frosts uses such forms as the parable, the tall tale, the dramatic narrative, the allegory, the gothic, the quest, the song, the apocalyptic prophecy, and the lyric. Argues that through these devices, Frost presents his philosophical vision of the world. Sees myth as the expression of the universal in the local. Frost is a mythmaker because he uses New England as a metaphor for the universe. Concludes that Frost's mythopoetic qualities make him a major poet and place him in the modern camp, like Faulkner, Joyce, Yeats, and Eliot.

Martin, Dellita J. "Langston Hughes's Use of the Blues." College Language Association Journal 22 (1978): 151-59.

Suggests that Hughes's Fine Clothes to the Jew relies extensively "on several genres of Afro-American oral tradition--the blues, field chants, shouts, spirituals, and work songs." Concentrates on "Suicide," "Lament Over Love," and "Young Gal's Blues" to show the poet's use of blues both structurally and thematically. Shows how Hughes adapts the three unit structure of the traditional blues genre to convey his moods of quiet despair.

Martin, Robert K. "Hart Crane's 'For the Marriage of Faustus and Helen': Myth and Alchemy." Concerning Poetry 9 (1976): 59-62.

Identifies the mythological significance of Crane's allusions to the cuckoo and the finch, which are references to the Greek gods. Discusses also the use of the Faust legend. Argues that Crane radically rewrites the Faust legend and eliminates the damnation of Faust in order to demonstrate his belief in transformation and his faith in poetry as magic art.

Martin, Terence. "Rip, Ichabod, and the American Imagination." American Literature 31 (1959-60): 137-49.

An unsophisticated treatment of Irving's partiality toward fairy tales, superstitions, and folk motifs.

Martin, W. R. "The Use of the Fairy-Tale: A Note on the Structure of The Bostonians." English Studies in Africa 2 (1959): 98-109.

Points out the incorporation of a "submerged archetypal 'tale'" in The Bostonians. Suggests James consciously adapts and parodies the traditional fairy tale plot of the hero and the maiden.

Martin, Wendy. "The Rogue and the Rational Man: Hugh Henry Brackenridge's Study of a Con Man in Modern Chivalry." Early American Literature 8 (1973): 179-92.

Identifies Teague as a con man (a traditional stereotype) and argues that Modern Chivalry criticizes the schemes of con men and profiteers in Post-Revolutionary America.

Mason, Julian. "Owen Wister: Observer in North Carolina." North Carolina Folklore 20 (1972): 163-68.

Gives biographical evidence of Wister's interest in folklore, particularly in folk music. Discusses a singing game and some folk music that Wister collected and employed in his writing.

Masterson, James R. "The Tale of The Living Fang." American Literaure 11 (1939-40): 66-73.

Notes de Crévecoeur's proficiency in using tall tales as illustrated in his story of a New Jersey rattlesnake in Letters from an American Farmer.

Matthiessen, F. O. American Renaissance: Art and Expression in the Age of Emerson and Whitman. New York: Oxford U. P., 1941. xxiv, 678 pp.

In a larger discussion of the American transcendentalists, some attention is given in Chapter XIV, "Man in the Open Air," to the need for mythology and to the incorporation of American folk characters and legends into American literature in an effort to meet this need.

Mawer, Randall R. "Classical Myth in Jewett's *A Marsh Island*." *American Notes and Queries* 14 (1976): 85-87.

Points out the connection between the love triangle in Jewett's novel and Homer's version of the myth Vulcan, Venus, and Ares. Suggests this allusion intensifies the sexual conflict and broadens the context of the novel.

Mayne, Winifred Florence. "The Native Sources of Hawthorne's Supernatural Material." M.A. English. Columbia University. 1928. 59 pp.

Mayoux, Jean-Jacques. "Myth et symbole chez Herman Melville." *Inventario* 15 (1960): 43-54.

Argues that Melville was brought up on the strongly symbolistic tradition of Biblical Calvinism, and that evidence of this heritage is found in Melville's use of Biblical motifs such as Sodom and Gomorah in his novels.

McAtee, W. L. *Studies in the Vocabularies of Hoosier Authors: Baynard Rush Hall (1793-1863)*. Chapel Hill: The Compiler, 1960. 90 pp.

Lists folk terms, expressions, and proverbs found in Hall's works.

McCarthy, Kevin M. "Witchcraft and Superstition in *The Winter of Our Discontent*." *New York Folklore Quarterly* 30 (1974): 197-211.

Analyzes myth, ritual, and superstition in Steinbeck's novel and concludes that his use of these folk beliefs is tinged with parody, irony, and humor.

McCarthy, Paul. "Sports and Recreation in All the King's Men." Mississippi Quarterly 22 (1969): 113-30.

Considers folk games in Robert Penn Warren's novel.

McClary, Ben Harris. "Melville, Twain and the Legendary 'Tennessee Poet'." Tennessee Folklore Society Bulletin 29 (1963): 63-4.

Briefly discusses Melville's and Twain's metaphoric allusions to a "Tennessee Poet" who appears not to have existed.

McCullen, J. T., Jr. "Ancient Rites for the Dead and Hawthorne's 'Roger Malvin's Burial'." Southern Folklore Quarterly 30 (1966): 313-23.

Draws a connection between "Roger Malvin's Burial" and classical folk burial customs and beliefs, specifically the Roman Lemuria, an expiation ceremony to appease spirits troubled by violent death. Argues that Hawthorne alludes to this tradition to enhance the ominous tone of the story and to suggest his religious theme.

McCullen, J. T., Jr. and Jeri Tanner. "The Devil Outwitted in Folklore and Literature." North Carolina Folklore 17 (1969): 15-20.

Briefly recounts examples of the popular motif of outwitting the devil, primarily from English literature.

McCune, Margorie W., Tucker Orbison, & Philip M. Withim, eds. The Binding of Proteus: Perspectives on Myth and the Literary Process. Lewisburg: Bucknell U. P., 1974. 350 pp.

A collection of essays primarily dealing with myth as a general thought process or organizing principle; Bateson's article "Myth-A Dispensable Critical Term" is perhaps the most useful essay, since his preferred definition and use of the term myth as referring to preliterate matter corresponds to folkloristic usage. By this definition, most of the essays in this study would be excluded.

McDowell, Tremaine. "Notes on Negro Dialect in the American Novel to 1821." American Speech 5 (1930): 291-96.

Surveys the slow adaption of Negro dialect by American authors. Concludes that early American novelists tended to reproduce a dialect that resembled the field-dialects of Maryland and Virginia.

McDowell, Tremaine. "The Use of Negro Dialect by Harriet Beecher Stowe." American Speech 6 (1931): 322-36.

Concludes that Mrs. Stowe's Negro dialect "is only a makeshift in Uncle Tom's Cabin and, in The Minister's Wooing, only an approximation."

McGhee, Nancy B. "Langston Hughes: Poet in the Folk Manner," in Langston Hughes, Black Genius: A Critical Evaluation, ed Therman B. O'Daniel (New York: Morrow, 1971), pp. 39-64.

Argues that Hughes celebrates the common folk through his use of blues style and themes in his poetry. Suggests that Hughes portrays "the poverty, injustice and inequities of black folklife." Notes examples of characters and scenes that are illustrative of black folklife.

McHaney, Thomas L. "Eudora Welty and the Multitudinous Golden Apples." Mississippi Quarterly 26 (1973): 589-624.

Views The Golden Apples as a complete and unified piece because it resembles a cycle of myth. Argues that Welty uses themes and variations based on Celtic and Graeco-Roman mythology and her stories "play out the timeless legends of love, wondering, struggle, defeat, and success again and again under different conditions and bearing different names." Identifies Welty's use of the stories of Danae and Leda and the Celtic tradition of Halloween. Concludes that Welty gives us "something that did not exist before: a unique glimpse of life, a new myth fashioned out of the old."

McKeithan, D. M. "Bull Rides Described by 'Scroggins,' G. W. Harris, and Mark Twain." Southern Folklore Quarterly 17 (1953): 241-43.

Short study identifying a Mike Fink anecdote as reported by 'Scroggins' as a possible source for Twain's description of a bull ride.

McLuhan, Marshall. The Gutenberg Galaxy; The Making of Typographic Man. Toronto: University of Toronto Press, 1967. 293 pp.

Suggests that typography has affected modern psychology and epistemology and has caused a split of head and heart. Traces the ways in which the forms of experience and of mental outlook have been modified, first by phonetic alphabet and then by printing. Is primarily concerned with a sociological and psychological comparison of oral and written cultural phenomena.

McMillan, Douglas J. "Folkways in Ovid Pierce's 'The Wedding Guest'." North Carolina Folklore 23 (1975): 125-28.

Points out that the folklore in The Wedding Guest is contemporary and is shared by blacks and whites. Lists examples of proverbs, folk beliefs, animal love, etc.

McNeill, William K. "Lafcadio Hearn, American Folklorist." Journal of American Folklore 92 (1978): 947-67.

A biographical account of Hearn's background and interests that traces his lifelong preoccupation with folklore, specifically folksong, legends, and fairy tales. Surveys Hearn's exposure to American, Afro-American, and Japanese traditions, and documents Hearn's collection and re-creation of these in his writing. Concludes that Hearn "was really a cultural historian who kept seeking the old Nippon traditions that could serve as positive values in a rapidly emerging industrial nation."

McPherson, Hugo. *Hawthorne as Myth-Maker: A Study in Imagination*. Toronto: Toronto U. P., 1969. xiii, 256 pp.

Investigates Hawthorne's reliance on different kinds of myths: classical, personal, cultural (Puritan). Shows how Hawthorne adapts these to communicate his own spiritual and moral vision.

Meister, Charles W. "Franklin as a Proverb Stylist." *American Literature* 24 (1952-53): 157-66.

Analyzes Franklin's attempt to coin proverbs and to translate foreign proverbs. Discusses his preference for balance, metaphor, and anticlimax.

Mellard, James M. "Faulkner's Jason and the Tradition of Oral Narrative. *Journal of Popular Culture* 2 (1968): 195-210.

Examines the style of the third section of *The Sound and the Fury* as evidence of the influence of oral narrative upon Faulkner and "sophisticated" written tradition.

Mellard, James M. "Malamud's Novels: Four Versions of Pastoral." *Critique* 9/2 (1967): 5-19.

Points out Malamud's reliance upon "the pastoral fertility myths of dying and reviving gods, of youthful heroes replacing the aged, of the son replacing the father, the primary expression of which is found in vegetation life rituals, myths of the Fisher King, and its historical successor, the Grail quest." Discusses allusions in Malamud's novels to this archetypal myth and its vegetation cycles. Argues that this motif conveys Malamud's pastoral vision.

Mendelsohn, Maurice. "Whitman and the Oral Indian Tradition." American Dialogue 7/3 (1972): 25-28.

Sees "a certain kinship between Whitman's poetry and the folklore of the ancient inhabitants of America--the Indians." Notes that Schoolcraft's translations of American Indian poetry were available and likely influenced Whitman. Notes the lack of rhyme or meter in Indian folklore and their corresponding emphasis on repetitions, parallelisms, and rich imagery. Suggests that Whitman, as well as Longfellow, borrowed these techniques.

Mengeling, Marvin E. "Irving's Knickerbocker 'Folktales'." American Transcendental Quarterly 40 (1978): 355-64.

Suggests that Irving's visit to Walter Scott prompted Irving to use legendary and folktale materials prolifically. Argues that Irving structured and stylized his Knickerbocker stories along the prescribed lines of European oral narratives. Identifies Irving's use of three-fold repetition in "Rip Van Winkle" and "Sleepy Hollow."

Merivale, Patricia. Pan the Goat-God: His Myth in Modern Times. Cambridge: Harvard U. P., 1969. ix, 286 pp.

Surveys literary treatments and allusions to the Pan myth in British and American literature and interprets the thematic implications. Includes discussion of Faulkner, Cabell, Pound, but concentrates on British literature.

Metzger, Deena Posy. "Hart Crane's Bridge: the Myth Active." Arizona Quarterly 20 (1964): 36-46.

Identifies two American Indian myths in The Bridge, Quetzalcoatl and the founding of Tenochtitlan. Documents the sources and interprets the themes of these myths.

Michelson, Bruce. "The Myth of Gatsby." Modern Fiction Studies 26 (1980-81): 563-77.

Examines the source of The Great Gatsby's mythic powers in two forms: the mythic heritage that Fitzgerald was schooled in and drawing upon, and the novel itself as a fulfillment of the mythic formula, "those immemorial needs of the teller and listener alike." Argues that The Great Gatsby is a modern retelling of the myth of "the skyborn mortal ascending towards the heavens" in a vain attempt for some glorious transcendence, emulating the stories of Icarus, Bellerophon, or in particular Phaeton. Traces the echoes of the legend of Phaeton in The Great Gatsby, which appear "most persistently and strongly." These include primarily the allusions to the golden car and the sun imagery surrounding Daisy and Tom.

Middleton, David. "Faulkner's Folklore in As I Lay Dying: An Old Motif in a New Manner." Studies in the Novel 9 (1977): 46-53.

Identifies the folkloric content of As I Lay Dying, "the substrata of folk matter on which the funeral journey is built." Concentrates on the mourning husband motif and on Faulkner's "skillful, inverted" use of it.

Mieder, Wolfgang, "Behold the Proverbs of a People: A Florilegium of Proverbs in Carl Sandburg's Poem 'Good Morning, America'." Southern Folklore Quarterly 35 (1971): 160-68.

Observes that the function of the proverbs in "Good Morning, America" is to describe the American people through their proverbial language. Identifies and annotates eleven proverbs in the poem.

Mieder, Wolfgang. "The Proverb and Anglo-American Literature." Southern Folklore Quarterly 38 (1974): 49-62.

Argues that merely listing the occurrence of proverbs in literature is not sufficient; " a literary proverb study must also include an explanatory essay concerning the various function of the proverbs in text." Includes a bibliographical list of 144 studies of proverbs in literature.

Mieder, Wolfgang. "Proverbs in Carl Sandburg's 'The People, Yes'." Southern Folklore Quarter 37 (1973): 15-36.

Sees Sandburg's heavy reliance on proverbs (322 cited in The People, Yes) as evidence of his democratic and populist philosophy. Lists the proverbs.

Milledge, Luetta Upshur. "Light Eternal: An Analysis of Some Folkloristic Elements in Faulkner's Go Down, Moses." Tennessee Folklore Society Bulletin 29 (1963): 86-93.

Suggests Faulkner utilizes "the raw material of folklore but he transmutes it into enduring literary creation." These materials include tall tales, exemplum, folk speech, folk ritual, custom, weather lore, and bootlegging lore.

Miller, James E. Jr., ed. Myth and Method: Modern Theories of Fiction. Omaha: University of Nebraska Press, 1960. 165 pp.

Reprints selections from Chase and Frye about the connection between mythic archetypes and literature.

Miller, James E., Jr. "Redburn and White-Jacket: Initiation and Baptism." Nineteenth-Century Fiction 13 (1959): 273-93.

Argues that "the two books tell one story of initiation into the evil of the world; observation, criticism, and sampling of that evil; and finally, baptism into evil." Points out the conformance to the pattern of initiation evidenced in the motifs in the narrative.

Miller, Jim Wayne. "Regions, Folklife, and Literary Criticism." Appalachian Journal 7 (1980): 180-87.

Examines the question of why some authors achieve national or "universal" recognition for their adaptation of folk materials, and why some are branded as regionalists. Concludes that it is the result of a dominant critical view that promotes a separation of art and life, an unfortunate perspective according to the author.

Millichap, Joseph R. "Carson McCullers' Literary Ballad." The Georgia Review 27 (1973): 329-39.

Identifies the coincidences between folk ballad form and McCullers' Ballad of the Sad Cafe including tangled relationships and economy of plot.

Millward, Celia and Cecilia Tichi. "Whatever Happened to Hiawatha?" Genre 6 (1973): 318-32.

Proposes that Longfellow was following the epic-heroic poetic tradition and not the pre-heroic, shamanistic poetry of the Kalevala. Examines the typical characteristics of epic-heroic poetry as they appear in Hiawatha.

Mitchell, Carol. "Ceremony as Ritual." American Indian Quarterly 5 (1979): 27-35.

Discusses ritualistic elements in Leslie Silko's novel.

Mitchell, Carol. "Rudolfo Anaya's Bless Me, Ultima: Folk Culture in Literature." Critique 22 (1980): 55-64.

Examines four different aspects of traditional life portrayed by Anaya in his novel: la familia; the roles of men and women; the curandera and the bruja; and the close ties between the sacred and secular life. Argues that understanding these folk traditions is crucial for an appreciation of Bless Me, Ultima.

Mitchell, Charles. "Mythic Seriousness in Lolita." Texas Studies in Language and Literature 5 (1963): 329-43.

Interprets Lolita as a mythic presentation and solution to Humbert's existential despair, a depiction of "the Quest Hero searching for the realization of the spiritual image of self which transcends despair." Sees Humbert as the Quest Hero and Lolita as the beautiful Princess.

Monteiro, George. "Fenimore Cooper's Yankee Woodsman." Midwest Folklore 12 (1962): 209-16.

Examines the folk type of the woodsman as Cooper employs it to describe Billy Kirby in The Pioneers and suggests it reveals Cooper's ambivalence about cultural progress.

Monteiro, George. "A Nonliterary Source for Hawthorne's 'Egotism; or The Bosom Serpent'." American Literature 41 (1970): 575-77.

Notes an article in New-England Magazine that relates a version of the bosom serpent legend.

Montgomery, Evelyn. "Proverbial Materials in The Politician Out-witted and Other Comedies of early American Drama 1789-1829." Midwest Folklore 11 (1961-62): 215-224.

Lists 48 proverbs and 18 proverbial expressions in <u>The Politician Out-Witted</u>, and discusses its relationship to the comic style of early American drama.

Moore, Jack B. "A Traditional Motif in Early American Fiction: "The Too Youthful Solitary." <u>Midwest Folklore</u> 12 (1962): 205-16.

An anonymous short story in 1798 uses the folk theme of "The Boy Who Had Never Seen a Woman."

Moore, Robert. "Hawthorne's Folk-Motifs and <u>The House of the Seven Gables</u>." <u>New York Folklore Quarterly</u> 28 (1972): 221-33.

Traces Hawthorne's preoccupation with witchcraft to written accounts of witchery, from which he borrowed many supernatural and superstitious motifs.

Moorman, Charles. "Melville's <u>Pierre</u> and the Fortunate Fall." <u>American Literature</u> 25 (1953): 13-30.

Argues that <u>Pierre</u> is Melville's considered and systematic reworking of the myth of the Fall of Man. Discusses the attendant Edenic imagery.

Morris, Harry C. "Eudora Welty's Use of Mythology." <u>Shenandoah</u> 6/2 (1955): 34-40.

Considers Welty's use of Greek mythology through three approaches: "the use of myth as a means for ordering contemporary history, the reestablishing of myths in modern terms and the linking of them to their ancient counterparts, and the use of myth as a movement toward structural control and sharply delineated form." Observes that Welty follows Joyce, Pound, and Eliot in the first approach, Yeats in the second, and Hawthorne and Poe in the third.

Morris, Harry C. "Zeus and the Golden Apples: Eudora Welty." Perspective 5 (1952): 190-99.

Suggests that Welty uses the golden apples to have symbolic reference to the ancient Greek myths, but that she works her symbol in such a manner as to fuse the legends of diverse mythologies.

Morris, J. A. "Gullah in the Stories and Novels of William Gilmore Simms." American Speech 22 (1947): 46-53.

Reviews Simms' use of Gullah Negro dialect; argues he is perhaps the first important American writer to use accurate Gullah.

Morrow, Lenna Vera. "Folklore in the Writings of Julia Peterkin." M.A. English. University of South Carolina. 1963. 101 pp.

Morrow, Patrick D. "Bret Harte, Popular Fiction, and the Local Color Movement." Western American Literature 8 (1973): 123-31.

Defines local color as the characteristic folkways, dialect, and lore of a specific area, and argues that while Harte saw California in mythic and archetypal terms, and his work included some folklore, he was not a true realist or regionalist; his fiction instead tends toward parable and satire.

Moses, W. R. "Where History Crosses Myth: Another Reading of 'The Bear'." Accent 13 (1953): 21-33.

Posits the notion that myth dramatizes the human situation and contends that Ike "refused to go with the historical drift of things and remained a myth man all his life."

Moyne, Ernest J. Hiawatha and Kalevala. Helsinki: Suomalainen Tiedeakatemia, (FF Communications, No. 192), 1963.

Investigates the controversy over the sources of Longfellow's epic poem. Traces its connection to Indian legend and the Finnish *Kalevala*. Concludes it borrows meter, structure, and other elements, but it is not a plagarism, it is a valuable reworking of "crude Indian legends and myths" into a poem that is "the work of a skilled artist."

Moyne, Ernest J. "Manabozho, Tarenyawagon, and Hiawatha." *Southern Folklore Quartery* 29 (1965): 195-203.

Details the confusion of the Ojibway demigod Manabozho with the Iroquois demigod Tarenyawagon and the Iroquois law giver Hiawatha and the consequent mixture of Algonquin and Iroquoi's legends; blames Schoolcraft, not Longfellow.

Moyne, Ernest J. and Tauno F. Mustanoja. "Longfellow's *Song of Hiawatha* and *Kalevala*." *American Literature* 25 (1953-54): 85-87.

Points out that Longfellow worked from Schiefner's translation of the *Kalevala*.

Muffett, D. J. M. "Uncle Remus was a Hausaman?" *Southern Folklore Quarterly* 39 (1975): 151-66.

Surveys word usage, syntax, narrative style, and plot motifs in *Uncle Remus* and finds suggestive evidence linking the *Uncle Remus* stories to Hausaman folk narrative tradition.

Mullen, Patrick B. "American Folklife and *The Grapes of Wrath*." *Journal of American Culture* 1 (1978): 742-53.

Examines all aspects of the traditional life of migrant farm workers of the 1930's in order to reveal the novel's popular appeal and its success in depicting the major social, political and philosophical themes of the time. Considers anecdotes, legends, folk dances, music, superstitions, customs and behavior.

Mullen, Patrick B. "Myth & Folklore in _The Ordways_" in _Hunters & Healers_, ed. Wilson M. Hudson. (Austin: The Encino Press, 1971), pp. 133-45.

Identifies a variety of folklore forms in Humphrey's novel, including mythic journeys, tall tales, folk stereotypes, and folk anecdotes.

Mulligan, Louise Griffith. "Mythology and Autobiography in E. A. Robinson's _Tristram_." Ph.D. University of Massachusetts. 1975. 231 pp. _Dissertation Abstracts International_ 36 (1976): 6102A.

Traces the roots of the Tristram legend and shows how Robinson significantly alters the traditional narrative. Argues that Robinson's motivation was to give his text an autobiographical dimension. Concludes that in retelling the Tristram legend, Robinson was writing his own lifelong love story.

Murphy, James K. "The Backwoods Characters of Will N. Harben." _Southern Folklore Quarterly_ 39 (1975): 291-96.

Surveys Harben's major characters and concludes that he was a memorable folklorist who wrote effective local color stories.

Murray, Henry A. _Myth and Myth Making_. New York: George Braziller, 1960. 375 pp.

Contains a number of articles on the literary use of myth and on literature in comparison to myth; the entries are separately indexed herein.

Murray, Peter B. "Myth in _The Blithedale Romance_," in Vickery, ed., _Myth and Literature_ (Lincoln: U. of Nebraska, 1966), pp. 213-220. Also in _PMLA_ 75 (1960): 591-96.

Proposes that "Coverly's story and vision are based on . . . the Greek season myths, and he employs the actions, metaphors, and symbols of those myths to give his work its structure, to characterize his people, and to describe human relations."

Myers, Karen Magee. "Mythic Patterns in Charles Waddell Chesnutt's The Conjure Women and Ovid's Metamorphoses." Black American Literature Forum 13 (1979): 13-17.

Notes a resemblance between Greco-Roman folktales collected in Ovid's Metamorphoses and Afro-American folk stories in Chesnutt's The Conjure Woman, specifically in their concept of the universe and in the "conscious interpretations which the authors imposed upon traditional materials to make them relevant to their contemporary audiences." Analyzes Chesnutt's use of the old myth of the fall of man in "The Goophered Grapevine," as well as his use of superstitions and conjure. Observes that Chesnutt takes advantage of the folktale's ability to express complex philosophical issues in neatly packaged and highly entertaining metaphors. Concludes that "Chesnutt's use of seemingly innocent folk stories . . . allowed him . . . to imply criticisms of white society which it would probably have never tolerated had the critiques been stated directly."

Nagy, Deborah K. "'Annabel Lee': Poe's Ballad." RE: Artes Liberales 3/2 (1977): 29-34.

Points out that the manner of expression and structure of "Annabel Lee" correspond to ballad composition. Finds common ballad themes in the poem, a grieving narrator and a thwarted love, and ballad techniques, hyperbole, stanzaic pattern, rhyming and phrasing. Argues that the repetition in the poem is a mimicking of oral tradition and that Poe is "borrowing musical elements from the ballad tradition."

Nänny, Max. "Oral Dimensions in Ezra Pound." Paideuma 6 (1976): 13-16.

Argues that Pound modeled himself on the poets in oral society whose task it is to transmit the vital heritage of their cultures in epics. Sees The Cantos, accordingly, as a kind of "neo-oral epic," which selectively presents the best elements of the world's cultural heritage in rhythmic formulae.

Nänny, Max. "The Oral Roots of Ezra Pound's Methods of Quotation and Abbreviation." Paideuma 8 (1979): 381-87.

Explains a number of Pound's puzzling proclivities by pointing out their oral roots. For example, Pound's tendency to copy a text in the original language is seen as paralleling the attempt to gain authenticity of statement in oral tradition by quoting lines verbatim.

Naples, Diane C. "Eliot's 'Tradition' and The Sound and the Fury." Modern Fiction Studies 20 (1974-75): 214-17.

Argues that Faulkner uses Eliot's "mythical method" and that The Sound and the Fury is based on the myth of Europa.

Newcomb, Mary. "Classical Mythology in the Poetry of James Russell Lowell." M.A. English. University of Kansas. 1927. 183 pp.

Newland, Lillian Hazel Neeta. "The Development of the Yankee Character in American Drama fom 1787 to 1860." M.A. English. University of Washington. 1942. 90 pp.

Noble, David W. The Eternal Adam and the New World Garden: The Central Myth in the Novel Since 1830. New York: George Braziller, 1968. xi, 226 pp.

Reworks R. W. B. Lewis's and Henry Nash Smith's arguments, but lacks sophistication in his conception of folklore or folk ideas (such as the American Adam or the Garden of Eden) and how they influence literature. Uses myth in a casually undefined way.

Noyes, Sylvia Gray. "Mrs. Almira Todd, Herbalist-Conjurer." *Colby Literary Quarterly* 9 (1972): 643-49.

Analyzes the connection between Mrs. Almira Todd, a character in Jewett's *The Country of the Pointed Firs*, and folk medicine. Suggests the character draws her power from her alliance with the natural herbal remedies.

Nyland, Waino. "*Kalevala* as a Reputed Source of Longfellow's *Song of Hiawatha*." *American Literature* 22 (1950): 1-20.

Analyzes the folk song poetry of *Kalevala* and concludes that Longfellow did not follow its poetic techniques, but took his meter instead from Indian songs, as Longfellow maintained. Discusses Longfellow's debt to Schoolcraft's legends and Herder's philosophy.

O'Connor, William Van. "Rhetoric in Southern Writing: Faulkner." *Georgia Review* 12 (1958): 83-86. Also in *The Tangled Fire of William Faulkner* (Minneapolis: University of Minnesota Press, 1954), pp. 125-34.

Classifies Faulkner's two major styles as "high rhetoric" and "folk language" and suggests the two styles meet in *The Hamlet*. Examines the folk style of sentences from *The Bear* and *The Hamlet*.

Oden, Gloria C. "Chesnutt's Conjure as African Survival." *MELUS* 5/1 (1978): 38-48.

Argues that Chesnutt ventured in the spiritual area of Black folk belief by "deliberately using folk material to expose to scrutiny 'the mundane, everyday life of the slave, the relationship of the master to the ordinary slave, and the attitudes of such a slave to both his daily experience and his seldom-seen master'." Proposes that "Chesnutt knew that conjure filled a deep need in the slave's life for a weapon to invoke against the arbitrary and often violent circumstances that made up his existence" and that "it gave him the vitality of his African heritage." Concludes that it was Chesnutt's familiarity "with both conjure and the simple folk that believed in it" that allowed him to present such faithful representations of character.

O'Donnell, Thomas F. "More Apologies: The Indian in New York Fiction." New York Folklore Quarterly 23 (1967): 243-53.

Surveys the literary treatments of the Indian figure, and concludes they are superficial caricatures without anthropological authenticity.

Okeke-Ezigbo, Emeka. "Buzzard/Eagle Symbolism in Ralph Ellison's 'Flying Home'." Notes on Contemporary Literature 9/5 (1979): 2-3.

Briefly notes the Negro's folkloristic motif of viewing himself as a Buzzard and the white as an Eagle. Points out the ironic relevance of this folk association for Ellison's story.

Okeke-Ezigbo, Felix C. "Eagle against Buzzard: The Dialect Poetry of Paul Laurence Dunbar and James Weldon Johnson." Ph.D. State University of New York at Buffalo. 1979. 391 pp. Dissertation Abstracts International 40 (1979): 2065A.

Argues against the dichotomized view that "Negro dialect" has been used as a means either of "groping for an authentic national speech" or of "poking fun at the 'nigger'." Sketches the Afro-American worldview and argues that the speech of Afro-America has as much integrity and literary potential as any formal literary language. Analyzes the use of the Eagle and Buzzard as symbols of too opposing worldviews in the poetry of Dunbar and Johnson. Concludes that dialect usage can effectively express the veracity of the Afro-American experience.

Olderman, Raymond M. Beyond the Wasteland: A Study of the American Novel in the Nineteen-Sixties. New London: Yale U. P., 1972. xi, 258 pp.

Uses the metaphor of a wasted land combined with the myth of the Fisher King and the Questing Knight (as expressed in Eliot's The Waste Land) as a paradigm for American literature of the 1960's. Focuses primarily on traditional literary (rather than folkloristic) analysis of works by Kesey, Elkin, Barth, Heller, Pynchon, Hawkes, Vonnegut, and Beagle.

Oliver, M. Celeste. "Invisible Man and the Numbers Game." College Language Association Journal 22 (1978): 123-33.

Investigates the role of the numbers in Invisible Man and argues that Ellison gives his book the general texture of a numbers game and that he puts a numbers runner into the story to show the protagonist that he has been a victim of the game himself. Shows how the hero's activities are an ironic illustration of the numbers game because he does not play the game wisely for his own ends but instead is made to play for the sake of others. Instead of submitting slips of paper with his choices he receives slips of paper with his instructions "which are designed to 'keep this Nigger-Boy Running'"; he is an unwitting runner in the numbers game of life. Points out the folk significance of the hero's winning number 1,369 and of his "fall" into the coal cellar as corresponding to a numbers hit.

Concludes that the hero ultimately realizes that understanding of the numbers game is crucial to understanding life.

O'Meally, Robert G. "Riffs and Rituals: Folklore in the Work of Ralph Ellison," in Dexter Fisher, ed., Afro-American Literature (New York: MLA, 1979), pp. 153-69.

Suggests that much of Afro-American literature has its sources in folklore. Points out Ellison's self-acknowledged debt to folklore, his exposure to spirituals, gospels, folk idiom, folk tales, blues, and jazz, and his involvement in a never completed Federal Writers Project on urban folklore. Notes Ellison's critical belief that folklore humanized the tragic situation of American blacks, that it provided a sense of community, and that it crystallized the wisdom of a people. Reviews Ellison's argument that folklore provides a basis for successful literary expression, and observes that in his own work, Ellison substantially incorporated folk materials. Suggests Invisible Man is an extended blues and his writing frequently uses sermons, folk song, and folk characters.

Ong, Walter J., S.J. "The Writer's Audience is Always a Fiction." PMLA 90 (1975): 9-21.

Examines the difference between oral and written verbalizations in the relationship of the "audience" to 1) the writing, 2) the situation that inscribed communication establishes, and 3) the roles the readers are consequently called on to play. Concludes that written art is characterized by the author's further remove from the audience and by the audience's limited participation. Focuses, consequently, on the rhetorical techniques writers must employ to capture the attention of a non-present audience.

Orians, G. H. "New England Witchcraft in Fiction." American Literature 2 (1930): 54-71.

Surveys a host of authors, including Hawthorne, and concludes that they relied heavily on New England witch lore and its history for their fiction.

Oriard, Michael. "Shifty in a New Country: Games in Southwestern Humor." Southern Literary Journal 12 (1980): 1-28.

Views the writings of the Southwestern humorists as the epic of a democratic people; the heroes of these comic tales and sketches are folk of the most common sort. States that the most distinctive characteristic of this democratic epic is the prevalence of games. Rather than focusing on war as in other heroic epics of other nations, the battle of this American national epic literature is one of play and games. Identifies the reliance upon horse races, cock fights, gander pullings, shooting matches, and other games in the fiction of the Southwestern humorists. Their favorite form of literary expression, tall tales themselves, are seen as a form of game; observes that in frontier life almost any activity can be made the occasion of a game. Concludes that "the Southwestern humorists, without pretension to high literary achievement but close to the mind of the common folk, perhaps best understood the myth of an emerging American people."

Osborn, Chase S. and Stellanova Osborn. Schoolcraft--Longfellow--Hiawatha. Lancaster: The Jacques Cattel Press, 1942. xix, 697 pp.

Traces the extensive connection between the Manabozho-Hiawatha legends as recorded by Schoolcraft and their poetic treatment in Longfellow's poem.

Osburn, Bonnie Fae. "An Examination of the Superstitions in the Works of Mary Webb." M.A. English. Texas Christian University. 1949. 109 pp.

Ostendorf, Berndt. "Ralph Ellison's 'Flying Home': From Folk Tale to Short Story." Journal of the Folklore Institute 13 (1976): 185-99.

Discusses the rationale for Ellison's use of folklore, which is seen in the context of his esthetics. Argues that Ellison does not re-arrange black folklore to fit current political platforms. Rather he uses it to portray the Afro-American identity and its social system of communication; he attempts to lift ritualized behavior from thoughtlessness into consciousness. Posits that the function of folklore in Ellison's fiction is "neither ornamental, nor comical, nor universal. Folklore is his semiotic cultural code, a system of shared meanings and a pragmatic charter of behavior." Illustrates this thesis in an analysis of folktales, myths, folk behavior, speech, and belief in Ellison's "Flying Home."

Oster, Harry. "Whittier and Folklore." M.A. English. Cornell University. 1950. 100 pp.

Owen, Guy. "The Use of Folklore in Fiction." North Carolina Folklore 19 (1971): 73-79.

Argues that Owen used folk speech from central North Carolina in The Ballad of the Flim-Flam Man and his other novels because he wanted to take advantage of the racy and fresh idiom of Southern dialect and because he wanted to preserve the folk language. Especially relied on folk sayings, anecdotes, and folktales.

Parker, Arthur C. "Who was Hiawatha?" New York Folklore Quarterly 10 (1954): 285-88.

Traces Longfellow's adaptation of an Iroquoian legendary hero, Hiawatha, to his Algonquin material, as a replacement for Manobozho.

Parks, Edd Winfield. "The Three Streams of Southern Humor." Georgia Review 9 (1955): 147-59.

Identifies the localized humorous sketch and the exaggerated, frontier tall tale as two main streams of Southern humor that are indigenous products of American folklore. Surveys examples from Crockett, Simms, and Harris.

Parsons, Elsie Clews. "Joel Chandler Harris and Negro Folk-Lore." Dial 66 (1919): 492-3.

Observes that Harris has caught the folktale spirit. Identifies the folktale types that Harris employs in Uncle Remus Returns.

Patrick, Nancy. "A Delineation of Folklore Elements in Jesse Stuart's Tales from the Plum Grove Hills." Jack London Newsletter 13 (1980): 66-71.

Provides a representative overview of Stuart's use of folklore by citing various examples of folk custom, superstitions, remedies, speech, and folktale found in Tales from the Plum Grove Hills. Concludes that Stuart's use of folklore gives the reader a glimpse of "the old, free, pastoral world of his father's--a nostalgic evocation of a vanished past."

Paul, Sherman. "Morgan Neville, Melville, and the Folk Hero." Notes and Queries 194 (1949): 278.

Briefly outlines the connection between Melville's heroes and Western folklore, specifically the Mike Fink legend.

Payne, Mildred Y. "Folk Characters in Two Kroll Novels." Tennessee Folklore Society Bulletin 31 (1965): 16-22.

Examines a Mike Fink character, a village idiot, and some "folk folk" in Fury in the Earth and Rogue's Company.

Payne, Mildred Y. "A Tennessee Judge Revived: A Study of Folk Elements in One of Opie Read's

Best-Known Novels." Tennessee Folklore Society Bulletin 32 (1966): 82-87.

Discusses stock characters and plots in Read's novel.

Payne, Mildred Y. "The Vanishing Folklorist." Tennessee Folklore Society Bulletin 31 (1965): 105-08.

Suggests folklore writers like Read are no longer read because America is becoming urbanized.

Pearce, Howard D. "Myth in Anderson's 'Winterset'." M.A. English. University of Florida. 1961. 82 pp.

Pearce, Howard D. "The Plays of Paul Green: Their Growth from Literary and Folk Traditions." Ph.D. Florida State Unviersity. 1967. 222 pp. Dissertation Abstracts International 29 (1968): 611A.

Explores Green's philosophical assumptions, his use of dramatic traditions, and his exploitations of folk materials. In this last investigation, Green is revealed to utilize Negro and poor white folklore as well folk materials related to Biblical and mythical figures. The spirit of the folk materials is viewed as being entirely consistent with Green's intellectual temper, in that both propose a sense of spiritual unity in a physical world.

Pearson, Carol. "Bellow's Henderson the Rain King and the Myth of the King, the Fool, and the Hero." Notes on Contemporary Literature 5 (1975): 8-11.

Traces Bellow's use of the myth of the traditional hero, who frequently begins as a fool and ends up as a king. Ses this pattern in Henderson the Rain King, where the protagonist acquires the virtues of the hero through his ordeal in Africa. As a result, Henderson becomes a hero who possesses a positive and fruitful attitude toward life and who attempts to bring his fertile vision back to the stagnant and sterile contemporary world, where science and rationality have overwhelmed myth.

Peavey, Charles D. "Faulkner's Use of Folklore in *The Sound and the Fury*." *Journal of American Folklore* 79 (1966): 437-47.

Analyzes folk beliefs concerning the jimson weed, the narcissus, the cornflower, birds, shadows, and names as they appear in *The Sound* and other works.

Pedrini, Lura and Duilio T. Pedrini. "Similes and Metaphors in Cooper's *The Pathfinder*." *New York Folklore Quarterly* 23 (1967): 99-108.

Suggests that Cooper is a folklorist and that his similes and metaphors convey his folkloristic dedication to nature, simplicity, and romance, but provides no folkloristic evidence.

Penrod, James H. "The Folk Hero as Prankster in the Old Southwestern Yarns." *Kentucky Folklore Record* 2 (1956): 5-12.

Discusses the mischievous rogues who appear in the printed tales of the Southwestern yarn spinners and who were drawn from the folktales of their region.

Penrod, James H. "Folk Humor in Sut Lovingood's Yarns." *Tennessee Folklore Society Bulletin* 16 (1950): 76-84.

Discusses rituals and customs, tall talk, rambling narration, and comic sayings that characterize mountaineer attitudes and that Harris employed in his Sut writings.

Penrod, James H. "The Folk Mind in Early Southwestern Humor." Tennessee Folklore Society Bulletin 18 (1952): 49-54.

Southwestern humorists transcribed with slight modification the rich storehouse of folk humor in their region.

Penrod, James H. "Folk Motifs in Old Southwestern Humor." Southern Folklore Quarterly 19 (1955): 117-24.

Examines the close relationship between Southwestern humor and universal folk humor and suggests they coincide in four categories: "origin of the colored race, speaking animals, giant animals, and remarkable persons (folk hero types)."

Penrod, James H. "Harden Taliaferro, Folk Humorist of North Carolina." Midwest Folklore 6 (1956): 147-53.

Examines Taliaferro's portrayal of folk characters, transcription of folk tales, and recording of folk history.

Penrod, James H. "Military and Civil Titles in the Old Southwestern Yarns." Tennessee Folklore Society Bulletin 19 (1953): 13-19.

Notes that the Southwestern humorists used pretentious titles for satiric purpose.

Penrod, James H. "Minority Groups in Old Southwestern Humor." Southern Folklore Quarterly 22 (1958): 121-28.

Considers the treatment of "Negroes and Indians of their period" by nine Southwestern yarnspinners. Briefly notes their stereotypical characteristics.

Penrod, James H. "Teachers and Preachers in the Old Southwestern Yarns." Tennessee Folklore Society Bulletin 18 (1952): 91-96.

Discusses the disparaging portrayal of the stereotypical characters of teacher and preacher by Southwestern humorists.

Penrod, James H. "Two Types of Incongruity in Old Southwestern Humor." Kentucky Folklore Record 4 (1958): 163-73.

Discusses shifts in diction and burlesques as common devices in oral and written humor as evidenced in the writings of the Southwestern humorists of 1830-1860.

Penrod, James H. "Women in the Old Southwestern Yarns." Kentucky Folklore Record 1 (1955): 41-47.

Examines the women characters in the writings of the Southwestern humorists, and notes their kinship to the women of humorous folktales and folksongs--sturdy, resilient, high-spirited.

Peppers, Wallace Ray. "Linguistic Variation in the Dialect Poetry of Paul Laurence Dunbar." Ph.D. University of North Carolina at Chapel Hill. 1979. 230 pp. Dissertation Abstracts International 40 (1979): 2639A.

Investigates three phonological features (final consonant clusters, post vocalic r, and initial, medial, and final th) and two grammatical features (suffixal-Z and negation) and their contribution to the structure of Dunbar's dialect poetry. The results complement and support recent linguistic research in American urban dialects.

Perloff, Marjorie. "Cinderella Becomes the Wicked Stepmother: The Portrait of a Lady as Ironic Fairy Tale." North Carolina Folklore 23 (1969): 413-33.

A character study of Isabel which, after the initial recognition that Isabel is an apparently and exceptionally kindly stepmother to Pansy, contrary to fairy tale models, basically eschews further discussion of the fairy tale connection.

Peterson, Richard F. "The Grail Legend and Steinbeck's 'The Great Mountains'." Steinbeck Quarterly 6 (1973): 9-15.

Argues that Steinbeck suggests his theme of the acceptance of the life-death cycle in The Red Pony by incorporating imagery from the Grail legend, specifically sword and grail symbolism.

Petesch, Donald A. "The Role of Folklore in the Modern Black Novel." Kansas Quarterly 7 (1975): 99-110.

Examines the black folklore available to Chesnutt, Dunbar, Hayden, Brooks, Hughes, and other black artists from the Midwest. Reviews the active role of oral tradition in black folk culture and discusses its various functions. Traces evidence of folkloristic forms, such as contest situations typical of the folktale, and folkloristic functions, such as promoting a group's feeling of solidarity, in black fiction. Compartmentalizes the folkloristic influence into four general areas: (1) the group milieu found in much fiction; (2) the persistence of certain themes; (3) the presence of certain character types; and (4) the explanation of events in certain scenes.

Petrus, Marianne Jean. "The Mythical Method of T.S. Eliot." M.A. English. Trinity College. 1959. 104 pp.

Phillips, Billie Ray S. "Robert Penn Warren's Archetypal Triptych: A Study of the Myths of the Garden, the Journey, and Rebirth in The Cave, Wilderness, and Flood." Ph.D. North Texas State

University 1971. 217 pp. Dissertation Abstracts International 32 (1972): 6998A.

Points out Warren's affinity for myth, which Warren defines as "a construct which expresses truth and affirms value." Reveals Warren's use of three general mythic motifs. Concludes that the archetypal image study illuminates aspects of Warren's philosophy of "cosmic osmosis."

Phillips, Robert L., Jr. "A Structural Approach to Myth in the Fiction of Eudora Welty," in Prenshaw, ed., Eudora Welty (Jackson: U. P. of Mississippi, 1979), pp. 56-67.

Investigates the "mythical method" of Welty and her use of "classical myth, folk tale, and Celtic and northern European legend." Argues that Welty's method begins with Mississippi; "she did not begin with myth and fantasy and make them native to Mississippi; rather, she found that fantasy and myth are expressions of things she found 'around [her] in life'." Identifies three categories of myth and fantasy in Welty's fiction: "in the first, the narrator uses allusions to traditional myth and fantasy to enhance realistic characters and settings"; in the second, the narrator defines character and setting almost entirely through myth; and in the third, some characters themselves consciously experience myth and fantasy. Goes on to discuss how examples of Welty's fiction fall into one of these three categories. "Shower of Gold" and "The Worn Path" illustrate category one; The Robber Bridegroom and "The Wide Net" are examples of category two; and The Golden Apples illustrates category three.

Pickering, James H. "Fenimore Cooper and Pinkster." New York Folklore Quarterly 22 (1966): 15-19.

Identifies Cooper's use in Satanstoe of traditional folk culture, specifically the Pinkster festival of New York blacks.

Pinkett, Lilly Louise. "Folk Elements in American Drama from 1870 to 1936." M.A. English. Howard University. 1939. 121 pp.

Pitavy-Souques, Daniele. "Technique as Myth: The Structure of The Golden Apples," in Prenshaw, ed., Eudora Welty (Jackson: U. P. of Mississippi, 1979), pp. 258-68.

Suggests that Welty uses Eliot's mythical method and fuses mythological allusions to various traditions, e.g., Greek and Celtic, in order to show the universality of myth and of the artist's quest to portray life. Argues that the myth of Perseus, which centrally underlies the book, illustrates the artist's function of holding up a mirror to life, and that ultimately, the mythological metaphor becomes an artistic motif: "literature is itself the endless repetition of the same stories," so that Welty's numerous mythological allusions are self-reflexive, serving not just to direct our attention outwards to analogous events but also to call attention to the process of reflection itself, which constitutes the nature of life and the literary mode.

Plater, Ormonde. "Before Sut: Folklore in the Early Works of George Washington Harris." Southern Folklore Quarterly 34 (1970): 104-15.

Examines trickster and sexual motifs in early works by Harris in order to appreciate Sut's folk milieu. Concludes that Harris is a popular humorist who uses material from narrative folklore.

Pockmann, Henry A. "Irving's German Tour and Its Influence on His Tales." PMLA 45 (1930): 1150-87.

Recounts Irving's experiences in Germany and traces his exposure to German folk-tales, legends, and traditions. Suggests that Irving was a keen collector of folk materials which he incorporated into his writings.

Pollack, Viviain R. "Emily Dickinson's Valentines." American Quarterly 26 (1974): 60-78.

Suggests that Dickinson's valentines were following a tradition of British folklore and American burlesque humor.

Porter, T. C. "Kalevala and Hiawatha." Mercersberg Review 8 (1955): 255-59.

Argues that Longfellow "transferred the form, metre, spirit, and some of the most striking incidents" of Kalevala to his poem Hiawatha; calls Hiawatha an imitation.

Porter, Thomas E. Myths and Modern American Drama. Detroit: Wayne State Univ. Press, 1969. 285 pp.

Discusses O'Neill, Eliot, MacLeish, Kingsley, Miller, Williams, Wilder, and Albee. Examines nine plays by these playwrights as expressions of our culture--"the play speaks from the culture to the culture." Argues that American drama incorporates traditional ideas and attitudes ("folk ideas" and "folk myths") as part of its presentation of culture.

Poulsen, Richard C. "Black George, Black Harris, and the Mountain Man Vernacular." Rendezvous 8 (1973): 15-23.

Examines the literary use of mountain speech in George Ruxton and Emerson Bennett.

Pounds, Wayne. "Symbolic Landscapes in 'The Bear': 'Rural Myth and Technological Fact'." Gypsy Scholar 4 (1977): 40-52.

Applies Leo Marx's concept of contrasting worlds, one rural and the other urban, to Faulkner's story. Finds that the conflicting rural and urban landscapes "are contrasting repository images of 'aesthetic, moral, political, and even religious values'." Concludes that although Ike makes the requisite "redemptive journey that the new-world must always make away from society to nature, he fails to return . . . he confuses the mythically ordered ritual of the hunt with life in history."

Powell, Aileen. "Classical Mythology in Emerson's Writings." M.A. English. University of Texas. 1929. 126 pp.

Powell, William E. "Motif and Tale-Type of Simms's 'Grayling'." _Southern Folklore Quarterly_ 35 (1971): 157-59.

Suggests Simms's story should be listed under Motif N271 "Murder will out" or Type 960 "The Sun Brings All to Light."

Power, Helen Laura. "The Development of the Folk Drama in North Carolina with Special Reference to the Plays of Paul Green." M.A. English. University of Southern California. 1945. 166 pp.

Prenshaw, Peggy Whitmann, ed. _Eudora Welty: Critical Essays_. Jackson: U.P. of Mississippi, 1979. xviii, 446 pp.

Contains two articles specifically focussing on Welty's use of myth and legend (Phillips and Pitavy-Souques) that are referenced separately in this bibliography. Contains as well a number of studies that inevitably discuss in passing Welty's extensive connection to folklore.

Pronechen, Joseph S. "The Making of Hiawatha." _New York Folklore Quarterly_ 28 (1972): 151-60.

Biographical sketch of Longfellow's interest in Indians.

Pry, Elmer. "Folk-Literary Esthetics in _The Country of the Pointed Firs_." _Tennessee Folklore Society Bulletin_ 44 (1978): 7-12.

Suggests that while initially in nineteenth-century American literature, folklore is ornamental, with the advent of literary realism in the 1890's folklore begins to play a more substantial role, producing ultimately a folk literary esthetic. Identifies four ways in which folklore functions in a literary text: (1) reconstructs folk communities; (2) provides realistic speech patterns for character development; (3) provides generic forms and structures for literaty adaptation; (4) provides symbols and analogues to give the literature universality. Points out how the folklore in Jewett's novel illustrates these functions and how the novel correspondingly promotes folk values.

Pry, Elmer R. "A Folklore Source for 'The Man That Was Used Up'." Poe Studies 8 (1975): 46.

Observes that Poe's source may well have been contemporary oral folk narrative, judging from some parallel Indian legends produced by Dorson.

Pugh, Griffith T. "George W. Cable's Theory and Use of Folk Speech." Southern Folklore Quarterly 24 (1960): 287-93.

Discusses Cable's sophisticated aesthetic and method of handling dialect in fiction.

Quinn, Bernetta. "Medusan Imagery in Sylvia Plath," in Gary Lane, ed., Sylvia Plath: New Views on the Poetry (Baltimore: Johns Hopkins University Press, 1979), pp. 97-115.

Sees four levels of analogy in Plath's use of Medusan imagery in her poem "Medusa," one of which is the mythological Gorgon. Traces Plath's fascination with the myth of Medusa (as evidenced by a letter to her mother) and its counterparts as described by Neumann in The Great Mother and Graves in The White Goddess. Identifies also Plath's use of the legendary siren Lorelei, who lured sailors to their destruction.

Rabkin, Eric S. "To Fairyland by Rocket: Bradbury's *The Martian Chronicles*," in Martin Harry Greenberg and Joseph D. Olander, eds. *Ray Bradbury* (New York: Taplinger, 1980), pp. 110-26.

Points out the parallel underpinnings of science fiction and fairy tale. Argues that "Bradbury's composite novel is more radically a fairy tale than many other works of art." It contains references to fairy tale literature, employs fairy tale description, includes an enchanted setting, and uses fairy tale omnipotence of thought. Traces the fairy tale allusions in *The Martian Chronicles* and concludes that Bradbury created fairy land on Mars in the face of crass America, "so that the American myth could have a second chance."

Rabkin, Eric S. *The Fantastic in Literature*. Princeton: Princeton University Press, 1976. xi, 234 pp.

Considers briefly the contribution of folklore to literary fantasy e.g., fairy tale conventions, and includes some American examples, e.g., Fitzgerald and Poe.

Rabson, Barrie. "Irving's Sunnyside." *New York Folklore Quarterly* 7 (1951): 205-16.

Describes Irving's house and the superstitions and legends attached to it, which Irving incorporated into his fiction.

Raizis, Marios B. 'The Prometheus Theme in British and American Poetry." Ph.D. New York University. 1968. 338 pp. *Dissertation Abstracts International* 27 (1966): 1064A.

Broadly surveys the mythological and legendary background of Prometheus and discusses numerous literary treatments, primarily British.

Ranald, R. A. "William Faulkner's South: Three Degrees of Myth." Landfall: A New Zealand Quarterly 18 (1964): 329-38.

Suggests Faulkner avoids first degree of myth that distorts reality and favors instead second degree of rendering reality intelligible and third degree of rendering reality bearable (through Christian symbolism).

Randall, Dale J. B. "Dialect in the Verse of 'the Hoosier Poet'." American Speech 35 (1960): 36-50.

Analyzes James Whitcomb Riley's dialect usage and concludes that he used it accurately and effectively, but he did "touch them up" a bit, despite his arguments to the contrary.

Randel, William. "Edward Eggleston on Dialect." American Speech 30 (1955): 111-14.

Examines the unpublished fragments that illustrate Eggleston's pioneering efforts as a student of dialect, specifically of the Hoosier and Southern Negro dialects.

Randolph, Vance. "Recent Fiction and the Ozark Dialect." American Speech 6 (1931): 425-28.

Surveys a number of Ozark novels that employ dialect.

Reaver, J. Russell. "Emerson's Use of Proverbs." Southern Folklore Quarterly 27 (1963): 280-99.

Suggests that Emerson regarded proverbs as evidence of intuitive wisdom among the folk, but that he revised proverbs to fit his own beliefs. Concludes that, in his prose style, Emerson borrows folk proverbs, revises and enlarges upon them, and returns them to the people with their wider associations.

Reaver, J. Russell. "Mythic Motivation in Willa Cather's _O Pioneers!_" _Western Folklore_ 27 (1968): 19-25.

Interprets Alexandra's vision of a vegetarian god as a mythic corn-god figure, "reflecting not only her impulses towards sexual union with a male but also the very power of fruitfulness that she has been trying to develop in the land."

Reeves, Paschal. "The Humor of Thomas Wolfe." _Southern Folklore Quarterly_ 24 (1960): 109-20.

Argues that Wolfe wrote in the oral tradition and that an appreciation of his heritage of oral tradition is necessary for proper evaluation. Traces Wolfe's connection to Southern comic oral tradition and details his use of oral anecdotes, tall tales, and other oral conventions.

Reeves, Paschal. "Thomas Wolfe and His Scottish Heritage." _Southern Folklore Quarterly_ 28 (1964): 134-41.

Finds a sensitivity for the national origins of Wolfe's characters, especially for Scottish heritage, presumably as a result of Wolfe's own Scottish ancestry.

Regan, Robert. _Unpromising Heroes: Mark Twain and His Characters_. Berkeley and Los Angeles: University of California Press, 1966. 246 pp.

Argues that the motif of the Unpromising Hero, the lad who succeeds despite any likelihood of success, is a favorite both of world folk narrative and of Twain's fiction. Gives examples from both traditions and analyzes the reason for the motif's popular appeal.

Reichart, Walter A. "Washington Irving's Interest in German Folklore." _New York Folklore Quarterly_ 13 (1957): 181-192.

Surveys the German collections of folktales and ballads acquired by Irving and traces his borrowings from those texts.

Reisman, David J. "The Oral and Written Traditions." Explorations 6 (1957): 22-28. Also in Edmund Carpenter and Marshall McLuhan, eds., Explorations in Communication (Boston, 1960), pp. 109-16.

Sets forth three goals: to determine what is the difference between oral and written cultures; to see what is the significance of the new oral mass media; to assess the effect of the new media on countries without an established book tradition. Discusses mostly the sociological and psychological differences between oral and written art.

Render, Sylvia Lyons. "North Carolina Dialect: Chesnutt Style." North Carolina Folklore 15 (1967): 67-70.

Analyzes how Chesnutt maintains the flavor of naturalness in his sensitive rendering of the distinctive speech patterns of his characters.

Rhodes, Carolyn Fay Avery. "An Analysis of the Effectiveness of Faulkner's Use of Folklore." M.A. English. Stephen F. Austin State College. 1963. 155 pp.

Rice, Michael. "Myth and Legend: The Snopes Trilogy: The Hamlet, The Town, and The Mansion." Unisa English Studies 14 (1976): 18-22.

Asserts that "not only does Faulkner use the traditional myths and legends of the Old South and Classical Mythology; he has created his own as well." Sees connections between Eula Varner and Aphrodite, Flem Snopes and the "crippled Vulcan." Argues that Faulkner presents these characters in a mythic manner; Eula is portrayed as a pagan goddess and Flem as "a sort of backwoods Faustus." Suggests that Ratliff emulates bardic tradition in altering the story to suit the situation. Identifies finally overtones of Helen's seduction by Paris in Eula's seduction by McCarron.

Richards, Lewis A. "Frank Dobie's Use of Folklore: The Lost Adams Digging Story." Western Review 7 (1970): 29-49.

Examines the actual history of mining in New Mexico in order to show that Dobie's narrative conforms more to folkloric depictions rather than to actual fact.

Richardson, H. Edward. "Faulkner, Anderson, and Their Tall Tale." American Literature 34 (1962): 287-91.

Summarizes the account of Anderson and Faulkner swapping tall tales about a descendant of Andrew Jackson who is half-horse and half-alligator.

Richardson, Robert D. "Margaret Fuller and Myth." Prospects 4 (1979): 169-84.

Recounts Fuller's interest in mythology, especially Greek and Indian, as evidenced in her Conversations, her journal, and in her travelogue, Summer on the Lakes. Suggests that Fuller used myth to reveal what was best in human nature and as a valuable expression of religious belief. Traces Fuller's exposure to myth and discusses her extensive readings and uses of myth. Argues that Woman in the Nineteenth Century relies heavily on myth to communicate its idea of woman. Concludes that Fuller's interest in myth "provided her with a cultural paradigm that was an alternative to the threadbare Christian one, and helped her formulate her concept of feminine individualism."

Richardson, Robert D., Jr. Myth and Literature in the American Renaissance Bloomington: Indiana U.P., 1978. viii, 309 pp.

Offers "an essentially historical view of nineteenth-century American conceptions of myth" and examines its use in the literature of the American Renaissance. Surveys a variety of myth theories present in the period in question and distinguishes two opposing camps--the positive and negative responses to myth, the former viewing myth as "authentic tidings of invisible things" and the latter seeking to purge literature and philosophy of its primitive and nonhistorical past. Finds a valuable counterpointing of these contradictory attitudes towards myth reflected in the works of Emerson, Thoreau, Whitman, Hawthorne, and Melville. Documents the use of Nordic, Oriental, and Indian myths in these writers, and finds that they all rely substantially on mythic materials and forms in the presentation of their art. Emerson has a mythic conception of history which inspires him "to create a worthy mythology for the America of his day." Thoreau employs myth, especially Indian and Greek, to broaden his point, "always leading his facts towards fable or myth." Whitman incorporates Egyptian mythology into his poetry. Hawthorne rewrites and modernizes myth and attempts "to renovate myths by removing their 'classical' quality and substituting a gothic or romantic tone . . . of folklore and fairy tale." Melville uses a technique of "mythic investiture . . . to piece together . . . a coherent view of myth" from his familiarity with "Greek, Egyptian, Indu, Nordic, Persian, Mohammedan, Peruvian, Polynesian, Gnostic, and biblical mythology." Concludes that Melville was "better informed about and more deeply interested in problems of myth than any other American writer of his time." Includes a "selected Bibliography of Works Pertaining to Myth and Literature in America Between 1760 and 1860."

Rickels, Milton. Thomas Bangs Thorpe: Humorist of the Old Southwest. Baton Rouge: Louisiana State University Press, 1962. 275 pp.

A comprehensive biography that examines among other topics, the contribution of oral anecdotes and vernacular style to Thorpe's fiction.

Righter, Willian. _Myth and Literature_ London: Routledge & Kegan Paul, 1975. 132 pp.

Provides a general discussion of myth that surveys primarily theoretical and critical approaches to the use of myth in literature. The examples focus mostly on British literature, with the exception of a brief section entitled, "Mythic Significance" which considers the allegorical and mythic quality of American literature in such examples as Twain's _Huckleberry Finn_, Melville's _Moby-Dick_, and Faulkner's _The Bear_.

Roberts, John Willie. "The Uses and Functions of Afro-American Folk and Popular Music in the Fiction of James Baldwin." Ph.D. Ohio State University. 1976. 214 pp. _Dissertation Abstracts International_ 37 (1977): 5126A.

Suggests Baldwin uses folklore in several specific ways throughout his fiction: "to characterize, to provide structure, to advance plot and to comment on existing social conditions." Identifies Baldwin's reliance on folk music, as well as folk sermons, religious conversion narratives, and the heroic concept.

Roberts, Warren E. "Some Folksong References in Kennedy's _Swallow Barn_." _Southern Folklore Quarterly_ 27 (1953): 249-54.

Examines folk ballads in Kennedy's 1832 novel in order "to throw some light on the length of time a few ballads and songs have been known in America." Considers a dozen examples.

Rodenberger, Molcie Lou. "Caroline Gordon, Teller of Tales: The Influence of Folk Narrative on Characterization and Structure in Her Work."

Ph.D. Texas A & M University. 1975. 272 pp. Dissertation Abstracts International 36 (1976): 5302A-03A.

Suggests that Gordon is primarily a raconteur who preserves the traditions, stories, and customs from her Southern past. Identifies oral family sagas, folktales, and folk narrative techniques in Gordon's fiction.

Rodes, Sara Puryear. "Washington Irving's Use of the Folk Tradition." M.A. English. Vanderbilt University. 1956. 126 pp.

Rodes, Sara Puryear. "Washington Irving's Use of Traditional Folklore." Southern Folklore Quarterly 20 (1956): 143-53.

States that Irving uses folklore in his portrayal of ghosts, in his accounts of the rules concerning the discovery of buried treasure, and in his reliance on local legends as a basis for his tales.

Rogers, Ivor A. "Robert Heinlein: Folklorist of Outer Space," in Joseph D. Olander and Martin Harry Greenberg, eds. Robert A. Heinlein (New York: Taplinger, 1978), pp. 222-39.

Tries to account for Heinlein's popularity by demonstrating that his fiction follows mythic and folkloristic formulas. The folkloristic analysis is sketchy however.

Romines, Ann. "The Powers of the Lamp: Domestic Ritual in Two Stories by Eudora Welty." Notes on Mississippi Writers 12 (1979): 1-16.

Argues that domestic ritual is central to Eudora Welty's fiction and that Welty illuminates its attractions and dangers for both sexes. Analyzes the household rituals found in "Death of a Travelling Salesman" and "The Demonstrators" and argues that these rituals embody the domestic values of a traditional society.

Rose, Alan H. "The Image of the Negro in the Writings of Henry Clay Lewis." American Literature 41 (1969): 255-63.

Suggests that Lewis's (Madison Tensas) writings portray two predominant Southern beliefs: the destruction that accompanies rebellion against authority, and the fear of Negro violence.

Rosenberg, Bruce A. Custer and the Epic of Defeat. University Park: Pennsylvania State University Press, 1975. 313 pp.

Traces the parallel impact of the Custer legend on oral and written traditions, primarily from a Euhemeristic point of view. Notes an underlying structure in oral and written versions of the Custer story similar to that found in other epic defeats (most notably The Song of Roland).

Rosenberg, Bruce A. "Olrik's Laws: A Judicial Review." Folklore Forum 11 (1978): 152-162.

Suggests that many of Olrik's "Laws" are equally characteristic of both recited or printed stories. Considers some examples from American literature including Melville and Faulkner.

Ross, Esther W. Bostleman. "The Rip Van Winkle Tradition in American Drama." M.A. Speech. University of Southern California. 1931. 70 pp.

Rothman, Abby B. "The Electra Myth from Aeschylus to Robinson Jeffers." M.A. English/Comparative Literature. Columbia University. 1954. 82 pp.

Rourke, Constance. American Humor: A Study of the National Character. New York: Harcourt, Brace, 1931. 324 pp.

Identifies some comic characters prevalent in American culture and literature, particularly the Yankee pedlar and the backwoodsman. Traces the contribution of oral humor to a number of major authors including Emerson, Twain, Melville, and Hawthorne.

Rourke, Constance. "Examining the Roots of American Humor." American Scholar 4 (1935): 249-52, 54.

Contradicts Ferguson's premise in "The Roots of American Humor" that American humor is essentially European in origin.

Rourke, Constance. The Roots of American Culture and Other Essays. New York: Harcourt, Brace & Co., 1942. xii, 305 pp.

Surveys early American cultural history and the contributions of folk character types, folk music, and folk expression to it.

Rovit, Earl. "The Ghosts in James's 'The Jolly Corner'." Tennessee Studies in Literature 10 (1965): 65-72.

Considers the supernatural occurrences in James's story as taking "place within a frame of moral ambiance and the introduction of the occult is atmospheric rather than casual." Interprets the ghosts as allegorical representations of the protagonist's alter ego, thus justifying James's realistic use of "the supernatural."

Rowell, Charles H. "Sterling A. Brown and the Afro-American Folk Tradition." Studies in the Literary Imagination 7/2 (1974): 131-52.

Identifies one major group of Afro-American writers as being concerned with rearing a "superstructure of conscious art upon 'the American Negro's cultural background and his creative folk art'." These include Hughes, Toomer, Hurston and Brown. Focuses on Brown's attempt to recreate the folk art, lifestyle, and aesthetics of the black folks he had known and seen in Washington and when traveling in the South. Details how Brown uses worksongs, spirituals, folk rhymes, ballad forms, folk characters, folklife, slave-secular cadence, black folk music, and blues forms, subjects, and idioms in Southern Road. Argues that Brown "had tapped the black folk ethos, . . . the essence of black folk life and culture," and that he used his folk acquired verbal art to show us how black folk can "confront and survive a hostile universe, in spite of the dehumanization they perpetually encounter."

Roy, Emil. "The Iceman Cometh as Myth and Realism." Journal of Popular Cutlure 2 (1968): 299-313.

Suggests that the "real autobiographical events" are balanced and ironically complicated by buried fragments of religious initiation, trial, and purgation and by romantic mythical forms in the play.

Ruland, Richard. "Melville and the Fortunate Fall: Typee as Eden." Nineteenth-Century Fiction 23 (1969): 312-23.

Assesses the idyllic world of Typee as a kind of ocean Eden to which Tommo escapes from the sterility of civilization represented by the ship. The folkloristic perspective is not developed beyond this initial connection to the Bible.

Rulewicz, Wanda. "Myth and Ritual in the Drama of T.S. Eliot." Studia Anglica Posnaniensia 7 (1970): 138-47.

Argues that Eliot employed myth and ritual to provide order in his art. Points out Eliot's use of expiation and rejuvenation rituals in a variety of his dramas. Concludes that "in his plays, Eliot was constantly referring either to the history of Church or to Greek mythology."

Rulon, Curt M. "Geographical Delimitation of the Dialect Areas in The Adventures of Huckleberry Finn." Mark Twain Journal 14 (1969): 9-12.

Claims that there are only two dialects in Huckleberry Finn, one spoken by blacks and the other by whites.

Rusch, Frederik L. "A Tale of the Country Round: Jean Toomer's Legend, 'Monrovia'." MELUS 7 (1980): 37-46.

Suggests that Toomer uses legend as his model for "Monrovia" because he felt that children "who were not exposed to traditional legends and fables would grow up to be 'incomplete lopsided human beings'." Points out how "Monrovia" conforms to the general form and style of legends as identified by Campbell.

Rushing, Nellie Georgia. "A Word Study of Mary Noailles Murfree's Stories of the Tennessee Mountaineer." M.A. English. University of Chicago. 1929. 63 pp.

Sackett, Samuel J. "E. W. Howe as Proverb Maker." Journal of American Folklore 85 (1972): 73-77.

Surveys Howe's publications and aphorisms, of which only "Better be safe than sorry" survived in oral tradition.

Sackett, Samuel J. "Poetry and Folklore: Some Points of Affinity." Journal of American Folklore 77 (1964): 143-53.

Argues that the use of metrical and rhetorical devices is similar in poetry and folklore; discusses especially the stylistic parallels between gnomic folklore and poetry.

Sale, Rodger. Fairy Tales and After: From Snow White to E. B. White. Cambridge: Harvard U. P., 1978. 280 pp.

A study of children's literature that alludes briefly to the allusions and interconnections between literary classics and their folkloristic precursors.

Samuels, Charles E. "Folklore in Eben Holden." New York Folklore Quarterly 13 (1957): 100-103.

Contends that Irving Bachellar's North Country novels are filled with animal stories and folk anecdotes.

Sands, Donald B. "Holman Day: His Ballad Books (1900-1904) and Their Lexical Features." American Speech 41 (1965): 17-27.

Lists rural terms from a Maine poet and concludes he was effective in recreating the regional dialect.

Sands, Kathleen. "The Mythic Initiation of Arthur Gordon Pym." Poe Studes 7 (1974): 14-16.

Suggests that the initiation motif provides Poe's work with unity. Traces the progression of Pym's initiation through the separation, transition, and incorporation patterns. Views Pym's death as a shamanistic transformation and the entire tale as a priesthood rite that is designed to draw in the reader as a participant.

Schechter, Harold. "Death and Resurrection of the King: Elements of Primitive Mythology and Ritual in 'Roger Malvin's Burial'." English Language Notes 8 (1971): 201-05.

Draws a connection between "certain primitive rituals and myths that deal with death, resurrection, free spirits, and vegetation" in The Golden Bough and Hawthorne's "Roger Malvin's Burial." Argues for coincidental, not conscious, use of this parallel imagery; the parallels include the kingly status of Malvin, his youthful successor, the sterility of the land, the blessing of fertility, the colored handkerchiefs on the tree, and ritual slaying of the king. Concludes that these parallels evoke an involuntary response in the reader and add a unique dimension.

Schmitz, Neil. "Tall Tale, Tall Talk: Pursuing the Lie in Jacksonian Literature." American Literature 48 (1977): 471-91.

Looks at Baldwin's The Flush Times and Thorpe's "The Big Bear of Arkansas" as examples of the philosophical stance underlying tall talk, that is, as a reflection of alienation and of secret knowledge. Interprets tall talk as a subversive critique of established values that can ultimately become an ironic attitude, as in Melville's The Confidence Man. Shows how these authors employ tall tales and tall talk as a narrative skill for their audience's pleasure and as a philosophical statement for their reader's edification.

Scholes, Robert. "Myth and Manners in Sartoris." Georgia Review 16 (1963): 195-201.

Suggests that Sartoris is about the decline and fall of an aristocracy in a disrupted society and that it is more a novel of manners than a novel of myths.

Scholes, Robert and Robert Kellogg. The Nature of Narrative. New York: Oxford U. P., 1966. 326 pp.

An important study of the history and forms of literary narrative. Proposes a dialectical, quasi-evolutionary model as representing the "developmental process" of narrative. Examines the heritage of written narrative in the orally composed narrative of Europe and concludes that all art is traditional and that oral literature greatly influenced written forms and style.

Schroeder, James. "_Redburn_ and Failure of Mythic Criticism." _American Literature_ 39 (1967): 279-97.

Argues that the mythic interpretation of _Redburn_ as a novel of initiation does not hold up--"that it is contradicted repeatedly by some of the most important tonal and structural features of the novel."

Schultz, Elizabeth A. "The Insistence upon Community in the Contemporary Afro-American Novel." _College English_ 41 (1979): 170-84.

Points out the contradictory tendencies towards isolation and community in various Afro-American novels. Observes that one way black writers portray a sense of community is to use black folk tradition, especially conjure, blues, and jazz. The folkloristic discussion is limited however.

Schultz, Elizabeth A. "To Be Black and Blue: The Blues Genre in Black American Autobiography." _Kansas Quarterly_ 7 (1975): 81-96.

States that black autobiography, like the blues, expands the solo; it is, as Ellison says, "an autobiographical chronicle of personal catastrophe expressed lyrically." Argues that black autobiographical narratives can be grouped in two camps: the written slave narratives that seek explicitly to change the destiny of the community, and the oral slave narratives that do not seek to change their listeners' destiny. Suggests that nineteenth and twentieth-century written autobiographies of blacks fall into one of these two camps, which are respectively termed, the testimonial autobiography and the blues autobiography. Analyzes a number of black autobiographies, e.g., by Wright, Angelou, Hurston, Hughes, McKay, and shows how they follow the formal criteria identified.

Schwendinger, Robert J. "The Language of the Sea: Relationships Between the Language of Herman Melville and Sea Shanties of the 19th Century." Southern Folklore Quarterly 37 (1973): 53-73.

Describes similarities in tone, symbols, figurative language, and subject matter between Melville's writing and 19th century sea shanties. Concludes that Melville captures the spirit and authenticity of his times.

Scott, Nathan A., Jr. "Judgment Marked by a Cellar: The American Negro Writer and the Dialect of Despair." Denver Quarterly 2 (1967): 5-37.

Identifies a "mythic, secularized Calvinist pattern of the 'wounded Adam'" as being the cultural basis of Hawthorne, Melville, and subsequent Black American writers.

Sears, Donald A. "Folk Poetry in Longfellow's Boyhood." New England Quarterly 45 (1972): 96-104.

Searches out the broadside balladry and folk poetry of Portland, Maine that influenced the themes, metrics, and tones of Longfellow's later work.

Serafin, Joan Michael. "Faulkner's Use of the Classics." Ph.D. University of Notre Dame. 1968. 264 pp. Dissertation Abstracts International 29 (1969): 3155A.

A concordance of classical allusions in Faulkner, some of which are to mythology.

Seshachari, Neila C. "Myth in the Novels of F. Scott Fitzgerald." Ph.D. University of Utah 1975. 220 pp. Dissertation Abstracts International 36 (1975): 2203A-04A.

Reads This Side of Paradise as the mythic quest for the Grail, The Beautiful and Damned as an anti-fairy tale, The Great Gatsby as a monomyth, Tender is the Night as a mythic scapegoat ritual, and The Last Tycoon as a mythological prefigurative motif of Lord Shiva.

Sharpe, Elinore Velma. "Willa Cather's Works as They Reflect Early American Folkways." M.A. English. University of Southern California. 1951. 138 pp.

Shelton, Frank W. "Barthelme's Western Tall Tale: 'Porcupines at the University'." Notes on Contemporary Literature 9/1 (1979): 2-3.

Notes the similarities between the Western tall tale of driving a frog, turtle bee, or turkey herd to market and the porcupine drive in Barthelme's story. Concludes that to Barthelme, significance lies in the absurdity of his juxtaposition of a Western tall tale with America's modern urban culture.

Simms, L. Moody, Jr. "Irwin Russel and Negro Dialect Poetry: A Note on Chronological Priority and True Significance." Notes on Mississippi Writers 2 (1969): 67-73.

Argues that even though Russel was not the first of the postwar poets to use Negro dialect verse, he was one of the most significant. He possessed "a spontaneity and a spark of genius which gave to his work a feeling of sharing intimately the emotions of the Negroes he described."

Skaggs, Merrill Maguire. The Folk of Southern Fiction. Athens: University of Georgia Press, 1972. xiii, 280 pp.

Examines the economic and social status, institutions, activities, and daily lives of a group the author calls "plain folk" found in a wide range of Southern American local color fiction. Considers these materials more as evidence of local color than as borrowings of folk tradition, a concept that seems to elude the author.

Slabey, Robert M. "Myth and Ritual in Light in August." Texas Studies in Literature and Language 2 (1960): 328-49.

Relates the life cycle and personal problems of Joe Christmas to the archetypal story of the dying god and his resurrection. Notes Faulkner's conscious use of Frazer's Golden Bough, and points out numerous likenesses between the Adonis myth and the story of Joe Christmas, including the circumstances of his birth and death. Concludes that the rebirth of Joe Christmas takes three forms, physically, spiritually, and poetically, and that Faulkner's use of the ritual of the dying god illustrates his view of the rhythm of life.

Slochower, Harry. "Moby-Dick: The Myth of Democratic Expectancy." American Quarterly 2 (1950): 259-69.

Identifies myth as the roots of folk memory and indigenous lore that answers universal questions, and suggests that Moby Dick expresses the American myth of expectancy, "a surfeit of opportunities," which is expressed in the quest journey.

Slochower, Harry. Mythopoesis: Mythic Patterns in the Literary Classics. Detroit: Wayne State University Press, 1970. 362 pp.

A consideration of myth, not as certain oral tales, but as a creative and poetic structure of expression that deals with problems and that illustrates ways to deal with those problems. Mythopoesis is the re-creating of ancient stories in modern literature. Analyzes examples from Western literature, including Moby-Dick.

Slotkin, Richard. Regeneration through Violence: The Mythology of the American Frontier 1600-1860. Middletown: Wesleyan U. P., 1973. viii, 670 pp.

Defines myth as "a narrative which concentrates in a single, dramatized experience the whole history of a people in their land." Examines a variety of materials including The Adventures of Colonel Daniel Boon and Moby-Dick by means of this loose conception of myth as the "intelligible mask" of the American "national character." Argues that "true myths are generated on a sub-literary level by the historical experience of a people and thus constitute part of their inner reality which the work of the artist draws on, illuminates, and explains." States that in "American mythogenesis the founding fathers . . . tore violently a nation from the implacable and opulent wilderness," and their "concerns, their hopes, their terrors, their violence, and their justification of themselves, as expressed in literature, are the foundation stones of the mythology that informs our history."

Smith, Henry Nash. Virgin Land: The American West as Symbol and Myth. Cambridge: Harvard U.P., 1970. viii, 305 pp.

Presents a literary history of the United States that focuses on the predominant themes of the frontier and the myth of the garden. Discusses a number of folkloristic topics, such as character types and cultural beliefs, but not from a folkloristic perspective. Argues that American literature has been significantly influenced by the westward expansion of its populace.

Smith, Robert. "A Note on the Folktales of Charles Chestnutt." College Language Association Journal 5 (1962): 229-32.

Identifies Chesnutt's stories in The Conjure Woman and The Wife of His Youth and Other Stories as falling under the category of ordinary folktales, because they deal primarily with magic and superstition that are the product of Negro folklife. Observes that the narrator in The Conjure Woman, Uncle Julius, uses the folktales as a means of watching out for his own welfare.

Snyder, Gary. "The Incredible Survival of Coyote." Western American Literature 9 (1975): 255-72.

Informal discussion of the popularity of the Coyote figure in Western culture, folklore, and literature. Suggests that Coyote's appeal is that he is an outsider and yet also a survivor, thus he is a natural symbol for alienated groups in our society. Gives examples of Coyote narratives and contemporary poems incorporating the Coyote motif.

Solensten, John M. "Hawthorne's Ribald Classic: 'Mrs. Bullfrog' and the Folktale." Journal of Popular Culture 7 (1973): 582-88.

Examines the connections between Hawthorne's short story and the German Märchen. Suggests that "Mrs. Bullfrog" reflects the oral tradition of the folktale and that "the structural device of the recollected wedding journey provides a convenient means of following the rite de passage of a priggish initiate to sexual knowledge." Argues ultimately that the story is a twist on the Adamic theme of the acquisition of sexual knowledge.

Solomon, Robert H. "Classical Myth in the Novels of William Faulkner." Ph.D. Pennsylvania State University. 1975. 230 pp. Dissertation Abstracts International 36 (1976): 7428A-29A.

Identifies a limited and consistent body of classical myth-figures in Faulkner's writing, including Pan, Poseidon, Aphrodite, Apollo, Persephone, Io, Phaeton, and Ares. Suggests Faulkner acquired these from Bullfinch and Graves and is indebted to contemporary anthropological interpretetions of myth as disguised fertility ritual. Sees the myth of Apollo-Phaeton in As I

Lay Dying and the rape of Io in _The Hamlet_. Argues that Faulkner used the folkloristic allusions because he believed "that man was a victim of a pattern of sacrifice of life and limb for brute fertility." Concludes that Faulkner layered myths from other areas and eras.

Sorsby, Gladys E. "Nathaniel Hawthorne's Use of Folklore in the _Twice-Told Tales_." M.A. English. Ohio University. 1956. 69 pp.

Southerland, Ellease. "The Influence of Voodoo on the Fiction of Zora Neale Hurston," in Roseanne P. Bell, et al., eds., _Sturdy Black Bridges: Vision of Black Women in Literature_ (Garden City: Doubleday, 1979), pp. 172-83.

Surveys Hurston's personal exposure to the voodoo tradition of Haiti, which was apparently substantial, and traces evidence of this influence in _Their Eyes Were Watching God_, _Moses, Man of the Mountain_, and _Mules and Men_. The allusions include the use of numerology (nine and six), colors (yellow and blue), and customs (conjuring). Concludes that the voodoo gives shape to Hurston's religious beliefs.

Spears, James E. "William Faulkner, Folklorist, A Note." _Tennessee Folklore Society Bulletin_ 38 (1972): 95-96.

Briefly surveys folk characters, speech, superstition, and behavior in _Sartoris_.

Spillers, Hortense. "Ellison's 'Usable Past': Toward a Theory of Myth." _Interpretations_ 9 (1977): 53-69.

Sees the novel as insisting that "the black American experience is vulnerable to mythic dilation." Uses the term myth to denote "a form of selective discourse" based on Barthes' definition of myth as "a type of speech." Does not confine myth to oral speech, however, but rather "mythic form is a kind of conceptual code, relying on the accretions of association which cling to the concept." Sees Invisible Man as mythic by this definition, and traces some archetypal resonances in the novel. Suggests that "invisible man repeats the moves of the hero which Joseph Campbell illustrates." More a psychological theory of myth, rather than a folkloristic analysis.

Spivey, Herman E. "Faulkner and the Adamic Myth: Faulkner's Moral Vison." Modern Fiction Studies 19 (1973-74): 497-505.

Connects Faulkner to Lewis's tradition of writers preoccupied with the Adamic myth and argues that the Edenic metaphor in "The Bear" characterizes Faulkner's moral vision. States that "Faulkner says that all God asks is 'pity and humility and sufferance and endurance and the sweat of his face for bread'." Deals with myth in general and non-folkloristic sense.

Stafford, John. "Patterns of Meaning in Nights with Uncle Remus." American Literature 18 (1946-47): 89-108.

Adopts Kenneth Burke's concept that literature, like folk proverbs, may be thought of as "strategies for dealing with situations." Applies this folkloristic sociological criticism to Nights with Uncle Remus and reveals four levels of significance, all of which rely on Negro folklore to make their point.

Stafford, William T. "'Some Homer of the Cotton Fields': Faulkner's Use of the Mule Early and Late (Sartoris and The Reivers)." Papers on Language and Literature 5 (1969): 190-98.

Links Faulkner's satiric treatment of the mule to Shaw's "Essa on the Mule" and the tall tale conventions of the Southwestern humorists. Suggests Faulkner uses the mule as a central symbol of ideal behavior.

Stahl, Sandra. "Style in Oral and Written Narrative." Southern Folklore Quarter 43 (1979): 39-62.

Outlines seven stylistic features found in folklore and literature that are manifested differently in the oral versus written format. Uses a tale teller and story writer from Huntington, Indiana as an illustration of the differences and continuities in oral and written mediums.

Stahlman, M. Lucille. "Folk Sources and Analogues of Irving's Alhambra: A Study of Three Representative Tales." M.A. Folklore. American University. 1966. 148 pp.

Stanonik, Janez. Moby-Dick: The Myth and The Symbol, A Study in Folklore and Literature. Ljubljana, Yugoslavia: Ljubljana University Press, 1962. 214 pp.

A comprehensive investigation of the folkloristic underpinnings of Moby-Dick, including plot, characterization, and dialogue. Argues that Melville modeled Moby-Dick on a folktale and interprets the mythic symbolism inherent in the novel.

Starbuck, Arward. "Cotton Mather's Relation to the Salem Witchcraft." M.A. English. University of Chicago. 1922. 59 pp.

St. Armand, Barton Levi. "Emily Dickinson's American Grotesque: The Poet as Folk Artist." Topic 31 (1977): 3-19.

Finds Dickinson's art resembles a homemade sampler or native folk painting and that she uses the plainstyle hymns of Isaac Watts as a metrical model. Identifies correspondences between Dickinson's descriptions and images from early primitive American art.

St. Armand, Barton Levi. "Emily Dickinson's 'Babes in the Wood': A Ballad Reborn." Journal of American Folklore 90 (1977): 430-41.

Points out Dickinson's general interest in folk materials and her specific reliance on Laws ballad Q34, "The Children in the Wood" for one of her poems.

Stegner, Wallace. "History, Myth, and the Western Writer." The American West 4 (1967): 61-62, 76-79.

Observes that Western writing is locked into past folklore and has become mythic, in the sense of being bound to a timeless past.

Stein, Allen F. "Return to Phelps Farm: Huckleberry Finn and the Old Southwestern Framing Device." Mississippi Quarterly 24 (1971): 111-16.

Argues that the ending of Huckleberry Finn follows the traditional framing device of Southwestern humorists, but that Twain uses it here not to insulate the audience from the narrative but to bring the reader and his world into the story and to comment critically on the negative influence of society. The "respectable" world of the framing device is satirized as morally bankrupt.

Stein, William Bysshe. Hawthorne's Faust: A Study of the Devil Archetype. Gainesville: University of Florida Press, 1953. vii, 172 pp.

A general study of the devil figure in Hawthorne, more as a Faustian archetype than as a folkloristic manifestation.

Stein, William Bysshe. "The Motif of the Wise Old Man in Billy Budd." Western Humanities Review 14 (1960): 99-101.

Traces Melville's use of the Wise Old Man motif in his depiction of the Dansker, and observes that Melville significantly alters the motif because the Dansker does not prepare Budd for the deceitfulness of Claggart.

Stein, William Bysshe. "The Motif of the Wise Old Man in Walden." Modern Language Notes 75 (1960): 201-04.

Points out that Thoreau alludes to the traditional sages of the great cultures of the world in explaining his move to Walden. Suggests that Thoreau believes his society has lost contact with the Wise Old Man, and that we must return to a deeper appreciation of traditional wisdom. Concludes that "every analogy of knowledge in Walden subsumes the presence of the Wise Old Man."

Stein, William Bysshe. "Walden: The Wisdom of the Centaur," in Vickery, ed., Myth and Literature (Lincoln: U. of Nebraska, 1966), pp. 335-48. Also in English Literary History 25 (1958): 194-215.

Sees in Walden a pattern of heroic virtue, a reiteration of the labors of Hercules, Theseus, and Perseus, which prepares the hero for "the influx of self-knowledge that is Chiron's wisdom."

Steinbrink, Jeffrey. "'Boats Against the Current': Mortality and the Myth of Renewal in The Great Gatsby." Twentieth Century Literature 26 (1980): 157-70.

The "myth of renewal" is presented as the eroded belief in "the possiblities of spiritual regeneration in a boundless New World" envisioned by the Puritans. This myth is not analyzed folkloristically however.

Stephens, Robert O. "Macomber and That Somali Proverb: The Matrix of Knowledge." Fitzgerald/Hemingway Annual (1977): 137-47.

Analyzes Francis Macomber's emergence into manhood as a conversion from one order of cultural belief to another "from that of a decadent, industrial, and commercial system of economic individualism to one of traditional and organic values." The new order of belief corresponds to Hemingway's hunter's code and is embodied in a Somali proverb that Macomber recites to himself. Observes that at his moment of transformation, "Macomber comes into awareness of a formal ritual code of feeling and conduct analogous to that glimpsed by Jack Barnes in Pedro Romero's behavior." Investigates the model of initiation and the function of proverbs in it and gives examples of the behavioral code into which Macomber is ultimately initiated.

Stevens, Annie Winn. "An Inquiry into the Sources of the Beast Tales of Joel Chandler Harris." M.A. English. Columbia University. 1921. 121 pp.

Stock, Ely, "Witchcraft in 'The Hollow of the Three Hills'." <u>American Transcendental Quarterly</u> 14 (1972): 31-33.

Shows that Hawthorne's early tale reflects biblical conceptions of witchcraft. Argues that "although Hawthorne's interest in Salem witchcraft undoubtedly stimulated his conception, the work is rooted in a web of biblical allusion," particularly in the story of Saul and the Witch of Endor described in I Samuel 28.

Stone, Albert E., Jr. "The Infernal Reminiscence: Mythic Patterns in 'The Celebrated Jumping Frog of Calaveras County'." <u>Satire News Letter</u> 1 (1964): 41-44.

Suggests that there are a number of hidden meanings in "The Jumping Frog." Reads Twain's tale as a metaphoric account of traditional conflict between east and west, and as an heroic quest by a Grail Knight. Argues that Twain uses allusions to the Grail legend and to folktale frog transformations to suggest the hidden message that America has declined from a search for the religious to a preoccupation with the political.

Stone, Edward. "The Tug of the Fairy-Tales," in The Battle and The Books (Athens: Ohio University Press, 1964), pp. 137-62.

Exposes James's affinity for fairy tales, legends, fables, and the mythic perspective, as evidenced by numerous allusions to them in James's fiction.

Stonsifer, Richard J. "Faulkner's 'The Bear': A Note on Structure." College English 23 (1961): 219-23.

Identifies a connection between Ishtar's descent into the underworld and Ike McCaslin's quest for the bear.

Strauch, Carl F. "Emerson's Adaptation of Myth in 'The Initial Love'." American Transcendental Quarterly 25 (1975): 51-65.

Surveys the literary treatments and philosophical significances of the classical myth of Cupid, and suggests that it underlies in a crucial way Emerson's poem. Explains the philosophical attitude towards love that Emerson presents in poem through his treatment of the Cupid narrative. Concludes that "Emerson saw in Cupid the possiblity of employing the god for his own mythic purposes."

Strelka, Joseph P., ed. Literary Criticism and Myth. University Park: Pennsylvania State U.P., 1980. xii, 306 pp.

A collection of essays dealing with myth as a general concept or structure, whose action is ritualistic, ceremonial, or compulsive. For the most part, the use of the term myth in these articles tends towards the abstract. Includes contributions by Block, Feder, White, and Vickery; contains no specific consideration of American literature.

Strickland, Carol Colclough. "Emmeline Grangerford, Mark Twain's Folk Artist." Bulletin of the New York Public Library 79 (1976): 225-33.

Identifies the folk art tradition of a "conventional mourning picture produced by amateur female artists in the first half of the nineteenth century" as an exact match for the graveyard scene drawn by Emmeline. Suggests that Twain's variation of the mourning picture as presented in Huck's description of Emmeline's other paintings about a dead bird and a woman with six arms reveals how he burlesques the tradition through the devices of exaggeration and fantasy. Twain satirizes sentimental romanticism through his use of the familiar mourning picture, "eliciting both laughter at humbug and outrage at false piety."

Stromme, Craig John. "Barth, Gardner, Coover, and Myth." Ph.D. State University of New York at Albany. 1978. 245 pp. Dissertation Abstracts International 39 (1978): 876A.

Contends that Barth, Gardner, and Coover all moved from realistic fiction to mythic fiction in the late sixties. Examines the reasons for and results of this change. Suggests Barth found myth to be a convenient vehicle for his exploration of the problems of faith, freedom, and responsibility. Reasons that Gardner found in myth a metaphor for the reconciliation of the conflicting needs of self and society by the heroic artistic consciousness. Concludes that Coover moves from relying upon traditional Christian mythology to creating the first American myth. Coover uses myth "not as a device to free the writer from the constraints of realistic fiction" nor "to heighten the importance of philosophical struggles in the novel" but "to reveal the true nature of American thought and the American experience by unveiling the mythic structure our country is based upon."

Stull, William L. "The Quest and the Question: Cosmology and Myth in the Work of William S. Burroughs, 1953-1960." Twentieth Century Literature 24 (1978): 225-42.

Argues that contrary to critical opinion, Burroughs does not reject myth, nor does he aim at freedom from mythology, nor does he invent a whole new mythology; rather, he incorporates the quest motif from the Holy Grail, thus tapping a primordial source of vitality. Notes Burroughs did graduate work in comparative anthropology, and traces the quest pattern through a number of Burroughs' works. Observes that along with the myth goes a cosmology, "a vision of the creation and destruction of the world," and that out of the waste land Burroughs creates a new world.

Sullivan, Francis W. "A Dictionary of Mythological Allusions in Certain Selected Novels of James Branch Cabell." M.A. English. University of South Dakota. 1950. 70 pp.

Sullivan, Phillip E. "Buh Rabbit: Going Through the Changes." Studies in Black Literature 4 (1973): 28-32.

Contends Buh Rabbit still persists in the works of Ellison and Cecil Brown in characters such as Stagolee, Mr. Jiveass Nigger, etc.

Sutton, Thomas. "Myth and the Short Stories of William Faulkner." M.A. English. Atlanta University. 1952. 57 pp.

Swanson, William J. "Fowl Play on the Frontier." West Georgia College Review 1 (1968): 12-15.

Discusses gander pulling as a frontier pastime that is described by Augustus Baldwin Longstreet.

Swink, Helen. "William Faulkner: The Novelist as Oral Narrator." Georgia Review 26 (1972): 183-209.

Finds that Faulkner's interest in Southwestern tales also led him to develop a prose style with a "'voice', i.e., the illusion of an oral story teller. Points out the rhetorical devices employed by Faulkner to sustain this impression, such as long rhythmical sentences and dialect speeches. Concludes that "he forced written rhetoric out of its conventional form and pushed it into new dimensions."

Tapley, Philip A. "Negro Superstitions in Children of Strangers." Louisiana Folklore Miscellany 4 (1976-80): 61-72.

Identifes superstitions in Lyle Saxon's work.

Taylor, Archer. "Folklore and the Student of Literature." The Pacific Spectator 2 (1949): pp. 216-223. Also in Alan Dundes, ed., The Study of Folklore (Englewood Cliffs: Prentice-Hall, Inc., 1965), pp. 34-42.

Identifies three relationships of folklore and literature: 1) folklore is often indistinguishable from literature; 2) literature contains elements borrowed from folklore; 3) writers imitate folklore. Cites examples, including some American authors (primarily Longfellow).

Taylor, Archer. "Proverbial Comparisons and Similes in On Troublesome Creek." Kentucky Folklore Record 8 (1962): 87-96.

Indexes some 200 folk sayings from the novel.

Taylor, Archer. "Proverbial Materials in Edward Eggleston, 'The Hoosier Schoolmaster,'" in W. Edson Richmond, ed., Studies in Folklore (Bloomington: Indiana University Press, 1957), pp. 262-70.

Lists over seventy proverbs in Eggleston's novel that give a picture of life in mid-nineteenth century Indiana.

Taylor, Archer. "Proverbial Materials in Two Novels by Harry Harrison Kroll." _Bulletin of the Tennessee Folklore Society_ 22 (1956): 39-52.

Lists over 200 proverbial expressions in Kroll's novels.

Taylor, Archer. "Proverbs and Proverbial Phrases in the Writings of Mary N. Murfree (Charles Egbert Craddock)." _Bulletin of the Tennessee Folklore Society_ 24 (1958): 11-50.

Lists over 400 examples.

Taylor, Archer. "Some Proverbial Expressions from Bayard Taylor's 'Story of Kennett'." _Keystone Folklore Quarterly_ 6 (1961): 23-24.

Annotates a dozen proverbs.

Taylor, Clyde. "Black Folk Spirit and the Shape of Black Literature." _Black World_ 21 (1972): 31-40.

Talks generally about Black folk spirit as surfacing in a wide range of cultural phenomena, which are successfully utilized by black artists such as Du Bois, Hughes, Brown, Hurston, Toomer, Bontemps, and Ellison.

Taylor, Marjorie Anne. "The Folk Imagination of Vachel Lindsay." Ph.D. Wayne State University. 1976. 284 pp. _Dissertation Abstracts International_ 37 (1977): 7133A.

Argues that Lindsay used the American resources of legends, local heroes, everyday events, and folk language to construct his poetry. Suggests that he employs American songs and chants, popular symbols, play games, and other techniques of folk culture in his poetry, in order to build a sense of national pride.

Taylor, Mary Eva. "The Merlin Legend in British and American Literature with Special Reference to Edwin Arlington Robinson." M.A. English. University of Alabama. 1925. 130 pp.

Tharpe, Coleman W. "The Oral Storyteller in Hawthorne's Novels." _Studies in Short Fiction_ 16 (1979): 205-14.

Suggests that Hawthorne's depiction of Holgrave's legend of Alice Pyncheon, Zenobia's legend of "The Silvery Veil," and Donatello's legend of the nymph of the fountain represent a unique refinement of Hawthorne's earlier experiments with oral folk narrators. Points out Hawthorne's affinity for oral folk legends, his belief in their timeless truth, and his attempt to emulate their form. Argues that Hawthorne casts Holgrave, Zenobia, and Donatello in the roles of oral storytellers in order to "transfer to them the folk narrator's ability to unite recollection and prophecy, history and the truth of the human spirit."

Therrell, Katheryne D. "Folklore in Mark Twain's Mississippi River Novels." M.A. Education. East Texas State University. 1967.

Thigpen, Kenneth A. "Folklore in Contemporary American Literature: Thomas Pynchon's _V._ and the Alligators-in-the-Sewers Legend." _Southern Folklore Quarterly_ 43 (1979): 93-105.

Suggests that folklore and literature can mutually illuminate one another, and investigates Pynchon's use of folktale and legend materials in his novel in an attempt to explain the current evolution of folkloric and literary taste.

Thigpen, Kenneth A. "Folkloristic Concerns in Barth's The Sot-Weed Factor." Southern Folklore Quarterly 41 (1977): 225-37.

Points out the extensive incidence of folklore in The Sot-weed Factor (including proverbs, oral legends, traditions, folk speech) and suggests Barth uses it to redefine traditional notions about history by undermining the veracity of recorded history and by encouraging a more vital folkloristic perspective.

Thomas, Gillian and Michael Larsen. "Ralph Ellison's Conjure Doctors." English Language Notes 17 (1979-80): 281-88.

Points out that Peter Wheatstraw fulfills the requirements of a conjure doctor and that Ellison's treatment of him reveals "his own reluctance to embrace black folklore." Argues that Ellison is ambivalent about his use of this black folklore because "the shaman cannot exert power in isolation, but only in a society that accords shamanic authority and which values its phenomena." Suggests that "by the end of the novel, the hero has himself acquired or experienced many of the attributes of shamanism: prophetic dreams, 'invisibility'," magical oratory, and shape-shifting of identity, but he is still excluded from possessing real power.

Thomas, W. K. "The Mythic Dimension of Catch-22." Texas Studies in Language and Literature 15 (1973-74): 189-98.

Suggests Chief White Halfoat is a vegetation god who is killed at the end of the year and that Orr is a sun god who crashes to rise again. Yossarian is a Promethean figure who urges us to accept the example of Orr as the way to salvation--through a cycle of birth, suffering, death, and rebirth.

Thompson, Judith J. "Symbol, Myth, and Ritual in The Glass Menagerie, The Rose Tattoo, and Orpheus

Descending," in Jac Tharpe, ed., Tennessee Williams: A Tribute (Jackson: U. P. of Mississippi, 1977), pp. 679-711.

Argues that many of Williams' plays are based on myths of dying gods, but unlike the original myth, they culminate in neither birth nor resurrection. For example, in The Glass Menagerie, the "failure of Jim to save Laura is also the failure of the fertility god to complete the initiation rite, the failure of Christ's second coming, the failures of Prince Charming, the Pirate, and Superman to rescue the maiden in distress." Thus, Williams' mythic echoes serve ultimately to extend the meaning of his works, to construct "an analogue of modern man's alienation from God and isolation from his fellow man." Concludes that Williams dramatizes man's existential angst as ritual, evoking archetypal and mythic images.

Thompson, Lawrence S. "Folklore in the Kentucky Novel." Midwest Folklore 3 (1953): 137-45.

Surveys numerous Kentucky authors and titles that incorporate folklore.

Thompson, Lawrence S. "Longfellow's Original Sin of Imitation." Colophon 1 (1935): 97-106.

Points out that Longfellow's "The Battle of Lovell's Pond" is indirectly based on an eighteenth-century ballad.

Thompson, Stith. "Folklore and Literature." PMLA 55 (1940): 866-74.

Surveys the field of folklore and its relation to literature in order to advance a plan for the future study of oral literature and its usefulness for written literature.

Thompson, Stith. "The Indian Legend of Hiawatha." PMLA 37 (1922): 128-40.

Compares Longfellow's version to the Indian legends and concludes that Longfellow violates the spirit of the Indian materials, by introducing romance, by humanizing the demigod hero, and by fabricating an artificial coherence, hence doing violence to the original myth and to the spirit of the life he depicts.

Thompson, Stith. "Literature for the Unlettered," in Newton P. Stallknecht and Horst Frenz, eds., Comparative Literature: Method and Perspective (Carbondale: Southern Illinois University Press, 1961), pp. 201-17.

Reviews the function and form of oral literature for the unlettered with the idea of comparing it to written literature's place in modern life. Includes a summary of oral literature's characteristics as distinct from written art.

Thorpe, Coleman W. "The Oral Story Teller in Hawthorne's Novels." Studies in Short Fiction 16 (1979): 205-14.

Argues that Hawthorne's later narrators in The House of Seven Gables, The Blithdale Romance, and The Marble Faun represent a unique refinement of Hawthorne's earlier experiments with folk narrators.

Thrift, Bonnie Beth Reading. "Harvey Ferguson's Use of Southwestern History and Customs in His Novels." M.A. English. University of Texas. 1940. 66 pp.

Tillepy, Inez. "The Evolution of the Yankee Character in American Drama." M.A. English. University of Alabama. 1939. 153 pp.

Tiller, Lessie. "Gullah in American Literature." M.A. English. University of South Carolina. 1923. 46 pp.

Tracy, Leng. "The Origin of the Rip Van Winkle Legend and the Different Manner of Its Presentation in the Media of the Short Story by Washington Irving and the Drama by Joseph Jefferson." M.A. English. University of Kentucky. 1933. 75 pp.

Traubitz, Nancy Baker. "Myth as a Basis of Dramatic Structure in Orpheus Descending." Modern Drama 19 (1976): 57-66.

Distinguishes five separate myth patterns in Williams's play: the loss of Eden, the battle of angels, Christ, Orpheus, and Adonis. Traces references in the play to these myths, and shows how Williams coordinates the disparate myths. Concludes that the play is a significant and worthwhile attempt to re-create myths in the context of our time and that the myths are integral to the structure of the play.

Travis, Bettye Texana. "Folklore in Julia Peterkin's Novels." M.A. Literature and Language. Colorado State College. 1936. 108 pp.

Tregeagle, Phyllis. "Edwin Arlington Robinson's Treatment of The Tristram Legend." M.A. English. Brigham Young University. 1934. 154 pp.

Tupper, Frederic, Jr. "The Comparative Study of Riddles." Modern Language Notes 18 (1903): 1-8.

A serious attempt to grasp the relationship of the folk use of riddles and the literary use of riddles by identifying the interaction and borrowing that goes on and by tracing the history and occurrence of some riddles in both literary and folk tradition.

Turner, Darwin T. "Black Fiction: History and Myth." Studies in American Fiction 5 (1977): 109-26.

Elucidates the function of myth and folklore to emancipate and valorize the downtrodden and surveys a significant tradition in Afro-American folk tales, drama, poetry, and novels that strives towards this end.

Turner, Darwin T. "Paul Laurence Dunbar: The Poet and the Myths," in Jay Martin, ed., A Singer in the Dawn: Reinterpretations of Paul Laurence Dunbar (New York: Dodd, Mead, 1975), pp. 59-74.

Argues against some distorted notions (myths) associated with Dunbar. Points out, for example, that Dunbar used two dialects, one black and one white. Concludes that Dunbar was an artist for the folk, not just black, but all people, but he was not a folk artist.

Turner, Frederick W., III. "Melville and Thomas Berger: The Novelist as Cultural Anthropologist." Centennial Review 13 (1969): 101-21.

Suggests that novelists may "distort or misrepresent historical facts and figures and yet tell the truth about the culture of which that history is one kind of record." Argues for the metaphoric truth of fiction and folklore as illustrated in discussions of Melville's Israel Potter and Berger's Little Big Man. In Berger's novel, we see the legend of Custer told from the context of Indian culture and folklore, which gives us a very different picture than the European-centered version.

Turner, Frederick W., III. "Myth Inside and Out: Malamud's The Natural." Novel 1 (1968): 134-139.

Argues that the "conflict between myths and the outer world" has been a persistently recurring theme of Malamud's fiction. Points out the use of the "ur-myth of the hero" in The Natural, and its correspondence to the paradigms suggested by Rank, Campbell, and Raglan. Discusses the characteristics of the mythological hero and shows how Roy Hobbes evinces them.

Twitchell, James. "Poe's 'The Oval Portrait' and the Vampire Motif." Studies in Short Fiction 14 (1977): 387-93.

Interprets "The Oval Portrait" as a vampire story, and argues that the "vampire-myth was an ideal paradigm for love that is too demanding or, in the case of 'The Oval Portrait,' art that is too life-consuming." Draws comparisons to other stories by Poe and concludes that the changes show Poe's final tightening of the vampire motif, "now applying it to the process of artistic creation" and creating his most sophisticated variation on the vampire theme.

Tyler, Ronald. "Mark Twain's Mythic Vision: An Affirmation of Man's Possibilities." Ph.D. University of Nevada. 1970. 419 pp. Dissertation Abstracts International 31 (1970): 1777A.

Defines mythic elements as those directly related to the Jungian concept of archetypes and to Campbell's monomyth quest pattern. Applies this general concept of myth to The Mysterious Stranger.

Tyler, Troi. "The Function of the Bear Ritual in Faulkner's Go Down, Moses." Journal of the Ohio Folklore Society 3 (1968): 19-40.

Examines bear lore and totemic rituals as expressions of Faulkner's moral concerns in Go Down, Moses.

Ujhazy, Maria. "Melville's Use of Mythology." Acta Litteraria Academiae Scientiarum Hungaricae 20 (1978): 53-63.

Suggests Melville discards all mythologies as equally fallacious and that he presents in Moby-Dick a "demythicized" world. Illustrates how Melville ironically subverts and explodes Biblical myths such as Jonah and Genesis by presenting them irreverently and sarcastically and by exposing their illogic.

Urie, Margaret Ann. "The Problem of Evil: The Myth of Man's Fall and Redemption in the Works of William Faulkner." Ph.D. University of Nevada, Reno. 1978. 219 pp. Dissertation Abstracts Interational 39 (1979): 4943A.

A general discussion of how Faulkner finds redemptive meaning in a sinful world. No folkloristic analysis.

Utley, Francis Lee. Bear, Man, and God: Eight Approaches to William Faulkner's 'The Bear.' New York: Random House, 1964. 429 pp.

A collection of short essays and excerpts, many of which consider the cultural and folkloristic roots of "The Bear." Utley's own essay, "Pride and Humility: The Cultural Roots of Ike McCaslin" (pp. 167-87) views "The Bear" as a tall tale of an epic hunt for an immortal Hunted Bear and as an expression of the Southern folk tradition of hunting and its values.

Utley, Francis Lee. "Folk Literature: An Operational Definition." Journal of American Folklore 74 (1961): 193-206. Also in Alan Dundes, ed., The Study of Folklore (Englewood Cliffs: Prentiss Hall, Inc, 1965), pp. 7-24.

Defines folk literature as "orally transmitted literature" and discusses briefly its relationship to printed literature.

Utley, Francis Lee. "From the Dinnsenchas to Proust: the Folklore of Placenames in Literature." Names 16 (1968): 273-293.

Examines Irish, French, and American examples and suggests placenames have a universal charm.

Utley, Francis Lee. "Oral Genres as a Bridge to Written Literature." Genre 2 (1969): 91-103.

Also in Folklore Genres, Dan Ben-Amos, ed. (Austin: University of Texas Press, 1976), pp. 3-15.

Reviews the generic distinctions of folk literature and examines "The Wife of Usher's Well" as an example of the ballad genre that may be used to foster appreciation of other related literary genres.

Utley, Francis Lee. "The Study of Folk Literature: Its Scope and Use." Journal of American Folklore 71 (1958): 139-148.

Postulates that the student of folk literature is concerned with three problems: what laws emerge from the study of communal or oral process; how these laws contrast with those of the individual or written process; and how a work of oral literature influences and is influenced by the work of the sophisticated writer.

Van Pelt, Rachel Elizabeth Stanfield. "Folklore in the Tales of Nathaniel Hawthorne." Ph.D. University of Illinois. 1962. 309 pp. Dissertation Abstracts International 23 (1962): 627.

Traces Hawthorne's biographical exposure to superstions, legends, and myth as a boy in Salem and Maine and his predisposition to reading chronicles and histories rich in superstition. Analyzes Hawthorne's preoccupation with the supernatural and witchcraft. Identifies also the mythological basis of the Tanglewood Tales, and Hawthorne's use of prophecy, curses, and tale types. Concludes that Hawthorne's preoccupation with folklore explains his reliance on character types and grotesque symbols, and it provides, though his transformation of it, the raw materials of his artistic excellence.

Vargo, Edward P. "The Necessity of Myth in Updike's The Centaur." PMLA 88 (1973): 452-60.

Argues that Updike's use of myth is comic in The Centaur. Sees myth as a central element in the structure of the novel, which "takes on the character of a complete ritual in itself." Suggests that Peter has in the life and actions of his father, "a myth that enables him to face the transcendent questions of time, life, and death." Points out the allusions to the Chiron myth, and suggests that the ritual actions of The Centaur provide a mythic consciousness for its characters. It is this mythic consciousness that makes the ritual meaningful and that enables Peter to receive "a new life and a new freedom."

Varnado, S. L. "Poe's Raven Lore: A Source Note." American Notes and Queries 7 (1968): 35-37.

Suggests Poe may have consulted Dalyell's The Darker Superstitions of Scotland in writing "The Raven."

Vernon, Dodd. "An Analysis of the Use of Folk Materials by Stephen Vincent Benet." M.A. English. University of New Mexico. 1949. 30 pp.

Vickery, John B. "Literary Criticism and Myth: Anglo-American Critics." Yearbook of Comparative Criticism 9 (1980): 210-37.

Rehashes the general arguments of the contributors to his collection of essays in Myth and Literature.

Vickery, John B. The Literary Impact of The Golden Bough. Princeton: Princeton U.P., 1973. viii, 435 pp.

Considers The Golden Bough to be "both the most encyclopedic treatment of primitive life available to the English speaking world and the one that is behind the bulk of modern literary interest in myth and ritual." Illustrates this contention with extensive discussions of the influences on and uses by major authors such as Yeats, Eliot, Lawrence, and Joyce. Presents a thorough picture of the intellectual roots and context of Frazer's work and an admirable analysis of its subsequent intellectual and literary influence.

Vickery, John B. Myth and Literature: Contemporary Theory and Practice. Lincoln: University of Nebraska Press, 1966. xii, 391 pp.

Presents a large selection of essays on aspects of the connection between myth and literature. A half-dozen studies focused specifically on the use of myth in American literary texts are referenced individually in this bibliography. Additionally, there are a number of valuable studies that comparatively analyze the nature of myth and literature and their interdependence, e.g., studies by Hyman, Wheelwright, Chase, Watts, Frye, Lytle, Rahv, Douglas, and Block.

Vickery, John B. "Ritual and Theme in Faulkner's 'Dry September'," in John Vickery, ed., The Scapegoat: Ritual and Literature (Boston: Houghton Mifflin, 1972), pp. 200-208.

Identifies a common ritual of the scapegoat as victim underlying a number of related characters in Faulkner's short story. Suggests that Faulkner presents an ironic treatment of the scapegoat theme because the innocent victim, Minnie Cooper, tricks the town into punishing another innocent victim, Will Mayes.

Vlach, John M. "Fenimore Cooper's Leatherstocking as Folk Hero." New York Folklore Quarterly 27 (1971): 323-38.

Argues that Cooper consciously chose to cast Natty Bumppo as a folk hero in the form of Daniel Boone and that this character reflects significantly the folklore of 19th century America.

Vorpahl, Ben M. "'Such Stuff as Dreams are Made on': History, Myth, and the Comic Vision of Mark

Twain and William Faulkner." Ph.D. University of Wisconsin. 1966. 540 pp. Dissertation Abstracts International 28 (1967): 698A.

Points out the connection to Southwestern humor in both Faulker and Twain, but does not explore the folkloristic roots.

Waddington, M. "The Function of Folklore in the Poetry of A. M. Klein." Ariel 10 (1979): 5-19.

Compares the function of a piece of folklore in a poem to its function in a given social group in order to shed light on both the poem and the group. Sees the initial function of folklore in literature to be as a rhetorical device, serving to affirm some collective belief of the group. Suggests an additional function is that it is a way of revealing psychological insights or values, sometimes through inversion or reversal of the traditional folk interpretations of the material being used. Illustrates the discussion with examples from Hath Not a Jew.

Walker, Jeanne Murray. "Rites of Passage Today: The Cultural Significance of The Wizard of Earthsea." Mosaic 13 (1980): 179-91.

Links the structure of Le Guin's fantasy novel to van Gennep's model of traditional rites of passage. Suggests that Ged's rite of passage is essential to the book's meaning; it portrays "the hero's slow realization of what it means to be an individual in society and a self in relation to higher powers."

Walker, Ralph Spencer. "Edwin Arlington Robinson and the Arthurian Tradition." M.A. English. University of Tennessee. 1936. 87 pp.

Walker, Robert G. "Another Medusa Allusion in Welty's 'Petrified Man'." Notes on Contemporary Literature 9 (1979): 10.

Briefly notes that Leota's sticking out of her tongue corresponds iconographically to Medusan imagery. Observes that Welty subtly signals an important change in her major character with a gesture "that is at once naturalistically appropriate and symbolically integral to the dominant allusive pattern of the entire story."

Walker, Warren S. "Buckskin West: Leatherstocking at High Noon." New York Folklore Quarterly 24 (1968): 88-102.

Considers Natty Bumppo a folk hero even if he is not in oral tradition, and compares him to the Southern cavalier and the Western cowboy hero.

Walker, Warren S. "The Frontiersman as Recluse and Redeemer." New York Folklore Quarterly 16 (1960): 110-122.

Investigates the mythic, ethical, and ethnic basis of Natty Bumpo , who, according to this study, is drawn from the character of the frontiersman.

Walker, Warren S. James Fenimore Cooper: An Introduction and Interpretation. New York: Barnes and Noble, 1962. 142 pp.

Chapter 2, "Quest for an American Novel" points out that Cooper relied heavily upon stock characters and their manners, habits, customs, beliefs, and dialects, including over a thousand proverbs. Focuses in the other chapters more on the literary history of Cooper.

Walker, Warren S. "Proverbs in the Novels of James Fenimore Cooper." Midwest Folklore 3 (1953): 99-107.

Lists several hundred proverbs found in Cooper's novels; suggests it is the most frequently used folklore in Cooper's writings.

Wallace, Paul A. W. "John Heckewelder's Indians and the Fenimore Cooper Tradition." American Philosophical Society Proceedings 96 (1952): 496-504.

Argues that Cooper "poured the prejudices of John Heckewelder into the Leather-Stocking mold, and produced the Indian of nineteenth-century convention." Specifically, Cooper borrowed the polarized view of bad Indians (Iroquois or Mingos) and good Indians (Delaware or Mohicans) for his characterization from Heckewelder's ethnographic field study.

Walser, Richard. "Ham Jones: Southern Folk Humorist." Journal of American Folklore 78 (1965): 295-316.

Reprints a number of humorous sketches with oral roots published by Jones, specifically "Cousin Sally Dillard."

Walser, Richard. "Negro Dialect in Eighteenth-Century American Drama." American Speech 30 (1955): 269-76.

Surveys the varied and uneven use of dialect by early American dramatists and concludes that the speeches are generally crude and distorted duplications of the sounds which the playwrights thought they heard. Suggests the distinctiveness of Negro dialect made it especially valuable for literature.

Walsh, Thomas F. "Xochitl: Katherine Anne Porter's Changing Goddess." American Literature 52 (1980): 183-93.

Examines Porter's depiction of a Mexican goddess in "The Children of Xochitl" and "Hacienda" and notes that Porter was very familiar with Mexican mythology. Argues that Porter's transformation of Xochitl from a goddess of life in the "The Children of Xochitl" to a goddess of death in "Hacienda" is a reflection of her downward path to wisdom. Concludes that in Porter's recreation of the legend of Xochital, we can trace the vicissitudes of "how Porter lost hope for happiness in this life."

Walters, Thomas N. "Thad Stem, Jr., and Folklore." North Carolina Folklore 17 (1969): 40-52.

Interviews Stem and reports his sources and his use of folklore.

Walton, David A. "Joel Chandler Harris as Folklorist: a Reassessment." Keystone Folklore Quarterly 11 (1966): 21-26.

Views Harris as a special case, a combined folklorist and storyteller who modified his material to make it more accessible but whose presentation of folklore materials is essentially reliable.

Walton, Ivan H. "Eugene O'Neill and the Folklore and Folkways of the Sea." Western Folklore 14 (1955): 153-69.

Argues that in his plays O'Neill made extensive use of sailor folklore, including shanties, superstitions, tales, and customs, with which he had become acquainted in his two years of seafaring.

Ward, Jerry W. "Folklore and the Study of Black Literature." Mississippi Folklore Register 6 (1972): 83-90.

Considers the use of folklore by black writers including Ellison, Killens, Hughes.

Warren, Austin. "Myth and Dialectic in the Later Novels." Kenyon Review 5 (1943): 554-68.

Argues that James's later novels demonstrate evidence of an oral style produced by the process of dictation James adopted. Argues further that he employs two major techniques--a "mythic" one that allegorizes, that describes by extended conceit, and a "dialectical" that depicts in world in opposites.

Washington, Mary Louise. "The Folklore of the Cumberlands as Reflected in the Writings of Jesse Stuart." Ph.D. University of Pennsylvania. 1960. 518 pp. Dissertation Abstracts International 21 (1960): 844-45.

Investigates the Kentucky hill community and affirms that Stuart provides an inclusive and authentic picture of their way of life. Discusses the hill speech, pioneering lifestyles, hill workways, and the folk literature and humor of the Kentucky hill community as it is reflected in Stuart's works.

Watkins, Floyd C. "Indiana Folklore in the Fiction of James Kirke Paulding." New York Folklore Quarterly 7 (1951): 217-25.

Points out that Paulding's Koningsmarke (1823) uses Indian myths and songs and that it appeared several years before Schoolcraft published his work.

Watkins, Floyd C. "James Kirke Paulding's Early Ring-Tailed Roarer." Southern Folklore Quarterly 15 (1951): 183-87.

Suggests Paulding used the folk stereotype of "the ring-tailed roarer in Letters from the South (1817), possibly the earliest treatment of this type.

Watson, Douglas. "Folk Speech, Custom, and Belief in Harold Frederic's The Damnation of Theron Ware and Stories of York State." New York Folklore Quarterly 3 (1977): 83-99.

Shows that Frederic was an astute student of folklife who knew the process by which folklore is born and transmitted. Finds accurate and vivid portraits of Mohawk Valley folklife in the author's two major publications. Observes that Frederic uses folk speech for characterization and setting, folk belief for ethnic identification and definition, and folk customs to help to draw the setting, to move the story along, and to provide ironic comparisons.

Waugh, Butler. "Structural Analysis in Literature and Folklore." Western Folklore 25 (1966): 153-64.

An analytic comparison of the methods of structural analysis proposed by Propp and Dundes to those proposed by Köngäs and Maranda; not about literature or its relation to folklore at all.

Webb, James Wilson. "Irwin Russell and Folk Literature." Southern Folklore Quarterly 12 (1948): 137-49.

Examines Russell's incorporation of folk songs and ballads into his dialect poetry.

Weiher, Carol. "Horatio Alger's Fiction: American Fairy Tales for All Ages." CEA Critic 40/2 (1978): 23-27.

Notes the similarities between Alger's stories and the fairy tales collected by the Grimms, Jacobs, and Moe in Europe; they include easily identifible character types and predictable conflicts. Describes Alger's fiction as repeating "the fairy-tale formula of a journey from rags to riches" and discusses comparisons in Ragged Dick to "Jack and the Beanstalk" and "Cinderella."

Weil, Dorothy. "Folklore Motifs in Arna Bontemps' Black Thunder." Southern Folklore Quarterly 35 (1971): 1-14.

Points out that Bontemps' novel is "pervaded by beliefs and customs ... from Negro folklore." Examines folk motifs concerning death and the spirit, the importance of signs and portents, and the use of magic and conjure.

Weisinger, Herbert. The Agony and the Triumph: Papers on the Use and Abuse of Myth. E. Lansing: Michigan State University Press, 1964. 283 pp.

Sixteen separate essays dealing with myth and literary criticism. Although most essays deal with literature from the English Renaissance, "The Mythic Origins of the Creative Process," pp. 241-265, discusses creative process as an analogue to the activities of a mythic hero and uses brief examples of American poets including W. D. Snodgrass and A.J.M. Smith.

Weixlmann, Joe, & Sher Weixlmann. "Barth and Barthelme Recycle the Perseus Myth: A Study in Literary Ecology." Modern Fiction Studies 25 (1979): 191-207.

Compares the esthetics of Barth and Barthelme and notes the similarities and dissimilarities in their use of the Perseus myth. Suggests that Barth uses it to point out the "discrepancy between art and reality" by acknowledging the artificiality of his story. Barth seeks to make his audience accept that literature is a distorted, but nevertheless valid, description of living: a "true representation of the distortion we all make of living." Barthelme, on the other hand, seeks to create a literary object that has the rhetorical power to leave its beholder forcibly modified and to communicate its creator's sense of play. Concludes that "Barthelme uses the myth to add a dimension to a contemporary character," while "Barth confronts the myth directly, adding to it and reinterpreting it."

Weldon, Roberta F. "Cooper's The Deerslayer and the Indian Myth of Nanabozho." New York Folklore Quarterly 2 (1976): 61-67.

Analyzes the parallels between Cooper's Tom Hutter and the Noah figure of Indian mythology, Nanabozho. Shows how Cooper reshaped the Indian deluge myth to his own ends, by inverting the positive potential of the narrative. In direct and ironic contrast to the myth, Hutter, called The Muskrat, goes down into the lake but he does not rise, revealing how ignoble and fallen the white man and his civilization have become.

Wellborn, Grace Pleasant. "The Golden Thread in _The Scarlet Letter_." _Southern Folklore Quartery_ 29 (1965): 169-78.

Examines the traditional and archetypal associations of the colors yellow (gold) and red in Hawthorne's novel. Concludes that as Hawthorne gives his version of the Eden story, his lovers move from sin and darkness to light and transformation.

Wellborn, Grace Pleasant. "Plant Lore and _The Scarlet Letter_." _Southern Folklore Quarterly_ 27 (1963): 160-67.

Observes that Hawthorne was very familiar with plant lore and that he used various plants in his settings for their symbolic associations.

Wentersdorf, Karl P. "The Element of Witchcraft in _The Scarlet Letter_." _Folklore_ 83 (1972): 132-53.

Insists that the witchcraft be taken literally, and discusses in some detail the realistic justification for Mistress Hibbins' actions and other intimations of witchcraft ceremonies in the novel. Suggests that allegorically the evil temptress is a satire on the Puritan aesthetic.

Werner, Craig. "Brer Rabbit Meets the Underground Man: Simplification of Consciousness in Baraka's _Dutchman_ and _Slave Ship_." _Obsidian_ 5 (1979): 35-40.

Suggests briefly that "*Dutchman* circles around several basic western myths: the fall, the flying Dutchman, and most importantly, the underground man." Concentrates discussion on literary treatments of these myths, including Dostoevsky and Ellison. Alludes also to the folktale model of Brer Rabbit and Brer Fox.

Wess, Robert C. "The Use of Hudson Valley Traditions in Washington Irving's *Knickerbocker History of New York*." *New York Folklore Quarterly* 30 (1974): 212-25.

Surveys folk traditions of the Hudson-Valley Dutch that influenced Irving, including folk tales, legends, and St. Nicholas.

West, Harry C. "Negro Folklore in Pierce's Novels." *North Carolina Folklore* 19 (1971): 66-72.

Finds, in addition to "Negro dialect, . . . a wealth of other folk materials [from] Negro culture: folk speech, sayings, remedies, signs, and superstitions [that] contribute to atmosphere and meaning in the novels."

West, Harry C. "Simon Suggs and His Similes." *North Carolina Folklore Journal* 16 (1968): 53-57.

Surveys the characteristics of Southwestern humor and identifies a range of folk expressions in Suggs' writings.

West, James L. W., III. "Early Backwoods Humor in the *Greenville Mountaineer*, 1826-1840." *Mississippi Quarterly* 25 (1971-72): 69-82.

Surveys four types of backwoods humor in a South Carolina newspaper, including tall tales, fight stories, marriage customs, and Crockett stories.

West, John Foster. "Mrs. Morehouse's Rain on the Just." North Carolina Folklore 19 (1971): 47-54.

Discusses the predominant types of folklore found in Rain on the Just ("dialect, folk speech patterns, superstitions, folkways, folk humor, folk maxims, and folk tales") and concludes that the folklore is well imitated but not authentic.

West, Victor Royce. "Folklore in the Works of Mark Twain". University of Nebraska Studies in Language, Literature, and Criticism 10 (1930): 1-87.

Argues that Twain had a keen interest in and deep appreciation of folklore and used it extensively in his writings. Argues further that the folklore materials were "natively his, and they come to his readers in all their original character, unimpaired by literary handling or artistic distortion." Concentrates on tracing examples of Mississippi Valley folklore in Twain's stories, including ghost lore, demonology, witchcraft, luck and unluck, signs, portents, omens, proverbs, and superstitions. Cites numerous examples of each genre, and concludes that at no time did Twain "swerve from the belief in the importance of folklore."

West, Victor Royce. "Folklore of Mark Twain." M.A. English. University of Nebraska. 1928. 128 pp.

Wheeler, Otis. "Some Uses of Folk Humor by Faulkner." Mississippi Quarterly 17 (1964): 107-22.

Focuses on Faulkner's appreciation of American humor and its important place in his art. Discusses four uses of folk humor in Faulkner's works, including As I Lay Dying, "Spotted Horses," The Hamlet, and The Town. The uses include: as moral satire, as a contrast to the frightening element, as a stylistic device, and as a way to manipulate the point of view.

Wheet, Geneva. "The Prometheus Myth in American Poetry." M.A. English and Classical Language. Tufts University. 1920. 116 pp.

Whitbeck, G. Paul. "Washington Irving's Treatment of Dutch Life and Customs." M.A. English. Columbia Universtiy. 1928. 72 pp.

White, John J. _Mythology in the Modern Novel: A Study of Prefigurative Techniques_. Princeton: Princeton U. P., 1971. xii, 264 pp.

Although primarily a study of the implementation of mythology in European literature, it examines some concepts crucial to folklore and literature scholarship. Discusses a wide range of issues relevant to the study of mythology in literature, and proposes four typological categories of mythological fiction.

White, John J. "Myths and Patterns in the Modern Novel." _Mosaic_ 2 (1969): 45-55.

White sees mythic "patterns" (or "limited parallels") in a number of novels with references to traditional myths (mainly Greek). Although he uses Joyce's _Ulysses_ as a main example, there are references to Updike's _The Centaur_, Malamud's _The Natural_, and Nabokov's _Pale Fire_. Ultimately, White concludes that these writers use myth as an analogy for a modern story and that "these modern novelists are using myths, not creating them."

Whiting, Bartlett Jere. "Guyuscutus, Royal Nonesuch, and Other Hoaxes." _Southern Folklore Quarterly_ 8 (1944): 251-75.

Calls attention to related hoaxes performed for financial profit in old Southwestern tradition, of which the Royal Nonesuch was a part.

Whiting, Bartlett Jere. "Partial Immersion in Georgia and Maine." _Southern Folklore Quarterly_ 11 (1947): 261-2.

Briefly points out a Maine analogue to a practical joke in Thompson's _Major Jones's Courtship_.

Whiting, Bartlett Jere. "Proverbial Sayings from Fisher's River, North Carolina." _Southern Folklore Quarterly_ 11 (1947): 173-85.

Lists some 200 examples of proverbs and folk speech from Taliaferro's _Fisher's Fiver_.

Whiting, Bartlett Jere. "Proverbs in Cotton Mather's _Magnalia Christi Americana_." _Neuphilologische Mitteilungen_ 73 (1972): 477-484.

Identifies some seventy proverbs in Mather's _Magnalia_.

Wideman, John. _Stomping the Blues_: Ritual in Black Music and Speech." _The American Poetry Review_ 7 (1978): 42-45.

Examines Afro-American folk traditions in A. Murray's poetry.

Wiggins, Eugene. "Benet's 'Mountain Whippoorwill': Folklore Atop Folklore." _Tennessee Folklore Society Bulletin_ 41 (1975): 99-114.

Demonstrates that Benet's poem shows knowledge of the folklore of mountain fiddling and of the native tradition of fiddle tune lyrics.

Wiggins, William H., Jr. "The Structure and Dynamics of Folklore in the Novel Form: The Case of John O. Killens." _Keystone Folklore Quarterly_ 17 (1972): 92-118.

Observes a development in Killens' use of black folktales in three novels, from ornamental in _Youngblood_ and _And Then We Heard Thunder_ to integral in _'Sippi_. Analyzes the structural correspondence between a black folktale and _'Sippi_.

Wiggins, William H. "The Trickster as Literary Hero: Cecil Brown's _The Life and Loves of Mr. Jiveass Nigger_." _New York Folklore Quarterly_ 29 (1973): 269-86.

Observes that Brown's novel includes literary revisions of black folktales, its hero is based on the trickster figure, and its form mimics folktale form with "the tale" sandwiched between the prologue and epilogue.

Wiley, Paul L. "The Phaeton Symbol in _John Brown's Body_." _American Literature_ 17 (1945): 231-42.

Argues that the character of Jack Ellyat in Benét's narrative is modeled on the mythic role of Phaeton.

Williams, Cratis D. "Linney's Heathen Valley." _North Carolina Folklore_ 19 (1971): 55-58.

Identifies mountain folk traditions in _Heathen Valley_ (folk speech, remedies, and wisdom) and concludes the novel is given the structure of a mountain square dance call.

Williams, Cratis D. "Mountain Customs, Social Life, and Folk Yarns in Taliaferro's _Fisher's River Scenes and Characters_." _North Carolina Folklore_ 16 (1968): 143-52.

Examines in detail customs, character traits, costumes, folktales, and anecdotes; concludes that Taliaferro presents an authentic and sympathetic view of Southern mountain life.

Williams, Leonard. "An Early Arkansas 'Frolic': A Contemporary Account." _Mid-South Folklore_ 2 (1974): 39-42.

Describes a play-party game found in a humorous sketch by Noland in the _Spirit of the Times_.

Williams, Sherley A. "The Blues Roots of Contemporary Afro-American Poetry ." Massachusetts Review 18 (1977): 542-54. Also, in Dexter Fisher & Robert B. Stepto, eds., Afro-American Literature (New York: MLA, 1979), pp. 72-87.

Examines the definition, forms, and functions of the blues in Afro-American tradition, and then illustrates how the blues have provided a structural model for Afro-American poets, such as Langston Hughes and Lucille Clifton. Suggests Hughes's "Young Gal's Blues" "is an example of an oral form moving unchanged into literary form" and is characteristic of classic blues at its best. Points out that Hughes and blues singers make the same assumption--that their audience shares the same reality as they do. Examines Clifton's Good Times as illustrating this same assumed knowledge of collective history and as operating "in much the same way that the communal pattern of statement and response plays . . . in the blues."

Willis, Lonnie Leon. "Folklore in the Published Writings of Henry David Thoreau: A Study and a Compendium Index." Ph.D. University of Colorado. 1966. 416 pp. Dissertation Abstracts International 28 (1967): 1412A-13A.

Assesses Thoreau as an active folklorist who ardently collected "antiquities" from his neighbors. Finds in Thoreau's writing an abundance of beliefs, practices, sayings, legends, proverbs, etc. Lists these with notations in a Compendium-Index. Concludes that Thoreau demonstrated considerable interest in the lore of New England folk, which reveals him to be a more warm, human and personable man than previously recognized.

Wilson, Barbara M. "Hawthorne's Use of Folklore in the First (1837) Edition of the 'Twice Told Tales'." M.A. English. University of Kansas. 1962. 101 pp.

Wilson, George P. "Lois Lenski's Use of Regional Speech." North Carolina Folklore 9 (1961): 1-3.

Defends Lenski's use of dialect and explains some of its various uses in her fiction.

Winkelman, Donald M. "Goodman Brown, Tom Sawyer, and Oral Tradition." Keystone Folklore Quarterly 10 (1965): 43-48.

Applies Dorson's method in order to find folklore forms in Hawthorne and Twain and decides they both incorporated numerous legends and beliefs.

Winkelman, Donald M. "Three American Authors as Semi-Folk Artists." Journal of American Folklore 78 (1965): 130-35.

Considers the general awareness and use of folklore by Twain, Chesnutt, and Wellman and concludes that although they are well removed from being folk artists, they do show the influence of folklore on the creation process.

Winslow, David J. "Hawthorne's Folklore and the Folklorists' Hawthorne: A Reexamination." Southern Folklore Quarterly 34 (1970): 34-52.

Surveys the scholarship about folklore in Hawthorne and concludes it is neither long nor impressive. Comments that "they point out what, but fail to answer questions of how and why." Argues that Hawthorne was a highly sophisticated literary artist who picked and chose the folklore he used to suit his moral and allegorical motives, and that his view of folk community was not completely accurate.

Withim, Philip M. "Mythic Awareness and Literary Form: Verbal Ritual in Whitman's 'Bivouac on a Mountain Side'," in Marjorie W. McCune, et al, eds. The Binding of Proteus (Lewisburg: Bucknell U. P., 1974), pp. 111-22.

Deals with myth in a very general way, as metaphor. "In the mythic world, the part stands for the whole." Primarily a phenomenological study. The verbal rituals identified are not folkloristic.

Witt, Stanley Pryor. "Harold Frederic as Purveyor of American Myth: An Approach to His Novels." Ph.D. University of Arizona. 1976. 226 pp. Dissertation Abstracts International 37 (1977): 7756A.

Suggests that three of Frederic's novels reflect a thematic structure comparable in nature to the monomythic adventure of the universal culture hero as described by Campbell.

Wolfe, Bernard. "Uncle Remus and the Malevolent Rabbit." Commentary 8 (1949): 31-41. Also in Alan Dundes, ed., Mother Wit From the Laughing Barrel (Englewood Cliffs: Prentice-Hall, 1973), pp. 524-40.

Describes the contrast between the format and the content of the Uncle Remus stories: the format supports racist attitudes, a black man "giving" to a white boy, but the content undercuts establishment values, the weak outsmarting the strong.

Wolfe, Gary K. "The Frontier Myth in Ray Bradbury," in Martin Harry Greenberg and Joseph D. Olander, eds., Ray Bradbury (New York: Taplinger, 1980), pp. 33-54.

Identifies Bradbury's interest in casting his stories "in the form of an American Indian legend" and points out some instances of this technique in Bradbury's fiction. Discusses how Bradbury recreates the perspective of the Indians facing the encroaching Western civilization in his depiction of space exploration. However, the folkloristic analysis is not emphasized.

Wolfsehr, Clifford. "Sandburg's Use of Folk and Native Materials." M.A. English. Washington State University. 1947. 58 pp.

Womack, Judy. "Daniel Boone--'Over the Velvet Falls'." Kentucky Folklore Record 18 (1972): 21-22.

Examines William Stafford's and Stephen Benet's historical concerns as evidenced in their literary poems about Daniel Boone.

Woodbridge, Hensley C. "Americanisms in Felix Holt's Gabriel Horn." Kentucky Folklore Record 2 (1956): 15-22.

Notes Holte's effective use of western Kentucky dialect, and lists local words and expressions found in his regional novel.

Woodward, Robert H. "Dating the Action of Rip Van Winkle." New York Folklore Quarterly 15 (1959): 70.

Briefly notes that Rip returns on the day of the election of the first President, based on evidence from folk custom.

Woodward, Robert H. "Harold Frederic and New York Folklore." New York Folklore Quarterly 16 (1960): 83-89.

Reviews folk expressions and historical lore in Frederic's nineteenth-century novels.

Woodward Robert H. "Harold Frederic's Use of British and Irish Folklore." New York Folklore Quarterly 17 (1961): 51-55.

Contends that in Frederic's stories about Great Britain and Ireland he made conscious, deliberate use of local or national legends.

Woodward, Robert H. "Harold Frederic's Woodchuck Story." New York Folklore Quarterly 17 (1961): 197-99.

Reprints the original text of a traditional anecdote employed by Frederic.

Woodward, Robert H. "Mohawk Valley Folk Life During the Civil War." New York Folklore Quarterly 18 (1962): 107-18.

Finds considerable folk "life" content in Frederic's regional novels, specifically folk beliefs, festivals, and farm activities.

Workman, Mark E. "The Role of Mythology in Modern Literature." Journal of the Folklore Institute 18 (1981): 35-48.

Proposes a tripartite framework for the study of the role of mythology in modern literature. Suggests that folklore in literature may classed as metonymic (the literary treatment is identical to the folkloric); metaphoric (the literary treatment is similar to the folkloric model but set in a factual world); and metamorphic (the literature undercuts or confuses the folklore). Illustrates the thesis in discussions of Hamsun's Pan and Pynchon's The Crying of Lot 49.

Wyld, Lionel D. "Fiction, Fact, and Folklore: the World of Chad Hanna." English Journal 56 (1967): 716-19.

Identifies briefly the folklore in Walter Edmonds' novel about circus life.

Yates, Irene. "A Collection of Proverbs and Proverbial Sayings from South Carolina Literature." Southern Folklore Quarterly 11 (1947): 187-199.

Culls roughly a hundred traditional phrases and proverbs from a dozen obscure novels from South Carolina.

Yates, Irene. "Conjures and Cures in the Novels of Julia Peterkin." Southern Folklore Quarterly 10 (1946): 137-49.

Investigates the charms and methods of conjure doctors as depicted in four Peterkin novels and concludes that this material enriches the novels' plots and characterizations.

Yates, Irene. "The Literary Utilization of Folklore in the Works of Contemporary South Carolina Writers." M.A. English. University of Virginia. 1939. 207 pp.

Yates, Norris W. William T. Porter and the Spirit of the Times: A Study of the Big Bear School of Humor. Baton Rouge: Louisiana State University Press, 1957. xi, 222 pp.

Discusses the Southwestern humorists' reliance upon tall tales and their conventions and identifies the most popular themes and topics of that frontier humor.

Young, Philip C. "Fallen From Time: The Mythic Rip Van Winkle." Kenyon Review 22 (1960): 547-73.

Finds historical predecessors in folklore for the Rip Van Winkle figure, such as the legends of Arthur, Merlin, John the Divine, Charlemagne, and the Seven Sleepers. Focuses on the Grimms' Teutonic Mythology for Irving's story. Analyzes Irving's treatment as emphasizing some form of spiritual transformation.

Young, Philip C. "The Mother of Us All: Pocahontas Reconsidered." Kenyon Review 24 (1962): 391-415.

Reviews the historical and literary treatments of Pocahontas, including Lindsay, Crane, and MacLeish. Concludes that she represents the "Dark Lady," the progenitress of all the erotic and joyous temptresses.

Young, Philip C. Three Bags Full: Essays in American Fiction. New York: Harcourt, Brace, Jovanovich, 1972. xvi, 231 pp.

The third section, entitled "American myth," contains two essays, one on treatments of the legend of Pocahontas, and one on Irving's use of legendary material in "Rip Van Winkle."

Yu, Beong-Cheon. "Lafcadio Hearn's Twice-Told Legends Reconsidered." American Literature 34 (1962): 56-71.

Discusses the esthetic and philosophical rationale underlying Hearn's use of Western and Japanese ghost-lore and legends in Stray Leaves from Strange Literature, Some Chinese Ghosts, and numerous retellings of Japanese legends. Concludes that Hearn believed ghosts and dream-life to be expressions of "man's aspiration for the impossible" and to be the very spirit of human existence.

Zajdel, Melody McCollum. "The Development of a Poetic Vision: H.D.'s Growth from Imagist to Mythologist." Ph.D. Michigan State University. 1979. 304 pp. Dissertation Abstracts International 40 (1980): 5445A-46A.

Traces H.D.'s philosophical and artistic development from strict Imagism in her early works to Freudian use of myth to pattern understanding in her later works. Explores H.D.'s growing interest in women characters and the problems of the woman artist and her use of dream-vision, psychological probing, and mythic materials to chronicle the woman's quest for identity, revelation and transcendence. Concludes that Imagistic and mythic concerns are all blended in the final syncretistic vision of H.D.

Zara, Bertha R. "The Figure in the Carpet: Patterns of Myths, Fairy Tales, and Bible Stories in the Fiction of Henry James." M.A. English. Hunter College of the City University of New York. 1960. 66 pp.

Zug, Charles G., III. "The Construction of 'The Devil and Tom Walker': A Study of Irving's Later Use of Folklore." New York Folklore Quarterly 24 (1969): 243-60.

Argues that Irving collected folk motifs from Germany and skillfully pieced them together in "Tom Walker"; concludes that Irving moved from merely repeating folk materials in earlier works to the actual mechanics of assembling traditional motifs into a successful narrative.

INDEX

I. AUTHORS

II. GENERAL STUDIES OF FOLKLORE GENRES

III. GENERAL THEORY

IV. REGIONAL AND ETHNIC STUDIES

AFRO-AMERICAN

GENERAL REGIONAL AND ETHNIC

V. HUMOR: GENERAL STUDIES

VI. MISCELLANEOUS: GENERAL STUDIES OF DIALECT, THEMES & CHARACTER TYPES: